MARCHAND, Donald A. Infotrends: profiting from your information resources, by Donald A. Marchand and Forest W. Horton. Wiley, 1986. 324p bibl index 85-29438. 24.95 ISBN 0-471-81680-9. T 58. CIP

Marchand (South Carolina) and Horton (Maryland) expand the traditional concept of economic resources to include information as a strategic asset. Beginning with a historical perspective of the shift from an agrarian to an industrial and finally to an information economy, the authors emphasize that "working smarter, not harder" is the new key to enhancing profitability. To this end, the authors examine the entire spectrum of creating, disseminating, and using information, such as employee retraining, educational curriculum, and selling information to customers. However, this is not a text on the mechanics of electronic data processing or management information systems. Rather, it is a compendium of contemporary thought related to an information society covering both the technological and humanistic factors. The writing and printing make the book easy to read and comprehend. Excellent use is made of charts and graphs. Extensive bibliography and index. An excellent resource for lower-division through graduate-level academic collections and for public libraries with extensive business holdings.—*S.R. Kahn, University of Cincinnati*

INFOTRENDS

INFOTRENDS

Profiting from Your Information Resources

Donald A. Marchand

and

Forest W. Horton, Jr.

567809

JOHN WILEY & SONS

New York • Chichester • Brisbane • Toronto • Singapore

This publication is designed to provide accurate and
authoritative information in regard to the subject
matter covered. It is sold with the understanding that
the publisher is not engaged in rendering legal, accounting,
or other professional service. If legal advice or other
expert assistance is required, the services of a competent
professional person should be sought. *From a Declaration
of Principles jointly adopted by a Committee of the
American Bar Association and a Committee of Publishers.*

Library of Congress Cataloging in Publication Data:

Marchand, Donald A.
    Infotrends: profits from your information resources.

    Bibliography: p.
    Includes index.
    1. Information resources management. I. Horton,
Forest W. II. Title.

T58.64.M37   1986   658.4'038   85-29438
ISBN 0-471-81680-9

Printed in the United States of America

10 9 8 7 6 5 4 3 2 1

To Lauren Elizabeth Marchand

and

Die Familie Dangel

Every company needs to plan its strategy for the transition from doing business in an industrial economy to doing business in an information economy. Most enterprises today are still unaware that the structural changes that have occurred in the economy of the United States and in other advanced Western societies not only have macroeconomic implications for the changing composition of the workforce, but, perhaps more importantly, have microeconomic consequences for the changing composition of traditional market sectors, competition, and the very way business is done.

At the core of such transition strategies is: (1) the need for businesses to treat information as a strategic asset, (2) the need to tie information management to strategic business planning, and (3) the need to raise responsibility for information resources to the top levels of the corporate structure. The whole category of white-collar information workers—from financial officers to inventory clerks—needs to be recognized for its critical role in productivity. Information workers must receive the same level of attention that has been given to traditional "blue-collar," production workers.

Most companies are only dimly aware of this shift to an information economy. And yet the changes, we contend, probably will be even more profound than those that accompanied our transition from an agrarian to an industrialized economy.

When America made the transition from the farm to the factory, the changes that occurred in the entire infrastructure of the country affected virtually every kind of business, not just agricultural producers. Whole sectors of the economy had to redefine themselves and the kind of business they were in, in order to succeed in an industrial economy. To succeed in the information economy as it matures, American executives will once again have to rethink the kind of business they are in, their strategic plans, and their management styles.

Moreover, our definitions of *productivity* and *competitive advantage* will have to change to suit the information economy. The earlier measures of output over input, where output is measured in terms of physical products produced from an assembly line, and input is measured in terms of labor manhours, must be revised to take into account that information itself is an input. Unlike traditional economic resources, however, information is not consumed as it is used. Productivity will expand as it embraces the speed and quality of decision making made possible by advanced information technologies and information-management approaches, and by new methods and concepts.

Every business, large or small, will be affected by the new information technologies as it faces keener competition, not just as measured by price performance in the marketplace, but in how information resources and technologies are employed in its offices, manufacturing plants, and laboratories. In short, competition will be as much won or lost at the executive workstation, at the laboratory work bench, and on the plant floor, as in advertising and marketing strategies, or financial planning strategies.

A few leading-edge companies, particularly those in the information-intensive industries such as banking, insurance, brokering, and related sectors, already have taken steps in this direction. Sears, Merrill Lynch, J. C. Penney, John Deere, and American Hospital Supply Corporation represent the leading edge of companies who are using information resources to gain competitive advantages in their markets. Automated databases are used to improve the number of customer subscriptions to maintenance contracts for retail appliances, develop new information products such as the Cash Management Account, automate their catalogs for the convenience of retail shoppers, and lock in dealers and suppliers to their automated networks. Many chief executive officers (CEOs) have been reading about the postindustrial society, but by and large, enterprises are still not even aware of the business reality of the information economy, much less have they identified the strategies and approaches they might use to cope with this phenomenon. This book's primary purpose is to address the business issues and management concerns that arise in an information economy, and to point medium- and large-sized businesses in the proper direction, so that they can manage information resources and assets to their competitive advantage. To deal with this complex topic we have structured this book into nine chapters.

In Chapter 1, we present the central theme of the historical shifts from an agrarian to an industrial, and now to an information economy. While the field of "information economics" is still in its infancy, we draw from the seminal works of such pioneers as Daniel Bell, Peter Drucker, Paul Hawken, Fritz Machlup, Marc Uri Porat, Kenneth Boulding, and others. Their intellectual contributions serve as a framework for our discussion of the information economy's impacts on business.

Next, in Chapter 2, we discuss the engine that is driving the information economy. Just as the use of chemical fertilizers served as the engine for the *green wave*, as the agricultural revolution of the late 1800s is known, and the steam, electric and gasoline engines became the driving forces behind the industrial revolution of the early 1900s, so silicon chips, fiber optics, lasers, and other basic technologies are making the information age a reality today. The information-processing industry is the business sector that is providing the impetus for this revolution, with its impressive array of hardware, software, and information products and services. These technologies, in turn, are having and will continue to have profound impacts on business management, competitive advantage, and productivity.

Having set the stage by describing the changing business environment of the information economy, we then move, in Chapter 3, to the need for each company to fundamentally rethink its corporate strategy. Just as the railroad industry in the late 1800s had to change its mindset from one of buying up large land tracts and laying railroad ties to one of moving goods and people from one place to another, so enterprises today must reconsider their traditional lines of business as they begin operating in an information economy. It is not just a question of selling a product, but of selling a solution to a customer's problem. This is where the lines between manufacturing and services and between traditional versus emerging markets are blurring and changing.

Chapter 4 examines alternative approaches companies can take once they've redefined their fundamental product lines, markets, production and distribution channels, and suppliers. For example, we examine the increasing use of acquisitions, mergers, and other forms of joint ventures, but retain our distinctive emphasis on the use of such strategies by companies operating in an information economy.

In Chapter 5, we take up the idea that data, information, and knowledge have themselves come to be regarded as valuable, costly corporate assets just like financial assets, physical assets, and human assets. We contrast the more conventional notion of using information as primarily a cost-displacement and productivity-improvement tool, with the more dynamic idea of visualizing knowledge itself as business assets: that is, as a critical success factor that will increasingly be the difference between winning or losing.

Chapter 6 looks at alternatives for organization and management structures, spans of control, leadership styles, and other factors every company should consider as it reorganizes and repositions itself in the information economy. Too many companies are blindly applying outmoded and inappropriate industrial-management theories (*scientific management,* for instance) to their operations, without thinking through the underlying validity of these approaches in changing business environments.

We examine the problem of redefining productivity in the information age in Chapter 7. Central to this discussion is the idea of adding value at each stage of the information life cycle. The qualitative dimension is as important in an information society as the quantitative dimension. Quality control must be built into the front end of the manufacturing cycle, not viewed as a last-minute check to be done just before goods are shipped.

Chapter 8 introduces the human factor into our discussion. We believe the essence of the information economy is a distributed network of human talent. Within the individual enterprise, outmoded human resources management philosophies must be replaced by modern approaches that maximize the brain contribution to the product, not just the brawn contribution. In short, we believe in working smarter, not just harder.

Finally, in Chapter 9, we look into the changing role of business in the information society. Clearly the shift to an information economy will require every business to rethink not just the elements of its economic milieu, but its political and social contexts as well. We do not suggest some kind of radical shift away from the profit motive to the quality-of-life motive. But we do endeavor to point out that there are both risks and opportunities for every business in the information society. Much of this discussion implicitly recognizes that doing business in an information economy forces suppliers, producers, and consumers into far closer proximity with one another than is the case in an industrial economy.

There is no need to panic. Companies still have time to consider if, how, and when they will reposition themselves in an information economy. But there is not all that much time. Even now some of your sharp-eyed competitors are moving their pieces on this new chessboard. How your company plans its initial counterattack strategies in the months ahead will, in all likelihood, determine how it rides out the competitive struggles of the late 1980s and 1990s. That is the timeframe within which the information winners will survive and flourish. The losers will be the dinosaurs still wondering why their "buggywhip" industrial-age policies and strategies didn't work. This book will help you to be a winner. Information is the key to profits.

DONALD MARCHAND
FOREST HORTON

Columbia, South Carolina
Washington, D. C.
April 1986

ACKNOWLEDGMENTS

We owe special thanks to John C. Kresslein, our research assistant, and Marjie Martens, for preparing numerous drafts of the manuscript. Elizabeth Shropshier assisted in the coordination of the research and drafting effort. Administrative support was also provided by Ann Brannon and Faye Henderson. Joyce P. Marchand gave us useful reviews and insights. We are indebted to Sena H. Black for providing an earlier analysis of the information-processing industry, which we have expanded and updated in Chapter 2. We wish to thank our colleagues Neil Burk, Pat Green, Green, Bruce Allen, and John Weitzel for their suggestions and comments in reviewing earlier drafts of the manuscript. Finally, we owe thanks to Michael Hamilton, our editor at Wiley, who had vision, patience, and dedication in seeing our ideas move from proposal to finished work.

D.A.M.
F.W.H.

CONTENTS

CONTENTS

INFOTRENDS

CHAPTER **1**

THE INFORMATION ECONOMY

Every business, whether service or manufacturing, traditional or emerging, or large or small, needs to plan its strategy for the transition from doing business in an industrial economy to doing business in an information economy. The structural changes that have been occurring in the economies of the United States and other advanced societies have major implications that affect every business firm. The composition of the work force, productivity, competitive battlefields, and business management philosophies, are all changing.

The key to competitive success in the information economy is to work smarter, not just harder. Labor, technology, capital, and *information resources* must be produced, consciously used, and effectively deployed. In the past, productivity improvement focused on labor, capital, and technology. Today, business must add an *information-oriented* approach to productivity improvement to be competitive in national and international markets. For example, for Citicorp and other leading banks and financial institutions, the strategy of using information resources for competitive advantage on a worldwide basis has been evolving for many years.

1

Although noted writers have done much to popularize the notion of an information economy,[1] the impact of this structural change on strategic management, and on competition in national and world markets, remains poorly defined and understood. American business and its senior corporate executives are just beginning to grasp and adapt to the basic changes in productivity, competition, and management required to succeed in an information economy.

The intent of this chapter is to provide a manager's guide to the evolution, definition, and business impacts of the information economy. We suggest that in order to fully comprehend them, it is necessary to plunge below the surface of short-term business and economic cycles and try to understand the deeper currents which are forcing a shift in the way American enterprise does business.

Accordingly, we have identified the following major features which constitute the foundation of the evolving information economy:

1. It is a business reality that is no longer novel or revolutionary.

2. Its impact on business management will continue to be profound both nationally and internationally.

3. It will affect traditional and emerging industries alike in the service, agricultural, and manufacturing sectors.

4. Its continued evolution will be significantly shaped and paced by business strategies and management decision-making styles.

5. It will continue to have a great impact on both the internal operations and external environment of the business.

EVIDENCE OF THE INFORMATION ECONOMY'S EMERGENCE

In 1900, an observer of the industrial economy would have found the task of accurately discerning the path of that economy during

---

[1] See for example Alvin Toffler, *The Third Wave* (New York: Morrow, 1980); John Naisbitt, *Megatrends* (New York: Warner, 1982); and Paul Hawken, *The Next Economy* New York: Holt, 1983).

the first half of the twentieth century very difficult. Similarly, the reality of the information economy has not burst on the business scene full-blown, but has evolved over some 25 or 30 years. Moreover, statistical evidence to define this emerging social and economic reality has lagged behind the writers and commentators who have identified the important features of this significant change.

In 1962, economist Fritz Machlup made the first attempt to measure the growth of what he described as the "knowledge industries": education, research and development, communications media, information machinery, and information activities.[2] Moreover, he identified more than 50 specific activities within these five broad classes. His education category included expenditures for all formal public and private education in the United States, as well as for public libraries, military and religious learning, and training on the job. In the communications media category, Machlup included radio and television broadcasting, telephone services, postal services, and printing and publishing. Information machinery involved computers, telecommunications equipment, printing presses, and information services including governmental, legal, financial, and business activities.

In measuring these activities for the year 1958, Machlup estimated that the knowledge industries accounted for roughly 29 percent of the gross national product.

Although Machlup's work was bold and innovative, the business impacts of this early research were not evident until Peter Drucker pointed out in 1968 that America after World War II had shifted from an economy of goods to a "knowledge economy."[3] Relying in large measure on Machlup's earlier work, Drucker contended that in 1955 one-fourth of the U.S. GNP could be attributed to knowledge industries, whereas a decade later this same sector was consuming a third of a far larger GNP.

In line with these pronounced occupational shifts in the economy, Drucker also suggested that knowledge was the key factor in a country's international strength. What distinguished a nation as advanced versus less developed was precisely the ability to

[2] Fritz Machlup, *The Production and Distribution of Knowledge in the United States* (Princeton: Princeton University Press, 1962).

[3] Peter Drucker, *The Age of Discontinuity* (New York: Harper & Row, 1968).

generate and use knowledge resources in the form of experts, scientists, libraries, information centers, and new technologies. In the end, he perceived the reality of the knowledge economy as a central "discontinuity" in all advanced economies.

A further advance in the development of the information-economy idea came in 1973 with the publication of *The Coming of Post-Industrial Society* [4] by the Harvard sociologist, Daniel Bell. Although Professor Bell was concerned with developing a "social forecast," a good deal of his basic argument for the evolution of societies rested on a three-stage hypothesis of economic development. As Table 1-1 indicates, Bell suggested that advanced economies have progressed from the preindustrial to industrial and finally to a postindustrial stage. As these historical stages have evolved, the basic strategic resources and tools of economic activity have shifted as has the nature of work and culture. In the *postindustrial economy,* a term he coined, the application of knowledge and intellectual technology in response to the organized complexity of economic, organizational and social institutions becomes the critical factor of production.

In 1977, when *The Information Economy,* [5] a nine-volume report published by the Department of Commerce and authored by Marc U. Porat with the assistance of Michael R. Rubin, was issued, his theories were vindicated. The Commerce study made use of the national income accounts published by the Bureau of Economic Analysis to create a computer model of the U.S. economy for the year 1967. The definition of the information sector used in the Commerce study was similar to that used by Machlup.

The Commerce study set up a six-sector economic model. There is a primary information sector which includes all industries that produce about 90 percent of the primary information machines or market information services. This includes the private sector, which produces about 90 percent of the primary information products and services, and the public sector, which contributes about 10 percent. There is also a secondary information sector with two segments: (1) the public bureaucracy, and (2) those

[4] *The Coming of Post-Industrial Society* from Daniel Bell, ©1973 by Daniel Bell. Reprinted by permission of Basic Books, Inc., Publishers.
[5] Washington, D.C.: U.S. Department of Commerce, 1977.

TABLE 1-1.   **Bell's Framework of Social Change**

	Pre-Industrial	Industrial	Post-Industrial
Regions	Asia Africa Latin America	Western Europe Soviet Union Japan	United States

Economic sector	Primary
	extractive:
	  Agriculture
	  Mining
	  Fishing
	  Timber
		Secondary
		goods
		producing:
		  Manufacturing
		  Processing
			Tertiary
			  Transportation
			  Utilities
			Quaterary
			  Trade
			  Finance
			  Insurance
			  Real Estate
			Quinary
			  Health
			  Education
			  Research
			  Government
			  Recreation

Occcupa-tional slope:	Farmer Miner Fisherman Unskilled worker	Semi-skilled worker Engineer	Professional and technical Scientist
Technology:	Raw materials	Energy	Information
Design:	Game against nature	Game against fabricated nature	Game between persons

Methodol-ogy:	Common sense
	experience
		Empiricism
		Experimentation
			Abstract theory:
			  models
			  simulation
			  decision theory
			  systems analysis

Time perspective:	Orientation to the past Ad hoc responses	Ad hoc adaptiveness Projections	Future orientation Forecasting
Axial principle:	Traditionalism: Land/resource limitation	Economic growth: State or private control of investment decisions	Centrality of and codification of theoretical knowl-edge

Source: See note 4.

private bureaucracies whose activities are not directly identified in the national accounts as information services, yet who actually engage in information and knowledge work. The three remaining sectors include: (1) the private productive sector, which produces goods; (2) the public productive sectors, which build roads and dams; and (3) the household sector.

The primary information sector included industries like computer manufacturing services, telecommunications, printing, media, advertising, accounting, and education. The Commerce study concluded that, in 1967, sales of information goods and services of this sector to the other sectors amounted to $174.6 billion, or 21.9 percent of the GNP. Moreover, the study found that more than 43 percent of all corporate profits originated with the primary information sector. (In 1967, all corporations earned $79.3 billion in profits while the primary information sector earned $33.7 billion.)

The secondary information sector included those aspects of industry that directly engaged in information work, but whose activities are not measured directly. While the goods produced may be sold in the market, the information work in these enterprises—the planning, scheduling, coordinating, and managing—are not factored directly into the GNP. In 1967, the Commerce study found that 21 percent of the GNP originated in the secondary information sector. The study concluded that, added to the contribution of the primary information sector, more than 46 percent of the GNP and 53 percent of labor income was accounted for through knowledge, communication, and information work.

In addition, as Figure 1-1 illustrates, the Commerce study examined the composition of the work force from 1860 and projected to 1980. Their analysis corroborated the evidence of Machlup and the historical-stage (postindustrial-society) theory of Bell. In tracing 100 years of change in labor in the four major sectors, it was observed that, at some point in the late 1950s, the U.S. workforce had shifted from a primarily industrial to an information workforce.

The findings of the Commerce study provided substantial evidence for the reality of the information economy in the United States and the transitional phases which the national economy has

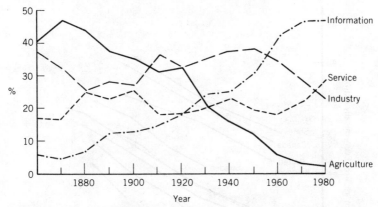

Figure 1-1. Four-sector aggregation of the U.S. work force, 1860–1980. *Source:* Dr. Marc Uri Porat, *The Information Economy: Definition and Measurement,* Washington, D.C.: U.S. Department of Commerce, May 1977, Vol. 1, p. 121.

moved through in progressing to the information economy.[6] Moreover, the study also provided support for the notion that the basic sources of wealth had shifted from capital to information and knowledge resources.

Emergence as a Global Phenomenon

If the Commerce study helped to define the United States as an information economy, a study prepared by the Organization for Economic Cooperation and Development (OECD) in Paris in 1981 provided a comparative view of the major advanced economies as they progressed from primarily industrial to information-oriented economies.[7]

As Figure 1-2 indicates, the study identified the changes in information workers for nine countries in the post World War II period. While the rates of change varied in each national economy, the trend to information occupations was unmistakable in advanced Western economies.

[6] Marc U. Porat, *The Information Economy* (Washington, D.C.: U.S. Department of Commerce, 1977).

[7] Organization for Economic Co-operation and Development, *Information Activities, Electronics and Telecommunications Technologies, Impact on Employment, Growth and Trade* (Paris: OECD, 1981).

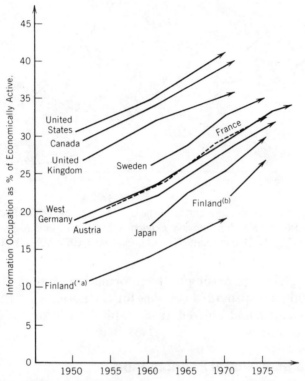

*Data for Finland was derived from two separate sources (a) I. Pietarinen; (b) The Central
Statistical Office of Finland, both sources using a rather more restricted definition. *

Figure 1–2.   Changes in the share of information occupations in all economically active over the post-war period. *Source:* Organization for Economic Cooperation and Development, *Information Activities, Electronics and Telecommunications Technologies, Impact* on Employment, Growth and Trade, Paris: OECD,
1981, p. 25. Used with permission.

Moreover, the size of the primary information sector varied
from 14.8 percent of the GNP in Australia to 24 percent of the
GNP in the United States in 1967 and 1968 respectively. In addition, the OECD assessed the relative contributions of the secondary information sectors in selected member countries. While
the U.S. economy continued to be the most information intensive
in both the primary and secondary information sectors, the
economies of Japan, the United Kingdom, and other countries
studied were also progressing in a similar direction.

As Peter Drucker had emphasized 13 years earlier, the OECD study and studies of individual countries such as the United Kingdom have provided evidence of the information economy's emergence as a global phenomenon, and of the significant role information activities would continue to have in international trade.

The Evolution of the Information Business Has Closely Mirrored the Development of the Information Economy

Almost all discussions or studies of the information economy have emphasized the catalytic role of computers and communications technologies in the transition from the industrial to the information economy. As the role of the information business has grown, so have the capabilities of information workers to process knowledge and information resources. In 1980, the historical evolution of the information business through the agricultural, industrial, and information economies in the United States was graphically illustrated in a report of the Harvard University Program on Information Resources Policy entitled *Mapping the Information Business.*[8] As Figures 1-3, 1-4, and 1-5 illustrate, the information business in terms of its products and services has continued to evolve over the history of the United States, parallel with the emergence of the nation as an agricultural, industrial, and now information economy.[9] As these changes have progressed, the landscape of the information business has become crowded with new services, technologies, products, and transmission media. As the information business has continued to evolve with the discovery of new technologies and the integration of "older" technologies such as computers and communications, new opportunities and markets within this business have opened up. Thus, not only have the tools available to information workers changed, but the contribution of the information business to the GNP has continued to increase, both directly, in the primary information sector, and indirectly, in the secondary information sector as the Commerce and OECD studies have suggested.

[8] Cambridge, MA: Program on Information Resources Policy, 1980.
[9] *Ibid.*

Figure 1-3. The information business in 1780. *Source:* John F. McLaughlin with Anne E. Birinyi, "Mapping the Information Business," in *Understanding New Media*, edited by Benjamin M. Compaine (Cambridge, MA: Ballinger, 1984). ©1985 Program on Information Resources Policy, Harvard University.

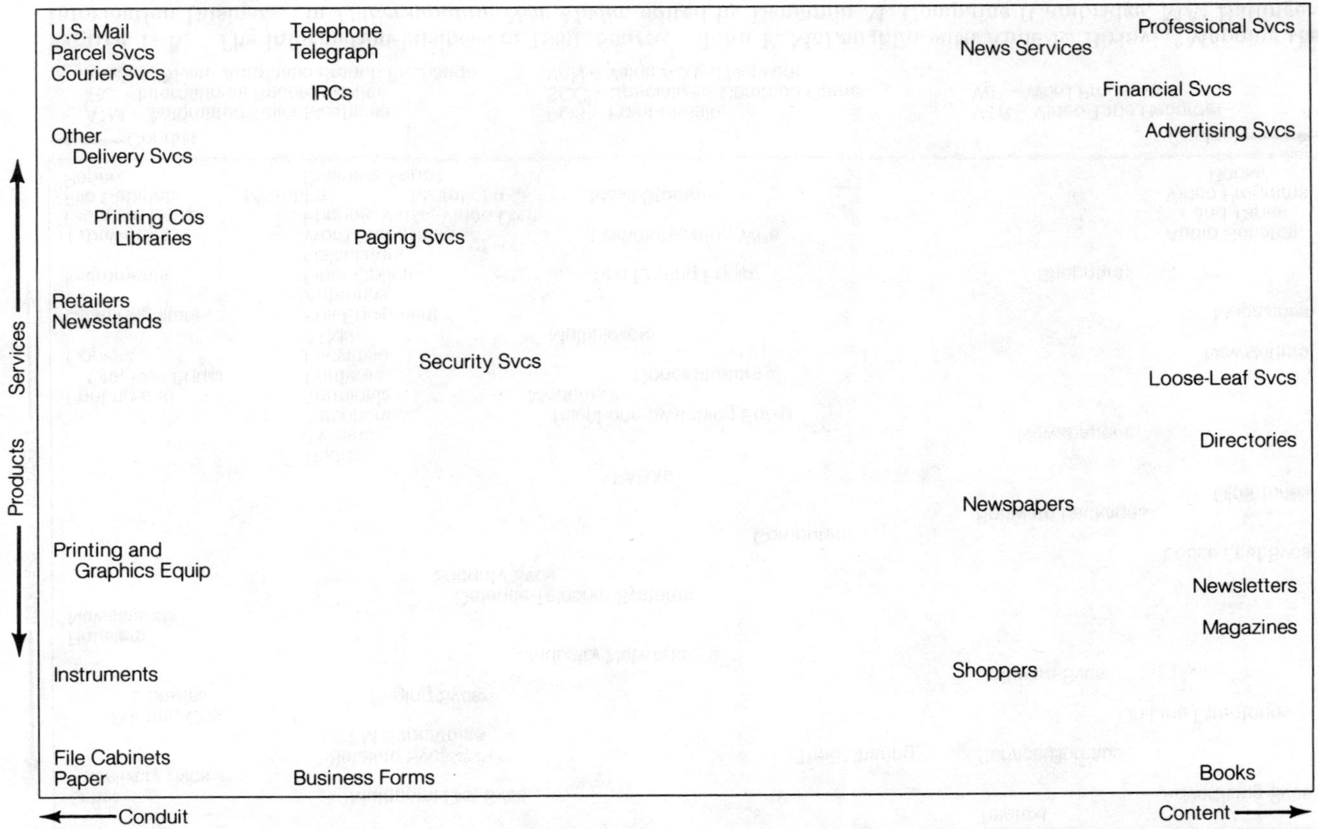

U.S. Mail
Parcel Svcs
Courier Svcs

Telephone
Telegraph

News Services

Professional Svcs

IRCs

Financial Svcs

Advertising Svcs

Other
Delivery Svcs

Printing Cos
Libraries

Paging Svcs

Retailers
Newsstands

Security Svcs

Loose-Leaf Svcs

Directories

Newspapers

Printing and
Graphics Equip

Shoppers

Newsletters

Magazines

Instruments

File Cabinets
Paper

Business Forms

Books

← Conduit →

Content

← Services | Products →

Figure 1–4. The information business in 1880. *Source:* John F. McLaughlin with Anne E. Birinyi, "Mapping the Information Business," in *Understanding New Media*, edited by Benjamin M. Compaine (Cambridge, MA: Ballinger, 1984). ©1985 Program on Information Resources Policy, Harvard University.

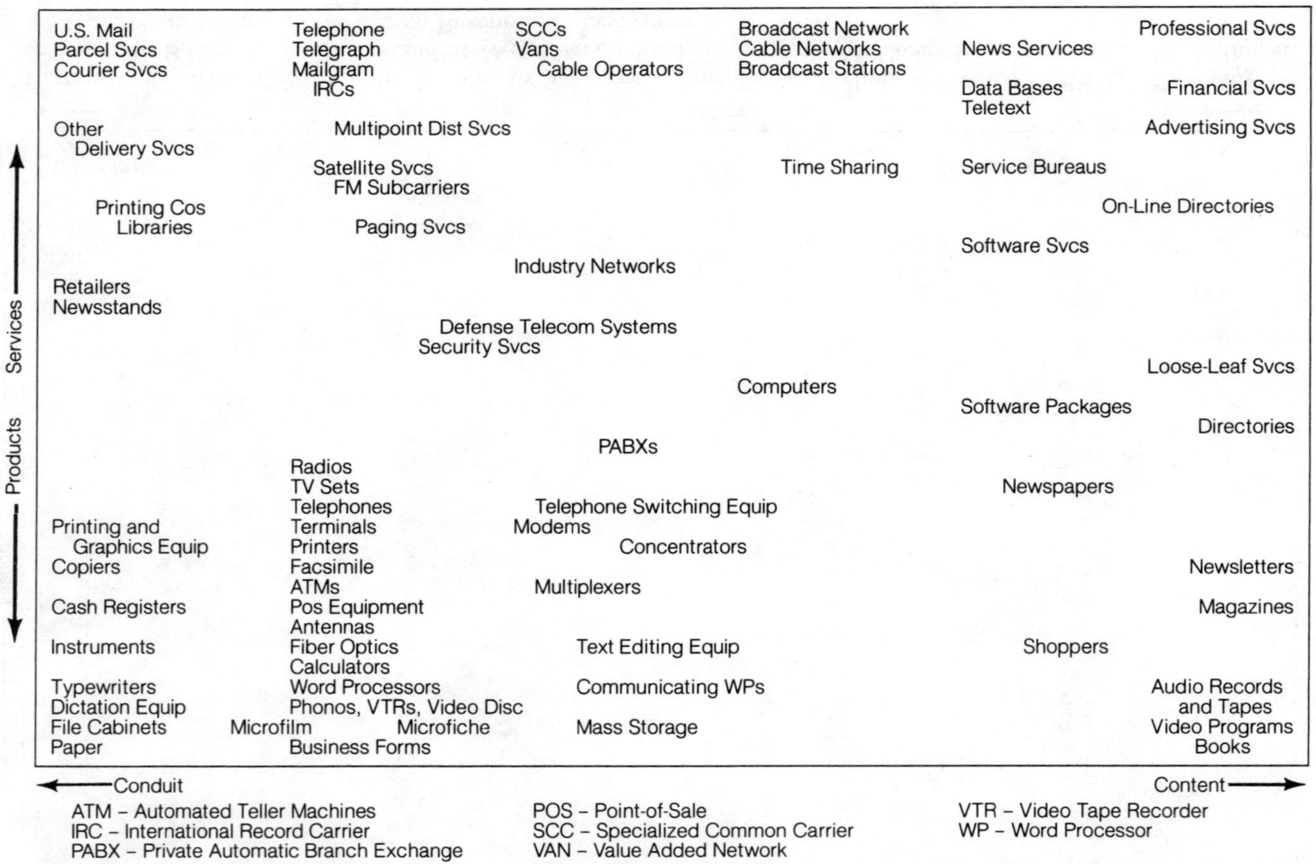

Figure 1–5. The information business in 1980.

Products — Services (left vertical axis)

Conduit → Content (bottom horizontal axis)

U.S. Mail
Parcel Svcs
Courier Svcs

Telephone
Telegraph
Mailgram
IRCs

SCCs
Vans
Cable Operators

Broadcast Network
Cable Networks
Broadcast Stations

News Services

Professional Svcs

Financial Svcs

Advertising Svcs

Multipoint Dist Svcs

Data Bases
Teletext

On-Line Directories

Other
Delivery Svcs

Satellite Svcs
FM Subcarriers

Paging Svcs

Time Sharing

Service Bureaus

Printing Cos
Libraries

Software Svcs

Industry Networks

Software Packages

Loose-Leaf Svcs

Directories

Retailers
Newsstands

Defense Telecom Systems
Security Svcs

Computers

Newspapers

Newsletters

Magazines

PABXs

Radios
TV Sets
Telephones
Terminals
Printers
Facsimile
ATMs
Pos Equipment
Antennas
Fiber Optics
Calculators

Telephone Switching Equip
Modems   Concentrators

Multiplexers

Shoppers

Audio Records
and Tapes
Video Programs
Books

Printing and
Graphics Equip
Copiers

Cash Registers

Instruments

Text Editing Equip

Typewriters
Dictation Equip
File Cabinets   Microfilm   Microfiche
Paper   Phonos, VTRs, Video Disc
Business Forms

Communicating WPs

Mass Storage

Word Processors

ATM – Automated Teller Machines
IRC – International Record Carrier
PABX – Private Automatic Branch Exchange

POS – Point-of-Sale
SCC – Specialized Common Carrier
VAN – Value Added Network

VTR – Video Tape Recorder
WP – Word Processor

Figure 1–5. The information business in 1980. *Source:* John F. McLaughlin with Anne E. Birinyi, "Mapping the Information Business," in *Understanding New Media*, edited by Benjamin M. Compaine (Cambridge, MA: Ballinger, 1984). ©1985 Program on Information Resources Policy, Harvard University.

THE INFORMATION ECONOMY TODAY

As evidence about the reality and basic features of the information economy continues to mount, there begins to be less concern about confirming that such a structural economic shift has continued historically, and more concern about understanding how the information economy is performing, and its impacts on productivity, investment, capital formation, labor force composition, and competition.

The relationship between the traditional manufacturing and "newer" information sectors on the one hand, and economic productivity on the other, is at the center of the economic problem confronting advanced economies today. Charles Jonscher, an MIT economist, has in recent years developed an economic model of the U.S. economy which provides insight into the nature of the economic forces at work.[10] As Figure 1-6 illustrates, the Jonscher model divides the economy into two sectors: an information sector (containing the Commerce study's primary and secondary information sectors), and a production sector (including all physical production and material processing operations). The solid lines represent the output of the production sectors and the broken lines the output of the information sector. Moreover, Jonscher divides *output* in three ways: "part goes to final consumption, part is used as input to the same sector, and part is used as input to the other sector."[11] Jonscher has calculated the size of these flows for two years, 1947 and 1972.

In analyzing the major implications of his model, Jonscher identifies key trends in the information economy which today are in part confirmed by the more current, independent analysis provided by Stephen Roach, a senior economist at Morgan Stanley and Company, Inc.[12]

First, the Jonscher model illustrates that the information

[10] Charles Jonscher, "Information Resources and Economic Productivity," *Information Economics and Policy,* Vol. 1 (1983), pp. 13–35.

[11] *Ibid.,* p. 17.

[12] Stephen S. Roach, "The Industrialization of the Information Economy," Unpublished hearing testimony, U. S. Congress, House Committee on Banking, Finance and Urban Affairs, Subcommittee on Economic Stabilization, June 12, 1984. Subsequently revised and published as "The Information Economy Comes of Age," *Information Management Review,* Vol. 1, Issue 1, Summer 1986, pp. 9–18. See, also, "A Productivity Revolution in the Service Sector," *Business Week,* September 5, pp. 106–108.

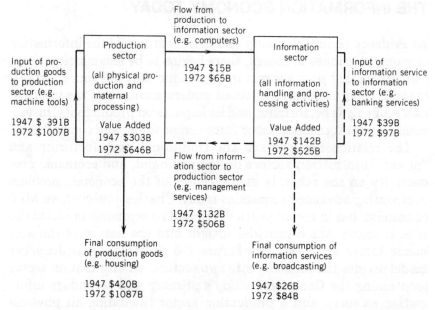

Figure 1–6. Schematic representation of the production and information sectors of the U.S. economy (in constant 1972 dollars). *Source:* see note 11.

sector has been growing at a much more rapid rate than the production sector: "The growth rate of the former has been almost double that of the latter; information sector value added increased by a factor of about 3.7 (in constant value dollars) between 1947 and 1972, while production sector value added grew by a factor of just over 2."[13] In Congressional testimony to the Committee on Banking, Finance and Urban Affairs of the U.S. House of Representatives, Stephen Roach has provided more recent confirmation of the relative performance of the information and "goods" sector (defined as Jonscher's production sector). As Figure 1-7 suggests, the share of output going to the goods sector has declined since the late 1960s to about 38 percent, while the information sector has filled the gaps: "Our projections suggest that this group of industries will generate close to two out of every three dollars of national output by 1985."[14] Moreover, Roach goes on to suggest

[13] *Jonscher,* "Information Resources," p. 17.
[14] Roach, "Industrialization," pp. 4, 14.

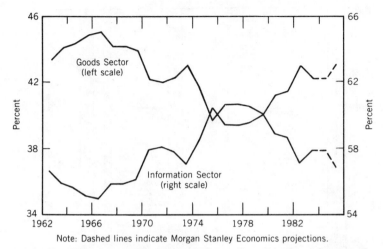

Note: Dashed lines indicate Morgan Stanley Economics projections.

Figure 1–7. The emergence of the information economy: Output shares in private nonform economy. Note: Dashed lines indicate Morgan Stanley Economics projections. *Source:* see note 14. Reprinted with permission of Aspen Systems Corporation. Copyright© 1984.

that "the information sector includes not only the fastest growing industries of the economy, but also a highly disproportionate share of the information workforce."[15]

A second implication that Jonscher draws from his model is that the output of the information sector is used primarily by industry rather than consumers: "Whereas final consumption of such information items as the media and printed matter had reached $84 billion by 1972, this figure is dwarfed by the $506 billion flow of information sector services required by the production sector."[16] The significance of this finding should not be underestimated. There continues to be a strong linkage between the rise of the information sector and the production sector. Indeed, the production sector is not displaced by the information sector as much as it is *transformed* by the products, services, and technologies underlying the information sector.

As Stephen Roach has indicated, the mix of employment and business fixed investments between the production and information

[15] *Ibid.,* p. 5.
[16] Jonscher, "Information Resources," p. 17.

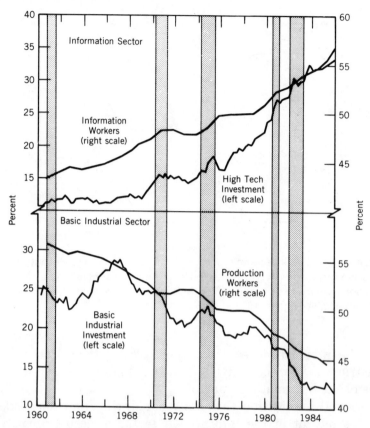

Figure 1–8. Structural Change and the information economy (investment and employment shares. Note: shaded areas indicate recessionary periods as designated by the National Bureau of Economic Research. Dashed lines indicate Morgan Stanley Economics projections. *Source:* see note 18. Reprinted with permission of Aspen Systems Corporation. Copyright© 1984.

sectors has shifted, and in so doing has contributed to the dramatic change in the nature of goods-producing rather than information work. In Figure 1-8, Roach illustrates the compositional trend in capital spending by mix in the workforce. The upper panel points out the rising share of the information workforce and that proportion of capital spending going into information technology: "From the Mid-Sixties through last year (1983), high-tech spending as a portion of total business fixed investment almost tripled—rising from about 12% to roughly a third. Similarly, over the same period, the employment share of information workers is estimated to have risen around 10 percentage points to about 55% of the nonfarm workforce."[17]

The lower panel paints the other side of the story. The decline in production workers has been accompanied by a decline in the basic industrial share of capital spending: "As a portion of total expenditures in plant and equipment, such outlays dropped to almost 12% in 1983—down almost two and a half times from the peak share of the late Sixties."[18] Moreover, in comparing the capital-labor ratio in production versus information work a similar picture emerges. In Figure 1-9, Roach again points out that, after peaking in the late 1960s, spending per production worker declined by about one-third through 1983. However, capital spending for information workers has risen relative to the increasing size of the workforce.[19] Thus, the dramatic shift in capital outlays reveals the significance of the information sector as both a source of economic growth and as a transforming force for the production sector as well.

What remains unclear in the mid-1980s concerning the linkage between economic production and the information economy, is the extent to which the rate of information-sector productivity will continue to rise in the face of slower advances in industrial productivity. The MIT economist Charles Jonscher suggests that while the proportion of information workers in the work force will peak at about 50 percent and possibly decline to 46 percent by the year 2000 (due in part to the application of information technology in the information sector), overall economic productivity will continue to rise with proportionally higher rates of productivity among information versus production workers. Jonscher attributes this optimistic forecast to four trends:

1. Continuing improvements in capabilities and cost-performance characteristics of information technology at the basic component and device level.

2. Improvements in capabilities and cost-performance characteristics of information technology at the system or application level.

[17] Roach, "Industrialization," p. 6.
[18] *Ibid.*, pp. 6–7.
[19] *Ibid.*, p. 15.

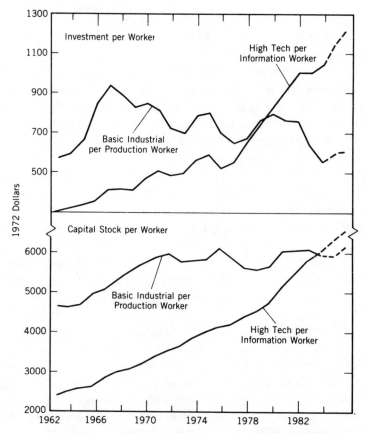

Figure 1–9.   Investment and Capital stock per worker: High technology versus basic industrial. Note: Investment and capital stock are expressed in constant 1972 dollars. Dashed lines indicate Morgan Stanley Economics projections. *Source:* see note 19. Reprinted with permission of Aspen Systems Corporation. Copyright© 1984.

3. Continual development of the telecommunications infrastructure.

4. Gradual reduction of institutional and social barriers to the introduction of information technology.[20]

[20] Charles Jonscher, "Information Resources and Economic Productivity," *Information Economics and Policy,* vol. 1 (1983), pp. 26–27.

Information's Impact on Business

If the information economy is a social and economic reality, then what is its impact on business? At the outset, it is clear that the information economy's impact on business will evolve over time and redefine our understanding of business management, competition, and productivity. While we have been living with the consequences of the information economy for many years, our understanding of these shifts in human events has lagged behind the reality.

Ironically, this delayed effect has been particularly acute in the United States in recent years, as compared to Japan and Western European nations. While American business in the 1960s was caught up in the heady industrial growth following the post-World War II era, and in the 1970s following the energy crisis and deep recession, other advanced economies were already assessing and planning their future in the information economy.

For example, in Japan, preliminary planning in moving that nation toward an information economy emerged as a national goal in the early 1960s and by the 1970s had been translated into a full-scale economic development strategy. Moreover, by the late 1960s, France, England, West Germany, and other European governments were beginning to study and assess their economic development strategies in the information economy, and the impacts such pronounced shifts in industrial priorities would have on business.

Even today, American business and political debates over industrial policy remain tied to traditional views of economic change. Many senior executives still remain skeptical or openly critical of the "fish and chips" economy. As the chairman of a large U.S. industrial corporation put it: "You can't build wealth creation on services and high tech and ship all our manufacturing, goods-producing capability off-shore." That and similar attitudes among corporate executives and senior managers betray some fundamental misunderstandings not only of the current state of the U.S. economy, but also of the terms and conditions under which the advanced economies of Japan and the Western European nations will compete with American business in the future.

Learning the Wrong Lesson

Business Week, Forbes, Fortune, and other leading magazines have called attention to the sweeping transformation of our economy, but too often characterize that transformation as traditional smokestack industries reeling from foreign competition able to apply high-technology comparative advantages better than we. Published statistics such as "200,000 auto workers or 20% of the industry's blue-collar work force on indefinite layoff," or "steel industry operating at only 42% of capacity," lead readers to write their congressmen with outraged cries for protectionism against unfair competition.

Some economists foresee mass joblessness with the only solution lying in stretching out vacations, shortening work hours, and sharing available jobs.

Educators and government bodies such as the National Commission on Excellence in Education note that only 20 percent of all 17-year olds can write a persuasive essay, and only 33 percent can solve a math problem requiring several steps. One U.S. Chamber of Commerce study found that 35 percent of companies surveyed had to provide remedial basic-skill training to new employees. AT&T alone spends $6 million each year to teach workers reading and math skills.

In short, policy makers in all fields, not just in economics, are forced into ill-considered conclusions and recommendations because they still view the economy in industrial terms. Moreover, they are still constrained by statistical calculations based on outmoded and obsolete classification approaches, as well as on invalid assumptions about the fundamental sources of wealth and capital formation.

The fact is that U.S. business continues to lose important sectors of the economy to international competition because senior managers have been slow to modify and rethink business strategy and management in an information versus industrial economy. Whether it is losing sectors of traditional markets such as television sets or autos to the Japanese, or being behind in adopting more productive manufacturing technology in steel or machine tools, U.S. business has largely chosen to interpret such losses in industrial economic terms, rather than to perceive these changes in the terms of doing business in an information economy. Seen in this light, the emergence of the information economy has had and will continue to have pronounced impacts on business management and strategy in the United States.

IMPACTS ON BUSINESS MANAGEMENT

First, there can be little question after 30 years of living in the information economy that information and knowledge are factors of production as authentic and as critical as capital and labor. While the contribution of information and ideas to productive behavior is no doubt difficult to define and measure, the linchpin of our market system is the strategic use of information. As Paul Hawken has suggested: "One of the great myths about economic behavior is that money is the language of the economy. The language of an economy is the information contained in manufacturing, products and services, money is only part of that information."[21]

Moreover, Hawken rightly points out that the Japanese emphasis on learning as an integral part of management has redefined how business success is measured in the information economy. This "requires more intelligence from everyone—management, labor, consumer, governments. Those who do not become learners again, regardless of age or rank, will find themselves at an increasing disadvantage as the information economy takes root."[22]

Transformation of Agriculture and Industry

A second impact that the information economy has on business revolves around the effects the new economy has on the agricultural and manufacturing sectors. The information economy does not supplant these sectors, but it does transform them. Just as the manufacturing economy industrialized agriculture during the nineteenth and twentieth centuries, the information economy is transforming manufacturing and agriculture through the use of automation, robots, computerized information services, and

[21] Paul Hawken, *The Next Economy* (New York: Holt, 1983), p. 79.
[22] *Ibid.*, p. 83.

communications networks. Thus, the demand for manufacturing and agriculture do not grow smaller; only the labor and material inputs are reduced and changed.

Through the skillful use of new "intellectual technology" such as more efficient planting practices on farms, better and more integrated factories, automated notebooks in the laboratory, combined with new uses of computers, robots, and computer numerical control devices, the productivity of research and development (R&D) in manufacturing and agriculture is changing in the information economy. Any argument that the industrial economy is in decline seriously misreads the nature of the transformations occurring.

Indeed, rather than wringing one's hands about the demise of the industrial economy, it is more appropriate to perceive that the information economy is leading to a more mature stage of agricultural and manufacturing development using new ideas and new technologies as critical factors of production.

Blurring Manufacturing and Services Lines

A third impact of the information economy on business is the blurring of the old boundaries between manufacturing and services. In the traditional view, services are merely an add-on to the manufacturing sector—they are by definition at least, "nonproductive." In the industrial economy, services either support the growth and survival of the manufacturing sector, or they are perceived as socially desirable but not economically essential. Thus, banks and financial services are important support services for the goods-producing sector, while McDonald's and Burger King's are perhaps nice to have for convenience but not essential to the survival of the economy. At the center of the economy and critical to its wealth-producing capacity is the goods-producing sector, around which ancillary services revolve.

What is commonly overlooked in this view is, first, the notion that the relationship between manufacturing and services is one of interdependence, *not* dependence. And, second, that the categories of service and manufacturing are not distinct and isolated domains, but represent two sides of a continuum:

"Certainly the economy is all of a piece. The distribution and general business services extend the manufacturing economy's reach, while the consumer and community services provide the social and human organization without which no economy can function. But the distinction between goods and services has become increasingly blurred. Many of the services—from transportation to television—can be provided only through the medium of goods, while the service content of goods production—from accounting and law to engineering and research—has been expanding steadily."[23]

Thus, contrary to the traditional view, in the information economy the growth of services helps support the growth of manufacturing and agriculture. As the economy evolves and becomes more complex, the need for new services and specialization in the division of labor continues to increase. Agricultural production migrates into food processing and distribution; manufacturing migrates into value-added services so that "a manufactured good becomes a service in package form."[24]

Blurring of Service Sector Internal Boundaries

A fourth impact of the information economy on business, which is related to the third, is that the boundaries between services also become blurred. In the industrial economy, the distinction between service sectors such as banking, investment, real estate, retailing, and insurance were clearly understood. Each domain had clear tasks in support of the goods-producing sector. Moreover, the lines between these services were written into law to assure the clarity of roles. Finally, the underlying technologies (largely manual and people-intensive) for delivering such services also contributed to a distinct set of work processes and service delivery modes in each industry. Bankers tended to money; brokerage houses tended to stocks and bonds; retailers tended to consumer goods; insurance companies to policies; and real estate firms to property transactions.

In the information economy, on the other hand, the artificial

---

[23] James Cook, "You mean we've been speaking prose all these years?" *Forbes* April 11, ("1983"), p. 143.

[24] *Ibid.,* p. 143.

walls between services begin to crumble as bankers, retailers, brokerage firms, realtors, and insurers conceive of their service as *information about* money, stocks, goods, houses, and the like. Moreover, as the technologies of computers and communications replace the paper-based work processes of the past, these changes put pressure on the laws and regulations separating the service domains as opportunities begin to arise for brokerage firms like Merrill Lynch to act like banks, for banks like Citicorp to act like investment firms and realtors, for retailers like Sears to integrate banking, investment, insurance, and realty services as a retail package for consumers. Moreover, even oil companies which deal in well-defined commodities begin to merge their fuel services with banking and retail services as the costs of opening full service gas stations on the corners of major intersections continue to rise.

As the information economy matures, the transforming technologies of computers and communications will continue to challenge our traditional definitions of specific services. Increasingly, the value-added aspects of services such as high quality information content and the effective delivery of that content at the point of cost-effective use will be the dominant criterion by which service domains are defined.

Entrepreneurial and Intrapreneurial Opportunities

A fifth impact closely related to the third and fourth is that with the boundaries between manufacturing and services blurring through the use of computer and communications technologies, the opportunities for entrepreneurism and intrapreneurism continue to increase. As the information economy matures, a premium is placed on ideas and strategic use of information for new business development, rather than on capital formation or cost displacement alone.

The entrepreneur, therefore, becomes the primary user of information resources and ideas for strategic advantage. As a premium is placed on innovative ideas, small businesses acquire an advantage in being flexible enough to evolve new products and services. Moreover, as such innovation proceeds, the role of small business as a source of employment continues to increase in significance, particularly in the service sector. For example, between 1980-1982, the U.S. Small Business Administration estimated that "the service industry continued to be the fastest growing job generator . . . accounting for about 52% (1.2 million jobs) of the total increase in new jobs, and small firms under 100 employees accounted for 89.6% of this growth."

Not to be left out, even large corporations in the information economy are providing opportunities for corporate entrepreneurs to test new ideas under conditions where "normal" corporate constraints on risk-taking and new investments in internal ideas are relaxed. Corporations as large as IBM are providing opportunities for entrepreneurism to flourish internally. The term "intrapreneur" has been coined to describe this internal entrepreneur.

Information Management a New Business Function

A sixth impact of the information economy on business administration comes in response to the phenomenal growth of the knowledge industries and the limited ability of individuals to absorb the information potentially available. In the information economy, a premium is placed on managing information and not just on automating information.

If corporate managers learned one lesson in the early phases of using computers, it was that the automation of information in and of itself is a mixed blessing that can be compared to the introduction of duplicating machines. Where the technical capability exists to copy anything and everything, the use of judgment in deciding what needs to be copied and why it needs to be copied becomes critical. Similarly, whether one discusses desktop computers or the use of large data processing centers, the same critical issues arise: The value and meaning of information can be lost in the proliferation of information services, if not well managed from the start.

Moreover, as information management grows in significance, it also influences management's definitions of competition and strategic advantage. Increasingly, the firm must employ new approaches to using its information resources, technologies, and people to define new markets or continue to profit in old ones. As this process advances, the firm evolves new ways of organizing itself to use information resources and new information technologies effectively and, in addition, begins to pay more attention to the management of its people, whose knowledge and experience represents a critical source of leverage for the firm. Thus, in the information economy, human resource management, financial resource management, and information resource management become closely linked as business managers pay increasing attention to ideas and information as sources of creativity, productivity, and profitability.

The remaining chapters of this book will serve to explore the specific effects of the information economy on business management, and will provide guidelines for successfully coping with the changing environment of business.

Next, in Chapter 2, we will discuss the impacts of the information processing industry as the source of the transforming technologies of computers and communications on business management. We will highlight the growing opportunities to develop new products and services provided by the information processing industry.

CHAPTER 2

THE INFORMATION PROCESSING INDUSTRY

In an agrarian economy, the transforming resource is capital; in an industrial economy, the transforming resource is energy; and in the information economy, the transforming resource is information. Its use and distribution influence the allocation of capital and labor. The tools that permit its efficient use—the silicon chips, the mainframe computers, and the telecommunications networks—become the engines of productivity improvement that both supplant and transform the tools of the industrial economy. Thus, those entrepreneurs and intelligent firms that provide for the efficient use, distribution, or processing of information in the new economy will emerge as the new centers of wealth creation and innovation.

Over the past 30 years of the information economy's evolution, the industry has grown and redefined itself as new technologies have come on the scene and old technologies have been displaced or transformed. In the 1960s, the impact of this industry on business centered on the development of large, mainframe computers and the significant investments in money and technical know-how required to operate these machines. In the 1970s, focus was on the convergence of computer and communication technologies, and the vast opportunities created for worldwide and local transmission of information among all types of computers, independent of time or place. In the 1980s, the impact of this industry is moving from an exclusive concern with processing and communications facilities to a focus on end-user software and information content.

In short, the era of pushing iron is coming to a close. The information processing industry is evolving into a software-based industry emphasizing the intelligent use of information assets and resources in business and consumer markets.

In this chapter, we will identify the industry's major components and discuss its impacts on every business. Like the auto, steel, and oil businesses in the industrial economy, the information processing industry is evolving as *the* basic or core industry of the information economy. Moreover, as it does so, this industry serves as a major source of productivity improvement and as the basis for the development of new kinds of goods and services. Indeed, in many ways, as the information processing industry develops, the best is yet to come; its major impacts on the economy and business have not yet been felt.

In providing an overview of the information processing industry and its major impacts on business, we will emphasize the following points in this chapter:

1. The information processing industry is the engine of the information economy.

2. No manufacturing or service business today can afford to ignore how trends in the information processing industry are affecting their traditional business.

3. The major impacts of this industry in the information economy, both nationally and internationally, have yet to be felt—since the industry is just beginning to come of age.

4. The industry is responsible for the creation of new kinds of goods and services throughout the economy that never existed before. Thus, it is a major source of innovation and entrepreneurial opportunity for the nation.

5. The transformation of the industry from primarily a hardware-driven to a software- and information-driven industry is just beginning to take hold. This will stimulate significant expansion and extension of its boundaries into traditional sectors.

6. If the industry is to continue to grow at or near a rate of 20 percent per year, four major markets will need to be penetrated significantly over the next 10 years: the office in large and medium-sized companies, small business, the factory, and the consumer market.

7. The information processing industry is changing both the external business environments of service and manufacturing businesses, as well as their internal business functions such as marketing, advertising, sales, finance, and production.

ENGINE OF THE INFORMATION ECONOMY

Before discussing the impacts of the information processing industry on business, it is necessary to provide a map for understanding the ever-changing landscape of this vast industry. (See Figure 2-1.) There are, of course, many ways of classifying this industry: by vendors and products; by specific applications; or by specific technologies. Here, however, we will take a simpler and more direct approach by providing an overview of the industry classified by its four major subsectors: (1) the computer industry, (2) the communications industry, (3) the information industry, and (4) the knowledge industry.[1]

To use a common analogy, the communications industry can be viewed as the transportation infrastructure of highways, roads, and bridges upon which information traffic travels; the computer

[1] The information processing industry classification portion of this chapter relied heavily on the innovative work of Sena H. Black in *The Information Economy and the Future of South Carolina* (Columbia, S.C.: Institute of Information Management, Technology and Policy, University of South Carolina, July, 1983). All estimates for growth rates of market sectors and values of market sectors have been updated based on 1983 as the baseline year.

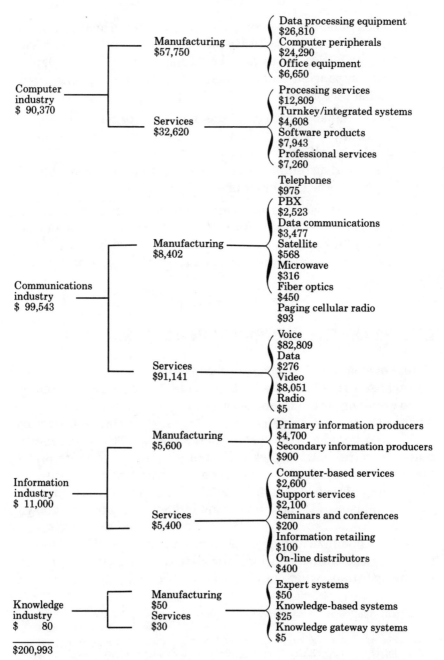

$200,993

Figure 2–1. The information processing industry; overview. ($000,000)

industry can be viewed as providing the traffic regulation function which facilitates the use by and processing of information vehicles; and the information and knowledge industries can be viewed as the traffic messages that flow over the communications networks and are processed in mainframe, mini, and personal computers.

In each case, we describe current trends in the traditional manufacturing and service sectors, as well as identify directions in which each sector is influencing the development of the other, interacting with the other, and helping to expand the boundaries and penetration of the information processing industry in the economy. Overall, in 1983, revenues in the information processing industry were estimated at $200 billion and growing at about a 20 percent compound annual rate, which means that revenues for the industry could top $1 trillion by the early 1990s. This means that 1983 revenues for the information processing industry were nearly three times larger than those of the steel industry, and almost twice as large as those of the automobile industry. Only the oil companies with 1983 revenues of $500 billion are larger. Moreover, by 1990, it is likely that the information processing industry will surpass the oil companies' prominent position and become the world's leading business. Before proceeding to discuss the industry's impact on business, let's look at the dynamics of each major information processing sector.

THE COMPUTER INDUSTRY

More than 30 years ago, few could have predicted that the computer industry would evolve as a $90 billion sector of the information processing industry in 1983, and that just one company, IBM, would receive $40 billion in revenues and project its growth so that by the mid-1990s it would be receiving around $180 billion in revenues. Moreover, the computer industry has provided the impetus for significant changes in the communications industry and the opportunity for tremendous growth in the information industry sector as well.

In terms of structure, the computer industry can be divided into two major segments: the computer equipment sector (manufacturing), and the computer service sector (services).

Manufacturing Sector

This segment consists of three types of markets: companies manufacturing data processing equipment ranging in size from supercomputers all the way down to microcomputers, companies involved primarily in the production of peripheral or ancillary equipment (e.g., printers), and the office equipment market.

Data Processing Equipment

At one end of a continuum, the mainframe computer market is by far the largest sector for manufacturers of different sizes of computers: It accounted for 55 percent of all computer sales in 1983. Its projected growth rate of 5 percent is the lowest in the entire industry, however. In part, this drop is due to past growth which has resulted in an extensive installed base. It is also testimony to a broad trend toward distributed processing, and the intense competition from minicomputers with increasing power in declining unit cost. Moreover, sluggish growth for the mainframe market will continue despite the fact that mainframes will retain an important role in major organizations and government agencies which have very large volume routine transaction applications such as cost accounting, inventory control, payrolls, and so forth.

At the other end of the continuum is the market for personal and desktop computers. For a specialty market that did not really exist until the late 1970s, growth has been tremendous. In 1983, revenues for personal computers were $8 billion and growing significantly more than the dollar value of shipments for the typewriters and word processors that PCs are destined to replace. In addition, the market for floppy disk drives was $400 million in 1983 and the market for the actual floppy disks was $200 million in 1983 and expected to be $1 billion by 1988.

Peripheral Equipment

The production of auxiliary hardware components that support or enhance the capabilities of the computer's central processing unit includes input devices such as keyboards, output devices such as printers, and storage mechanisms such as disk drives and diskettes.

As an industry, peripheral equipment manufacturing needs to be distinguished from the manufacture of mainframe computer equipment because the companies included in this sector are not always identical to the manufacturers of the computers themselves. Since the peripheral industry manufactures enhanced components, it is heavily influenced by trends in the mainstream computer market. As an industry, it has grown at a very rapid rate over the past few years.

There are three main areas where the growth should be especially strong. One area is the demand for disk storage systems, particularly for small (8″ and 5¼″) hard disks (Winchester disks), which is primarily propelled by the growth of the desktop and personal computer market. The floppy disk market will also be very strong, particularly as technology enables the storage of greater amounts of information on increasingly smaller disks such as the emerging microfloppy market (3″ to 4″ sizes).

A second area of market strength is that of input and output peripherals, particularly the production of printers for desktop and personal computers. Finally, the third area is the explosive growth in color graphics. But unlike the first two areas, which are dependent primarily on the desktop computer market, this third sector will be tied to the increasing use of computer-assisted design and computer-assisted manufacturing (CAD/CAM) in a variety of contexts. The estimates for the graphics terminal market range from 25 to 40 percent compounded annual growth with more than one-third of this market (30 to 35 percent) dedicated to CAD/CAM applications.

Office Equipment

Although the data processing and office automation industries are generally merging, there are sufficient differences between them to consider the manufacturers of office equipment as a separate category. The major components of this industry are word processors, electronic typewriters, and plain paper copiers. In 1983, revenues for these three sectors totaled $6.5 billion.

The fastest growing sector is the electronic typewriter market, which represents the transition between traditional office equipment such as typewriters and state-of-the-art technologies such as multifunctional workstations that process text as well as enhance information management functions. Over the next five years, this market is expected to remain strong.

Computer Services Sector

Although the computer hardware industry tends to be better defined and understood than the computer services industry, there are more than 6000 companies currently in the computer services market, and future prospects for this industry are excellent. In 1983, the industry's total revenues exceeded $32.6 billion.

In this highly specialized industry, the successful strategy appears to be one of exploiting innovative niches by beginning with a specific focus and then expanding the range of services offered. The overall industry classification represents the following four types of companies with concentrations in unique services.

Computer Processing Services

In this marketplace, firms purchase or lease and maintain their own computers, using them to provide data processing services to their clients. Two major types of services are offered: time-sharing (customers use the firm's computer for a fee), and facilities management (firm provides support services for the management of a data processing operation). The primary market for this sector is that of functioning as a service bureau for data processing needs.

In 1980, there were almost 2000 firms in this market. Traditionally, this has been the largest of all the computer service sectors: in 1981, it constituted about 57 percent of the total computer services market. However, due primarily to the advent of distributed data processing (whereby computing power tends to be dispersed to users within an organization), this sector is slowly declining. In 1986, it is estimated that this sector will constitute about 40 percent of the total computer services industry.

Turnkey or Integrated Systems Services

This complete package normally consists of an integrated computer system which includes hardware, custom software, professional assistance, and maintenance services. Three different types of companies exist in this industry sector: turnkey or integrated systems vendors, who act as brokers buying original equipment from manufacturers and repackaging systems and software together to meet specific client needs; hardware manufacturers, who expand their services to include software and other support facilities; and computer processing companies, which expand into this market.

The primary markets for this industry are computer-aided design and manufacturing and information processing systems for small and medium-size businesses. A relatively new market, this sector is expected to grow rapidly at an estimated annual rate of 32 percent.

Software Products

Although not the largest sector in terms of current market share, the software products industry promises to be the fastest growing of all the computer services in the next five years. The estimates vary widely in terms of annual growth rates, ranging from 30 to 45 percent. One way to understand the growth of this market is in terms of systems versus applications software. While demand for applications software will grow rapidly (27 percent), it is the systems software end of the industry which will lead the market with a growth rate of 30 percent.

There are almost 5000 companies operating in this marketplace, ranging from industry giants to small software companies. Those that operate primarily as software developers (as opposed to software firms that derive only part of their revenues from software products) tend to be medium- to small-sized firms.

In particular, it is the applications software market targeted to particular user industries and to the smaller microcomputers, that offers the best prospects for small firms and new entrants. The applications software market is expected to grow from $800 million in 1980 to more than $3 billion in 1986. No one vendor commands more than 2 percent of this market.

Professional Services

Firms in this sector are primarily involved in three types of products: custom computer systems and programming; data processing and management support; and a variety of consulting services ranging from management assistance to education and training. The primary users of these services are the banking and finance industries. As a whole, the professional service sector accounted for 23 percent of the total computer service market in 1981. In 1986, it is projected to account for over a third of that market. Estimates of annual growth rates vary widely, however, ranging from 17 to 30 percent.

This particular industry has several primary characteristics. First, this market is populated by a large number of individual and independent contractors. The average annual revenue of the approximately 2000 firms in this sector is $250,000. Second, this sector tends to be localized since it depends upon physical proximity to clients. Third, as an industry it is the most labor-intensive of all the computer services. And finally, because of high labor costs, shortage of programmers, and the increasing availability of standard off-the-shelf software packages, this sector is expected to show uneven rates of growth.

THE COMMUNICATIONS INDUSTRY

This industry has been undergoing rapid change in recent years. Like the computer industry, it is characterized by steadily declining prices and significantly improved software capabilities. However, the main variable in the communications industry has been the deregulation of the industry and the breakup of AT&T. The result is that companies have entered the marketplace not only as common carriers on long distance routes, but also as manufacturers and retailers of telephone equipment that interconnects with the local service offered by the seven Bell operating companies.

If the distinction between goods and services is less than clear for the computer industry, it is even more complex for the communications industry. In part, this is because telecommunications has been traditionally understood as a service industry. Moreover, value-added or innovative services are now emerging as an adjunct to the development of new communications technologies. However, even though the distinction between manufacturing and services is sometimes blurred, we shall first discuss the manufacturing component of the industry, and then consider the service component in order to sketch this changing marketplace.

Manufacturing Component

For purposes of discussion, we can divide this field into three major components: voice communications, data communications, and the "newer" technologies such as satellites and cellular radio.

Voice Communications Hardware

The manufacture of voice communications equipment is the dominant sector of this industry. Telephone instruments and private branch exchanges (PBX), which are centralized switching mechanisms for business organizations with the need for a large number of phones, have been dominated traditionally by AT&T as a regulated utility. However, with federal deregulation and AT&T's divestiture, this industry is facing increased competition, particularly from other industry giants. Furthermore, as an illustration of the convergence between computer and communications firms, IBM has entered this industry.

The major trends in the voice hardware industry are increased competition by major vendors, technological advances in terms of enhanced features such as call forwarding, automatic dialing, and voice messaging, and projections of vigorous growth.

Data Communications Hardware

This industry produces a diversity of hardware components to enhance the efficiency of data communications. When compared to voice communications, this sector is miniscule. The projected growth rates are higher, however. One conservative estimate is an annual compound growth rate of 25 percent. IBM dominates the production of front-end processors and AT&T dominates the modem market. The network/node controller and multiplexor markets, however, offer considerable scope for smaller businesses and independent firms. In many respects, these two sectors are similar to the computer peripherals market. Both are characterized by rapid growth, with good prospects for medium to small businesses which concentrate on particular market niches.

Other Technologies

The use of satellite communications is rapidly changing. Until now, the primary use was to deliver video entertainment signals to cable operators and individual homes. However, more complex applications have recently emerged, particularly with the transmission of integrated voice, video, facsimile, and data signals for business networks.

The major users of satellite communications are the military and government. Defense and government contractors are also expected to be the major clients for microwave communications equipment. Generally, the demand is for very advanced communications as well as for integrated communications systems that combine voice, data, video, and radio signals.

The fiber optics industry is still an emerging one. However, it is anticipated that technological advances in this field will be a major force in replacing traditional voice and data lines for short-distance routes. All three of these sectors, (satellites, microwave, and fiber optics) are dominated by established companies. Consequently, there is little opportunity for new entrants, let alone smaller businesses, in this marketplace.

In contrast, the paging and cellular mobile radio industry may offer more opportunities for new entrants. Like telecommunications, the world of radio common carriers has been changing because of two forces: new paging frequencies approved for use by the FCC, and the increased price-performance ratio of new paging products. As a result, paging services alone are expected to grow at a rate of 25 percent annually. These products, in conjunction with the development of cellular radio (whereby calls can be made from portable telephones to virtually any other telephone worldwide), have the potential of transforming the "electronic office" into the "mobile communications office." In this emerging industry, it is estimated that 40 percent of the growth will be dedicated to manufacturing, 40 percent to enhanced services, and 20 percent to retail distribution services, including installation and maintenance.

Service Component

Just as the traditionally separate telecommunications and computer companies are beginning to enter each other's territories, so too are the formerly distinct markets of telephone, data, video, and radio communications companies coalescing in terms of services offered. Three major trends can be identified when classifying this industry. First, telecommunications and radio common carriers, both of which are regulated by the Federal Communications Commission, have been subject to less restrictive laws in recent years. As a result, competition has been increasing. Second, with changes in technology and with increases in competition, "enhanced or value-added services" will be the major growth area of the future. These services include access to commercial databases, videotex, computer conferencing, and teleshopping. And finally, major portions of this industry, particularly enhanced services offered by common carriers, are dominated by established industry participants.

This service industry can also be analyzed in terms of two distinct types of services: wholesale communications services usually offered by common carriers; and retail distribution, installation, and maintenance services. The former is dominated by established telecommunications and other companies. The latter lends itself to competition from smaller businesses, however. In the past, retail services had not been a significant component of an independent industry, primarily because AT&T as a utility encompassed retail and maintenance costs. With the development of an "interconnect" industry and the increased application of innovative technologies (such as teleconferencing), the retail service component will grow rapidly, with significant possibilities for new businesses.

THE INFORMATION INDUSTRY

The third major component of the information processing industry is the information industry, which is based on the idea that information (that is, the message or intellectual content) is itself a valuable commodity. While it is true that information has always been the basis of numerous industries in the past, such as the printing and publishing trades, it is also evident that the production, transmission, and use of information has been radically transformed by the evolution of the information economy, and by the migration of more and more ink-print products and services from paper media to electronic data.

Whereas in the late 1970s the information industry was a loosely organized group of large and small firms employing many different types of technologies, by 1983 the industry was composed of 1153 U.S. firms. Its revenues of more than $11 billion were second only to those of newspaper publishing and surpassed telecommunication broadcasting and book and periodical publishing. Moreover, growing at about 16 percent per year, the information industry will surpass the newspaper industry by the mid-1990s in total revenues. By 1990, the firm of Paine Webber Mitchell Hutchins Inc. expects that the information industry's revenues will be about $46 billion worldwide, with $36 billion in U.S. revenues.

While the products of the information industry are quite diverse, a 1982 survey by the Information Industry Association indicated that 51 percent of the U.S. information business still consisted of print products. The survey estimated further that about 85 percent of the print products were primary or original products, while 15 percent were indexes, abstracts, and directories (secondary information). However, in terms of growth, secondary print products at 16 percent were expanding at a significantly higher rate than primary print products at 10 percent.[2]

In contrast to both these print information categories, computer-based services in 1982 were growing at 25 percent per year. In this category, about 60 percent of the products were secondary, while 40 percent were primary information products—indicating healthy opportunities for the creation of innovative information products using new information technologies.

In terms of subject categories, the information business is dominated by firms that specialize in market research like A. C. Nielsen, economics like Data Resources Inc., and credit-check information

[2] Information Industry Association, *The Outlook for the Information Industry,* volume II of *The Business of Information 1983* (Washington, D.C.: Information Industry Association, 1983), p. 6.

like Equifax and Dun & Bradstreet. Machine-readable databases such as those of Dow Jones News/Retrieval, CompuServe Information Service, and The Source offer a variety of services, including financial information, banking, bulletin boards, consumer tips, electronic shopping, and entertainment. The primary growth market for these services are users of micro- or personal computers.

Moreover, although consumer-oriented information services are expected to expand with the convergence of personal computers and videotex services, the most rapid growth will be in business-oriented information services targeted for specialized groups of users.

THE KNOWLEDGE INDUSTRY

This fourth industry traces its emergence to the multidisciplinary fields of artificial intelligence, expert systems, knowledge-based systems, knowledge gateway systems, and decision support systems. Since this industry is still so new, few reliable quantitative indications are available; our discussion, therefore, is mainly descriptive.

According to the Information Industry Association, knowledge resources will be the single most important source of dynamic change and innovation in our society by the end of the twentieth century. Knowledge centers will serve a critical role in breaking down barriers of cost, of information literacy, and of user confusion about how to identify, access, and effectively use these resources.

In the business world the history of knowledge management begins with the corporate library, which was established largely as a relatively static repository or archive of books, periodicals, technical literature, and similar materials. Then in the late 1970s the information center idea came along; it had become apparent that companies needed a specially equipped place for demonstrating new technologies and training employees on end-user hardware and software. Existing company in-house training facilities were simply inadequate to do the job.

Now we are entering the third stage of in-house information facilities development as companies begin to marry their finding aids to their traditional document and literature resources, using the PC as an access tool. The new resulting facility is often called the information resource center or knowledge center. The problem thus far, however, is that the tools ('primarily software'), needed to help end-users identify, access, and use all of the internal and external data, document, and literature resources efficiently and effectively are just beginning to move from the drawing boards into the marketplace.

Artificial Intelligence (AI)

In 1677 Gottfried Wilhelm Leibniz put forward the beginning of an idea for a "calculus of reasoning." He dreamed of such a calculus for reasoning processes in 211 fields of inquiry including grammar, mathematics, physiology, politics, theology, philosophy, and all the arts of discovery.

Only in the last decade has a gathering momentum of applied research turned Leibniz' dreams into practical reality through the development of highly complex and sophisticated computer programs that make inferences from knowledge bases.

Clark Holloway defines artificial intelligence as a nonhuman "black box" which possesses the facilities of knowing, reasoning, and understanding.[3] A robot is any machine that performs jobs previously done by a human, is self-operating, and is "intelligent," that is, contains a logic function in the form of a microprocessor.

According to Holloway, the first American robot was made in 1961, the first Japanese robot in 1969, and the first Russian one in 1971. While Japan's definition of a robot is broader than that in the United States, even by the U.S. definition there were 11,250 robots in Japan at the end of 1980 as compared with our 4370. Forecasted U.S. growth is as high as 40,000 by 1990, however.

Expert Systems (ES)

Here the focus shifts from making a "smart machine" such as a robot (the domain of AI), to the information system. What the

---

[3] Clark Holloway, "Strategic Management and Artificial Intelligence," *Long Range Planning,* October 16, 1983, p. 89.

expert system field does is apply the more advanced and sophisticated knowledge learned from AI theory to the more difficult data organizing, indexing, and searching challenges inherent in these complex domains of knowledge. Contributions to ES from AI include: the use of predicate calculus as a basis for the so-called "inference engine" which is at the heart of an ES; knowledge representation languages; interactive classification of conceptual knowledge; semantic simplification; and heuristic searching. Expert systems are good at interpretation, prediction, diagnosis, design, planning, monitoring, debugging, repair, instruction, and control.

In the near term, AI-based systems in the information industry will most likely be used in information classification systems, intelligent data base front ends, and information analysis support. In the long term, we will see speech recognition, story builders, and natural language analysis.

Knowledge-Based Systems (KBS)

In this instance there is no "knowledge base," as such. Instead, there are masses and masses of data. But data alone is not knowledge. Knowledge implies a set of rules that govern how information should be used to convey meaning. In short, not all ES systems are knowledge-based. Conversely, not all KBSs are expert systems.

When an entire domain of knowledge is confronted by the KBS designer (knowledge engineer), the problem rather quickly breaks itself down into two parts. The first part deals with the logical characterization of the particular domain of knowledge (e.g., medicine, geology). The second concerns itself with developing a set of rules or inferences by which sense or meaning can be extracted by users out of the domain of knowledge.

Knowledge Gateway System (KGS)

Just as ESs and KBSs attack a specific domain of knowledge and "cut it down to size" so that inexpert users can access and use the information, the KGS, a special kind of ES and KBS, takes as its domain of knowledge the learning and information finding-seeking-using process itself. Recognizing that no two users are alike and therefore never go about solving their information problem in precisely the same way, the KGS challenge is to produce knowledge industry products and services that take into account the vagaries of the learning process and the information discovery process.

Decision Support Systems (DSS)

This field is the latest iteration of management information systems development. The basic idea is to produce software for middle-level managers faced with semistructured tasks. Thus, the line becomes fuzzy in trying to decide whether Visicalc, for example, is a DSS or just "smart software." Presumably DSS devotees would see this system going a step further than Visicalc, dBase III, and Lotus 1,2,3. Years ago when MIS theorists first talked about what the MIS was supposed to do, they said many of the same things DSS theorists are saying today. The difference, however, is that we now have far more powerful hardware and software to help make these promises closer to a reality.

THE INDUSTRY'S IMPACT ON BUSINESS

If the information processing industry is emerging as the leading or basic industry of the information economy, then what are its impacts on business? In developing a response to this critical question, two pitfalls must be avoided.

First, it is clear that the industry's impact on specific businesses and markets will vary: some businesses and industries will prosper, others will survive with mediocre performance, and some will not be profitable at all. At the level of the individual firm, many external and internal factors will influence the firm's capacity to be productive and profitable. The competitive strategy the firm adopts, the quality of its management and workers, and its ability to assimilate and use the services and products of the information processing industry will, as we will point out in subsequent chapters, determine its ability to succeed in the information economy.

Second, the evolution of the information processing industry will not be determined by market or technological forces alone, but by the interplay of economic, political, cultural, and social forces on the services and products of this industry. Therefore, it would be foolhardy to try to forecast the long-term development of the industry by extrapolating entirely from current trends. Linear extrapolations and projections will do little good in an industry as dynamic, innovative, and complex as the information processing industry. Assessing this emerging industry's long-term impacts on business is a little like it would have been to assess the long-term future of the auto and trucking industry in the 1920s. Thus, our analysis will err on the side of being conservative.

Our view is that business will try to assimilate the services and products of the information processing industry gradually. Businesses will seek to avoid high-risk ventures as well as ventures that require massive capital investments up-front with no clear prospect of profitable returns within three to five years. Moreover, a company's existing investment in people and information technologies will usually make radical shifts in business strategies and technologies impossible.

Nevertheless, at the aggregate level, several major impacts of the information processing industry on business in the information economy are discernible. As a group, these impacts define the *context* in which businesses will have to live.

Scaling Down Productivity

The first impact of the information processing industry on business has to do with a profound shift that is occurring in the definition of productivity. In the industrial economy, large profits are made by applying vast amounts of capital to the production of mass physical goods. The operative definition of productivity in this economy is "the bigger, the better." Thus, in their productive activities, the lead industries of this economy such as autos, steel, and textiles reflect a clear bias toward scaling up their mass-produced products. The evolution of the automobile in terms of size, fuel consumption, and cosmetics, particularly in the 1950s and 1960s, provides one of the clearest examples of this phenomenon.

In the information economy, on the other hand, the operative definition of productivity involves scaling down. The watch words of productive activity in this economy are "the smaller and cheaper, the better," or "less is more." Moreover, the basic technologies which drive change in the information processing industry reflect this redefinition of productivity. Some 36 years ago, the first really powerful computer (ENIAC) cost $3 million, contained 18,000 constantly overheating vacuum tubes, and filled a large room. Today, the processing capacity of ENIAC can be put into a single integrated chip that costs about $30. Furthermore, the direction of the semiconductor industry in developing logic chips that pack 10,000 circuits on a chip, or memory chips that contain 256 thousand bytes of memory, or microprocessors that process 32 bits of data at one time, provide illustrations of the new definition of productivity at work. Producing more with less is given new meaning by the information processing industry.

In addition, not only do the products of this industry exhibit the imperative to scale down, but the raw materials going into these products—light-weight, more sophisticated plastics and metals—displace the need for vast amounts of heavy steel, copper, lead and zinc, which are some of the basic materials in demand in the industrial economy. Thus, in a certain sense, the information processing industry is the nemesis of the traditional materials industry. For example, consider the technology of fiber optics—hair-thin glass fibers having the capacity to process data and voice signals at the speed of light—which is replacing the technology of twisted-pair, coaxial, and heavy copper cabling in the telecommunications industry.

Finally, as the downsizing trend continues in the basic technologies underlying the information processing industry (e.g., semiconductors, fiber optics, and lasers), the value-added products and services based on these technologies also exhibit this scaling down effect. Calculators that once cost hundreds of dollars cost just a few dollars today. Personal computers that cost several thousand dollars in the early 1980s will cost a few hundred dollars by the late 1980s.

In addition, as computer technology continues to be embedded in production processes ("through the use of computer-assisted design and computer-assisted manufacturing"), and in the end products themselves ("the cars, appliances, and other electromechanical devices"), the imperative of the cheaper, the smaller, the better continues to ripple through emerging and traditional industries. Whether a company is producing robots or television sets the imperatives are the same: they must manufacture the product more cheaply using the least possible amounts of the required materials and energy, and improve the product's performance constantly.

Blurring Industry Boundaries

The second impact of the information processing industry on business concerns the tendency of this industry's boundaries to expand as its products and services are used in more innovative and creative ways. As we noted in Chapter 1, the growth of the information processing business has closely mirrored the evolution of our economy from an agricultural to industrial, and now to an information economy. However, what we did not indicate then is that as the information economy matures, the boundaries of the information processing business will continue to expand.

Two major reasons serve to account for this expansion. The first reason is that technologies that were previously considered quite separate and distinct are converging. As we noted earlier not only are computers embedded in the communications networks of the economy but, more importantly, the technologies of communications (e.g., satellites, facsimile, telephones), are increasingly being used to "digitize" more and more voice, data, video, and even radio communications.

In the 1980s, the convergence of technologies has continued; including the integration of video and broadcast technologies with computers and communication technologies. Video discs, audio discs, videotex, and teletext represent the first wave of products that merge computers with video technology to produce stand-alone products, new graphic services (such as the production technologies that helped George Lucas produce "Star Wars"), and new ventures to merge personal computers and video discs to produce the technology package to automate the Sears catalog or to allow consumers to shop at home.

A second, and perhaps in the long run, more compelling reason for the expanding boundaries of the information processing industry is the common denominator—information. As the tools and transmission facilities of the information processing industry continue to interact, the distribution of information in its many forms—electronic and manual—provides increasing opportunities to create, package, and disseminate information through multiple and diverse media.

The key to these expanding services is the creative repackaging of the intellectual *content* of information. As more and more people are involved in knowledge work, the quantity and variety of information continue to expand and interact with the proliferation of new media to distribute information. Thus, the information processing industry continues to evolve.

Paul G. Zurkowski, the President of the Information Industry Association, has termed this interaction between information content and media the "info-structure" which he and Larry Day, Vice-President of Business International Corporation, have "mapped" into eight industry segments: content services, content packages, facilitation services, information technologies, integrating technologies, communications technologies, communications channels, and broadcast channels. For Zurkowski and Day, the info-structure denotes "the myriad elements necessary to support the sophisticated information handling capability that distinguishes the United States economy, enhances its productivity, and challenges our available human talent to be all that it can be."[4]

In less sweeping terms, as more and more businesses begin to treat information as a strategic resource, the boundaries between being in the information business and being in a service business begin to blur. Moreover, even in the goods producing sector the effective marketing of goods comes to depend on the appropriateness of the information used to advertise, market, service, and maintain the goods.

As increasing emphasis is placed on the quality of goods, the information content surrounding their production, marketing, and

---

[4] Paul G. Zurkowski, *Integrating America's Info-structure* (Washington, D.C.: Information Industry Association, 1983), p. 1 (Reprint).

use becomes a significant competitive advantage. In turn, more and more businesses in the information economy can be expected to perceive themselves as being at least indirectly if not directly part of the information processing business.

Producing New Goods and Services

The third impact of the information processing industry on business is that it has significant multiplier effect on the rest of business by generating new products whose range of potential uses are vast, as well as by stimulating existing businesses to use these goods in new ways to deliver their services or to fabricate their products.

The clearest example of this multiplier effect is in the area of the personal computer. Like TVs in the 1950s and 1960s, the PC has in less than a decade gone from a hobbyist gadget to a major business tool and an emerging mass consumer product. Moreover, unlike the TV, the PC's penetration of the U.S. market will take half as long, that is, 10 years versus the TV's 20. Moreover, the emergence of desktop and portable computers has in turn caused a proliferation of new software companies that write programs for the PC, and has also offered whole new opportunities for office furniture manufacturers to design new chairs, desks, and other accessories for the PC market.

Another example of the information processing industry's capacity to stimulate new services has to do with the proliferation of cash management accounts in the financial services market. Underlying the ability to offer consumers a high quality integrated financial service personalized to their need to retain accurate, timely records on numerous transactions, is use of on-line, interactive computerized networks between customer offices and regional or national service centers.

The ability of Merrill Lynch and other brokerage houses to offer such comprehensive, yet personalized service for individuals requires a nationwide network of communication facilities, data centers, and linkages with stock exchanges, credit card vendors, and banks. Thus, the information processing industry strongly influences through its technologies and services the opportunity to offer competitive products and services in other industries.

A third example of the industry's impact on innovative business products concerns the emergence of videodiscs. Originally designed to provide alternative media in consumer markets to video cassettes, these new products have been integrated with personal computers. That in turn has led to the growth of the computer-assisted instruction opportunities where full-motion video is coupled with the interactive processing capabilities of desktop or portable computer. Today, medical training packages are being sold as turnkey units which provide a PC, videodisc player, and the necessary software and information content in an integrated mode. Thus, while not all new technologies are successful in their original intended markets, they may find new uses in specific market niches which have yet to be discovered.

Offering Entrepreneurial Opportunities

The fourth impact of the information processing industry on business is closely related to the third. Despite the fact that computers are more than 30 years old and phones and other technologies are much older, the information processing industry as a whole is still in its infancy. Many of the most dynamic sectors of the industry are less than 10 years old, while others are still on the drawing boards or in experimental stages.

As we noted earlier, the PC market, the audio disc-video disc market, the fiber optic and laser markets, to name a few, are all products of the mid-1970s. In addition, the full effects of electronic banking, point-of-sale terminals, smart cards, and videotex services have yet to be felt in the mid-1980s. Finally, the physical limits which govern how many circuits can be placed on a silicon chip have not yet been reached, and may not be reached until the year 2000. In other words, the information processing industry offers tremendous entrepreneurial opportunities for the foreseeable future. The size of the pie in this industry is continuing to expand and thus the opportunities for risk-taking are as well.

Increasing International Character

Related to the information processing industry's youth is the fifth impact of this industry, which is its increasing international character, as the industry continues to penetrate foreign markets, and also as it grows as a proportion of international trade. Although the U.S. market remains by far the largest and most dynamic, the industry's impacts on international business are pronounced.

For example, as a market for information processing services and products, Western Europe is second in size only to the United States. The information processing industry receives a lot of attention in Europe because a major share of each country's market is already held by U.S. companies, particularly IBM, while Japanese companies threaten to capture most of the rest. National interest has produced national plans to assist the information processing business within individual nations. Some have openly promoted the importance of the information processing industry to business growth and productivity within their countries, and have raised the stakes involved in international trade.

Moreover, the Japanese have evolved a major strategy to penetrate the information processing industry in the United States and Europe, and have been met with aggressive counter-actions by U.S.-based vendors to penetrate the Japanese market. In addition, American, Japanese, and Western European vendors have targeted the developing world nations and the rich Middle Eastern states (and their business and government markets), as major avenues of potential growth.

Thus, as the information processing industry has become more worldwide in marketing its services and products, the value of these goods and services has begun to occupy a particularly critical role in the balance of payments. In the United States for example, the information processing industry is second only to farm products as a major source of international trade and export revenue.

Expanding Business Markets

The sixth impact of the information processing industry focuses on the major business markets in which the industry will need to target its marketing strategies in the years ahead to sustain an average growth rate of 20 percent. For example, a popular subject among industry watchers is the question of just how IBM can sustain a 20 percent annual rate of growth over the next 10 years and move from being a $40 billion to a $180 billion per year firm in the 1990s. If IBM is to accomplish this rather Herculean feat, it will have to penetrate four major markets in an unprecedented manner: the office in medium and large businesses, small business, factories, and consumers. In each of these major market areas, the pie is just beginning to expand to accommodate the information processing industry's products and services.

For example, in 1984 the management information systems departments of medium and large American corporations spent more than $100 billion in personnel, equipment, software, and facilities. Although growing at an annual rate of 15 percent, the penetration of workstations of all types into corporate offices remains rather limited (the current ratio is approximately one keyboard to three office workers). Moreover, most of the installed base of keyboards fall into the category of dumb terminals attached to mainframe computers. The real growth remains in the area of improving the ratio of workstations from 1:3 to 1:1 and substituting integrated office automation systems and intelligent workstations in the form of desktop and portable computers for dumb terminals in offices in medium to large corporations.

Similarly, the small business market remains largely untapped. Most of the 5.5 million small businesses in America still employ only limited data processing services or own their own computers. The rise of minicomputers in the mid-1970s and of the personal computer in the 1980s has opened vast opportunities to market low-cost hardware and software to small businesses. Moreover, since more than 400,000 small businesses are created each year the market is constantly turning over with substantial new, first-time customers. Finally, since most small businesses are in services, retail trade, and the white-collar sector generally, the information intensity of these firms provides an appropriate market for the services and products of the information processing industry.

The third major market opportunity for the industry lies in the automation of the factory. The United States leads the other advanced economies in the age of its manufacturing plants with 34 percent of its machine tools older than 20 years. Eighteen percent of Japan's equipment is similarly old. Moreover, 61 percent of Japan's machine tools are under 10 years old, compared with 31 percent in the United States. In 1979, according to International Data Corporation, the manufacturing sector had $750 of computer support per worker while the financial services sector had $2000 of support per worker. While U.S. factories are not unaccustomed to automation, many of the computerized tools sold today are upgrades of electro-mechanical equipment: "They speed up the process of turning out a single type of part or product—but tooling is always expensive."

Thus, the market for factory automation is large, but fragmented into separate domains such as floor automation, design automation, and inventory control. Even so, the worldwide revenues in this market were $8.2 billion in 1983 and are expected to grow to $38 billion by 1989.

While this is by no means an insignificant market, the real possibilities for growth in factory automation lie ahead with the evolution of robot-run factories, integrated manufacturing resource planning systems, flexible manufacturing systems, and group technology (that is, the design and fabrication of parts in families, rather than one-by-one in linear order with other parts that go into final assembly). The integration of information resources and technologies in the plant and between plants and front offices will expand opportunities for selling integrated systems at higher margins than stand-alone technologies. As the manufacturers of goods in the information economy continue to adopt these integrated technologies, the competitive market for their goods and services continues to expand. Moreover, as more American companies come to believe the popular General Electric slogan of "automate, emigrate, or evaporate," the movement toward factory automation will increase in industries that need to stay competitive in international as well as domestic markets.

The final major market opportunity for the information processing industry resides in the vast opportunities implied in the adage, "a computer in every home." Moreover, it is likely that by 1990, many homes will have several computers embedded in appliances, energy control devices, and autos. In addition, aggressive efforts are underway in the cable and telecommunications industries to provide two-way interactive networks to homes in order to permit high-speed data communications.

Finally, the ongoing ventures to establish videotex services for the home will pick up momentum in the next five years, as more and more companies begin entering the consumer information services market. While today there are only a handful of companies offering consumer videotex services, key industry actors such as IBM, Sears, and AT&T have begun to commit substantial investments in providing electronic information services to consumers.

Providing New Tools

The seventh and final impact of the information processing industry is related not only to the changes in the external environments of business, but also to the impacts of the industry on traditional business functions. While we will discuss these impacts in more depth in subsequent chapters, it is important to recognize from the outset that innovations such as telemarketing, teleconferencing, automated catalogs, videotex, and teletext are opening up new opportunities for transforming the tools available to marketing, advertising, and sales departments.

Moreover, innovations in factory automation such as manufacturing resource planning (MRP) and flexible manufacturing systems are redefining the production function in business. Still other innovations such as automated cash management, financial services systems, and human resource information systems are providing tools to modify the financial management and personnel functions within small and large companies alike.

CHAPTER 3

RETHINKING YOUR BUSINESS IN THE INFORMATION ECONOMY

Effective business strategy requires awareness of the customer, the competition, and your company's field of distinctive competence. In addition, insight about the economy in which one does business and the underlying shifts occurring in customer needs, attitudes, and perceptions requires a keen set of directional antennae. Moreover, to develop and pursue an effective business strategy requires the intellectual flexibility to come up with realistic responses to changing situations, "not simply to discriminate with great precision among different shades of gray."[1]

In an economy with a relatively stable structure, the main concern of business is to do more with less and to do this in a clearcut direction. In a turbulent economy undergoing major structural change, a principal concern of managers is to know what business they are in; to understand enough about the business environment to establish an appropriate vision and strategic direction for the firm.

[1] Kenichi Ohmae, *The Mind of the Strategist,* New York: Penguin, 1982, p. 13.

In this chapter, we will integrate the impacts of the information economy and the information-processing industry on business, to understand the changes in business environments which require manufacturing and services companies alike to rethink the businesses they are in. What aspects of the business environment today make pinning down a strategic business direction such a challenging and, at times, perilous task? This chapter will address this critical question.

THREE LEVELS OF STRATEGY DEFINITION

Within most businesses, there are three levels at which business strategy must be defined as indicated in Figure 3-1.[2] At the highest level, *corporate strategy* specifies two areas of overall interest to the company: the definition or view of the kinds of businesses in which the company will participate, and the allocation of key corporate resources to each of those businesses.

How a corporation defines what lines of business it is in will determine, or at least influence, its acquisition and use of people, money, manufacturing capability, and information resources. In a turbulent economy, the identity of a company may change over time and in turn alter the priority given to its mix of resources. For example, over the last 10 years, Citicorp has shifted its corporate identity from a bank, to a financial-services firm, and finally to an information company that provides diverse financial information and investment services.[3]

Every shift in identity a company makes results in significant changes at the second level of strategy identified in Figure 3-1 as that associated with the strategic business unit (SBU), which can be a subsidiary, division, or product line in the firm. A business-unit strategy specifies: (1) the scope of that business in a way that links the strategy of the business to that of the company as a whole, and (2) the basis on which the business unit will achieve

[2] Robert H. Hayes and Steven C. Wheelwright, *Restoring Our Competitive Edge*, New York: Wiley, 1984, pp. 28–29.

[3] Walter B. Wriston, "The Citi of Tomorrow: Today," (unpublished speech). New York: Citicorp, 1982.

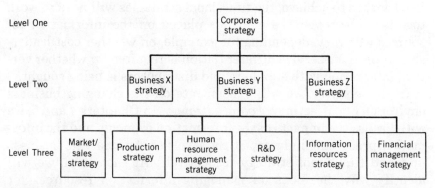

Figure 3–1. Levels of business strategy. Reprinted by permission of John Wiley & Sons. From R. H. Hayes and S. C. Wheelwright, *Restoring Our Competitive Edge.* Copyright© 1984 by John Wiley & Sons.

and maintain a competitive advantage. Specifying the scope of the business requires a view of the products, markets, and/or services to be provided. Such definition is required to avoid unnecessary competition among the firm's business units, but also to focus the efforts of each business unit on activities that are likely to enhance the competitive position of the unit in the markets it serves. As the corporate strategy of the firm evolves, the resources allocated to existing or new SBUs may change dramatically. Going back to the Citicorp example, it is clear that the rising star over the last 10 years at Citicorp has been the domestic-services market, so those SBUs offering effective financial, credit card, and insurance services to the U.S. consumer have received a good deal of attention and resources within the corporation.[4]

Finally, the third level indicated in Figure 3-1 is that of *functional strategies.* Once a business unit has defined its strategy, each functional area must develop approaches to support that strategy. While different functional strategies may exist for various business units, the appearance of a functional strategy for exploiting information resources and technologies to support the SBU and the other functional strategies, is occurring with increasing frequency. Depending on the competitive advantage the

---

[4] Leslie Wayne, "Citi's Soaring Ambition," *New York Times,* June 24, 1984.

SBU wishes to achieve, the functional strategies will need to work together. Moreover, the demands placed on the information resources will vary, depending for example, on whether cost leadership or product-service differentiation is required, or whether vertical integration with suppliers and distributors is being sought.

In this chapter, we will concentrate on the changing business environments affecting *corporate strategy*. In Chapters 4 and 5, we will discuss the impacts of the information economy and the information-processing industry at the levels of the strategic business unit and functional strategy respectively. At each level, we will identify why the focus on managing information resources for competitive advantage is becoming so inclusive and vital to successful businesses in the information economy.

We begin with a consideration of the overall business environment in which the company operates.

THE BUSINESS ENVIRONMENT FOR CORPORATE STRATEGY IN THE INFORMATION ECONOMY

There are eight major characteristics of the business environment in the information economy affecting the development of corporate strategy. These characteristics, individually and collectively, not only affect the ability of a company to maximize profit or shareholder wealth, but more importantly, they affect what Donaldson and Lorsch in *Decision Making at the Top* have called *corporate wealth:* "which includes not only the firm's financial assets reflected on the balance sheet, but also its important human assets and its competitive positions in the various markets in which it operates."[5] Moreover, in their study of how top executives formulate the strategy to achieve corporate wealth, Donaldson and Lorsch go on to suggest that, while "there are clearly pressures on management for quick results, corporate executives are primarily concerned with long-term corporate survival. In those instances where they have failed to adapt their company's strategy to a changing competitive environment, the explanation lies not in a short-term focus, but rather in *their*

---

[5] Gordon Donaldson and Jay W. Lorsch, *Decision Making at the Top,* New York: Basic Books, 1983, p. 7.

inability to read environmental trends accurately as in their adherence to traditional beliefs about consumer preferences and competitive practices."[6] (Emphasis added.)

Nathaniel H. Leff of Columbia's business school makes the point "what you don't know can hurt you."[7] He points out that effective management has always required strategic planning, but too often strategic planning was developed at a time when key features of a company's market environment were stable, or could be anticipated with some certainty. But now, stability and reliable forecasting are rare. Leff points out that uncertainty surrounds new basic issues like medium-term market growth, the identity and characteristics of future competitors, currency changes that impact the profitability of investment and financing decisions, and the increasing pace of technological developments.

Better business intelligence therefore becomes not just a "nice-to-have" luxury, but a critical tool to help dispel external uncertainties. Leff also believes outside directors and consultants can play a useful role in preventing companies from becoming captives of their own obsolete assumptions. He urges systematic thinking about the information needs of strategic management because the process forces questioning of old assumptions that have become "ossified" in company thinking.

As mentioned in Chapter 1, a real hazard for the evolution of corporate strategy today is to fail to read the environmental characteristics embedded in the information economy, rather than in an industrial economy. Sticking to traditional beliefs about one's industry and about the competition can be bad for business.

The Boundaries of Industries and Markets Are More Fluid and Blurred

The first characteristic of the business environment of the information economy is that the boundaries between industries and between market sectors are becoming increasingly fluid and blurred. In Chapter 1, we discussed the blurring of the boundaries between services industries, and between service industries and

---

[6] *Ibid.*, p. 8.
[7] Nathaniel H. Leff, "What You Don't Know Can Hurt You," *BusinessWeek*, March 14, 1983, p. 12.

manufacturing industries. As information resources become integral to increasing the value-added dimension of services or products, the key distinction is no longer between services and goods, but rather between enterprises where information resources are critical to success and enterprises where they are not (that is, where information resources may play an important but not crucial role in the presentation of the service, or in the production of the good). Thus, the increasingly fluid nature of boundaries in industry today is a condition which corporate executives must plan for and manage. However, there is no guarantee that recognizing this condition in your industry will lead to success; indeed, the inability to direct a firm through the shifting boundaries of specific industries has already become a popular sign of business failure. Thus, the leading question to ask for the development of corporate strategy in the information economy is: What business am I really in? Moreover, the signs of change affect large and small businesses alike. In the banking and financial-services industries, the blurring of boundaries between traditionally distinct service lines for business customers and consumers has redefined the identities of major banks and brokerage houses. Furthermore, the boundaries between industries are expanding and shifting even in traditional industries such as mail and transportation services, small-business retailing, and automobiles.

Figure 3-2 provides some examples of just a few strategies for firms in manufacturing and service industries, where boundaries are being extended and redefined. For example, in 1984, Federal Express moved from being the nation's leading overnight mail and package service, to developing a telecommunications strategy called Zap Mail, which moves messages and documents electronically in its national delivery system. Moreover, over the last 10 years, Sears, Citicorp, Merrill Lynch, and American Express, among others, have moved to becoming "full service" or "one-stop" customer outlets, and have aggressively blurred the boundaries between banking, insurance, brokerage, credit card, retailing, and real estate services. Starting from different positions, each corporation has sought to gain a competitive advantage by redefining the lines of business they are in as well as establishing themselves as comprehensive "financial planners" or as "one-stop" outlets to meet multiple customer needs.

Mail and package services / Transportation services / Telecommunication services

    e.g., Federal Express

Banking / Insurance / Brokerage / Credit Cards / Retailing / Real estate

    e.g., Sears, Citicorp, Merrill Lynch, American Express

Mail order services / Telemarketing

    e.g., New Process Co., Smith & Hawken, Ltd.

Publishing / Software retailing / Electronic-information services

    e.g., McGraw-Hill, Los Angeles Times, United Press International, Knight-Ridder Newspapers, Prentice-Hall, Inc.

Automobile and truck manufacturing / Computer-assisted manufacturing / Software services / Communications

    e.g., General Motors, Ford

Figure 3–2.   Selected Cases of Shifting Business Boundaries.

In retail services, firms have migrated from being essentially mail-order houses to full-service telemarketing firms. In 1910, the New Process Company entered the mail-order business by selling black raincoats to undertakers. Today, the $300 million firm has a customer base of 12 million, and a computer-based telemarketing strategy which allows the company to generate 1.4 million personalized information packets and process 40,000 orders per day.[8] Similarly, Smith & Hawken, Ltd. grew from $40,000 in 1980 to over $4 million in revenues in 1984 by offering durable, finely crafted, imported garden tools to a mixture of affluent horticulturists and organic gardeners.[9] Founded by Paul Hawken, the celebrated author of *The Next Economy*, the firm employs both a telemarketing and mail-order strategy with a customized educational and information service. Using a very detailed catalogue and a group of well-informed employees, the company provides its customers with carefully developed information on methods and schools of thought in gardening, as well as the imported tools themselves, and additional information on where they came from,

[8] Jeff Blyskal, "Mail order for the masses," *Forbes,* July 16, 1984, pp. 35–36.
[9] Ralph Whitehead, Jr., "Planning for the "Next Economy," *INC.,* June 1984, pp. 44–53, 53.

how they are made, how they can be used, and why they are good. Thus, consistent with the theme of his best-selling book, Paul Hawken adds information value to the telemarketing of gardening tools to enhance the overall image of the firm, as well as to develop a competitive edge on other mail order firms offering products with no advice.

A similar strategy is being pursued on a larger scale by leading book and newspaper publishers as companies move from paper-based publishing to electronic publishing and retailing.[10] Major publishers, such as McGraw-Hill and Prentice-Hall, are moving into software retailing as well as electronic publishing and electronic distribution of data services, newsletters, and even books. Major newspaper chains such as Knight-Ridder and the Los Angeles Times are implementing customer-oriented videotex services in their markets to capture opportunities for extending enhanced information services to customers, and to avoid erosion caused by the loss of revenue for classified advertising to electronic services they might not own.

In traditional industries such as auto/truck manufacturing, both Ford and GM are moving aggressively into computer-assisted manufacturing, software services, and even satellite communications. GM's acquisition in 1984 of Electronic Data Systems from Dallas, Texas, and Ford's entry into the satellite and aerospace communication businesses, are both indicators of major new corporate strategies tied to the emerging information-processing industry. Moreover, they represent clear examples of industrial-age firms moving into information-age markets.

Irving D. Canton points out that Borg-Warner is just one of many old-line manufacturing companies that have made the transition into services from manufacturing, only after overcoming serious internal-management resistance. Canton identifies 10 routes of entry into services businesses:

1. *Systems Selling in Business Markets.* A shift in management's point of view from selling a product to selling a solution is a customer's problem. Example: the fertilizer

---

[10] "Publishers Go Electronic," *Business Week*, June 11, 1984, p. 84.

industry's developing of "back blending" and "custom application" systems to help solve a whole range of the farmer's problems, not just fertilizer needs

2. *Systems Selling in Consumer Markets.* Example: Ticketron's computerized ticket-vending services including entertainment events and lottery tickets

3. *Capitalizing on Corporate Knowledge.* Examples: DuPont's establishment of a business unit to provide customized health and safety services to other corporations; Olin's offering of water testing, consulting, and on-going full-service water treatment contracts to its customers; Barber-Greene's establishment of an information-systems subsidiary to sell computer software systems to highway-construction equipment customers

4. *Capitalizing on Corporate Physical Resources.* Examples: Kimberly-Clark's exploitation of its in-house corporate aircraft know-how into a subsidiary (KC Aviation) that employs a staff of about 500 at bases in Appleton, Wisconsin and Dallas, Texas, to offer services beyond just corporate passenger transportation, including the installation of customer interiors and avionics in new corporate aircraft

5. *Financing Customer Purchases.* Example: GMAC's financing of dealer inventories and providing installment loans to customers to facilitate the distribution and purchase of GM products

6. *Contract Management and Shared Services.* Example: Hospital suppliers offering hospitals patient care, pharmacy, respiratory therapy, and emergency room care well beyond traditional janitorial, financial, data processing and food services

7. *Creating National Chains.* Example: Southland's 7-Eleven convenience chain with 6000 plus locations

8. *Integrating Forward to Distribution.* Example: Fanny-May Candy Shops owning their own distribution outlets and selling only company products

9. *Privatizing Public Services.* Example: using private companies to process health claims and running libraries and information centers

10. *Responding to Unplanned Events.* Example: Brunswick's assumed ownership of two financially troubled bowling centers

Canton emphasizes that "more than anything else, what is required [to enter the services sector] is the entrepreneurial spirit to look beyond manufacturing as the sole method of profiting from existing assets, resources and knowledge."[11]

Structural Economic Change Requires Strategic Planning and Management

The second characteristic of the business environment in the information economy arises from the opportunities and risks associated with the economy's structural change. As the information economy continues to evolve and transform the industrial and agricultural sectors, the requirements for integrating a firm's external and internal business strategies increase in importance. Whether the firm is in a declining industry such as textiles, or an emerging industry such as software development, the firm's formulation of corporate strategy is dependent on identifying opportunities and threats in existing and prospective markets, as well as evaluating basic strengths and weaknesses in existing operations and management systems. Moreover, strategic management today is no longer limited to tight financial control over business units as it was in the 1940s and 1950s, or confined to long-range forecasts of projected sales as in the 1960s. As industries have become more competitive in national and international markets in the 1970s and 1980s, the need for articulating the competitive strategy of a firm in an explicit manner has also grown in significance.[12] Moreover,

[11] Irving D. Canton, "Learning to Love the Service Economy," *Harvard Business Review,* May–June 1984, pp. 89–97. Reprinted by permission of the *Harvard Business Review.* Excerpt from "Kratylus automates his urnworks" by Tolly Kizilos (May–June 1984). Copyright© 1984 by the President and Fellows of Harvard College; all rights reserved.

[12] See Arnoldo C. Hax and Nicolas S. Mayluf, *Strategic Management,* Englewood Cliffs, N.J.: Prentice-Hall, 1984.

in recent years even manufacturing processes have been perceived as a "competitive weapon."[13]

In the textile industry today, for example, cost leadership through the aggressive management and use of office and factory automation has become a key to competitive strategy. In contrast, cosmetics firms have sought to use computer-based customer-profiling techniques to differentiate their cosmetic products from those of their competitors. Software companies have sought to focus their competitive efforts in selected market niches such as database management systems, financial software, or consumer games.

In each of these cases, formally and explicitly developing a competitive strategy has become a necessity. In addition, companies in these industries have had reduced time cushions for product cycles and market shifts, which have placed more importance on flexible planning and entrepreneurial management styles.

Scanning of External Business Environments Is More Complex and Demanding in the Information Economy

As interdependencies between manufacturing and service industries, and between domestic and international markets increase, the task of accurately reading and gauging the pace of events and opportunities becomes more demanding. A company's competition may not arise from known competitors in traditional markets. Indeed, as the lines between market sectors blur, the range of potential competitors may grow significantly.

Despite the fact that most companies are involved in a continuous struggle with inter- and intraindustry competition for market share, profits, and capital, few companies evaluate their existing and potential competitors as carefully as they study new production processes or product proposals. The automated management-information systems of most companies are geared primarily to deriving information from internal operations and to assist in the internal allocation of resources. Rarely do these information systems incorporate effectively the companies' use of external information resources:

---

[13] Hayes and Wheelwright, "Competitive Edge."

When management tries to add a competitive perspective to the company's strategic planning process, it often discovers that its knowledge of key competitors is extremely incomplete, widely scattered throughout the corporation, and generally not coordinated. What is perhaps even more frustrating is that the available internal assessments and opinions about competitors are frequently in conflict, unsubstantiated by facts, and often based on assumptions and intuitive hunches that are partially right, partially wrong, and usually out of date. [14]

Most companies possess what William L. Sammon has labeled an "informal competitor intelligence system." [15] As Figure 3-3 indicates, "pools" of competitor information are scattered throughout the business units and functional staffs of the company. [16] However, as Sammon also points out, these pools of uneven information about competitors may be worse than no information at all:

The manufacturing vice-president who tracks a competitor's capacity investment announcements may overstate the potential threat inherent in the capacity additions because he or she does not realize that competitor X lacks the cash flow to carry through these plans. If the finance staff has run a survey of sensitivity profiles on competitor X, it may realize that rising interest payments will probably compel the competitor's management to delay or perhaps cancel key capital projects. The marketing staff in business unit B may be certain that their individual adhesives are technically superior to those of competitors yet be unaware of new patents competitor X has filed on a radically new adhesive, that business unit B's corporate R & D staff knows is a technological breakthrough. In the course of labor negotiations, the corporate industrial relations staff may learn that the national union is planning to strike competitor Y's plants in the Southeast. However, this information which business unit A could use in its campaign to take market share from competitor Y in the East Coast regional market, is not passed on. [17]

[14] William L. Sammon, "Competitor Intelligence: An Organizational Framework for Business," in William L. Sammon, Mark A. Kurland, and Robert Spitalnic, eds., *Business Competition Intelligence,* New York: Wiley, 1984, p. 62.

[15] *Ibid.,* p. 64.

[16] *Ibid.,* p. 65.

[17] *Ibid.,* pp. 64, 66.

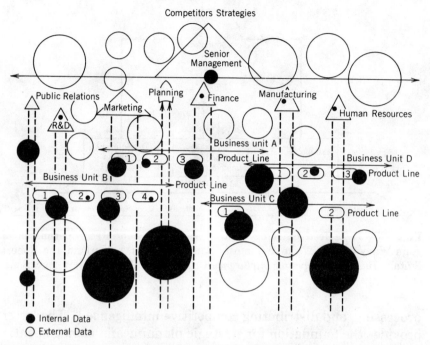

Figure 3–3.   Pools of competitor information. *Source:* see note 16. Reprinted by permission of John Wiley & Sons. From William L. Sammon, Mark A. Kurland and Robert Spitalic, *Business Competitor Intelligence.* Copyright© 1984 by John Wiley & Sons.

As the risks associated with corporate misinformation accelerate through companies, the need for developing a systematic approach to corporate competitor intelligence tends to grow as well. As James Gardner points out, effective corporate strategy is based on competitive intelligence that incorporates three dimensions: (1) evaluation of environmental trends, (2) competitor analysis, and (3) assessments of market dynamics.[18] While corporate strategy today may be influenced by entrepreneural insights or by opportunistic decisions, as Figure 3-4 illustrates, it nevertheless cannot succeed over the long term without effective systems of collecting,

[18] James R. Gardner, "Competitor Intelligence: The *Sine Qua Non* of Corporate Strategic Planning," in Sammon, Kurland, and Spitalnic, eds., *Business Competitor Intelligence,* New York: Wiley, 1984, p. 18.

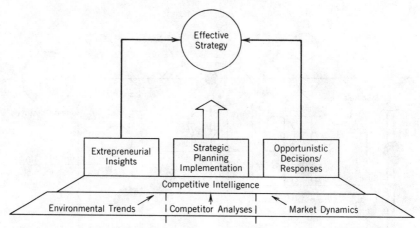

Figure 3–4.   Effective strategy. *Source:* see note 19. Reprinted by permission of John Wiley & Sons. From William L. Sammon, Mark A. Kurland and Robert Spitalic, *Business Competitor Intelligence.* Copyright© 1984 by John Wiley & Sons.

processing, and distributing competitive intelligence.[19] The latter provides the foundation for strategic planning and management.

Just what is *competitor intelligence?* An innovative Washington, D.C.-based information company, Washington Researchers, has for years mounted a special seminar series called "Competitor Intelligence: Research Aids and Reporting Skills." The seminar's goal is to teach participants how to tap the right sources and deliver solutions to their companies' business-intelligence needs.

Topics covered include:

1.   An understanding of why business intelligence is important and how it can be applied.

2.   How to influence and define information requests correctly so that the information-seeking process is not sidetracked.

3.   Uncovering sources of competitor intelligence, including: industry watchers (trade associations, trade press, government experts); industry suppliers, distributors, agents, customers, producers; competitors' public filings (federal,

[19] *Ibid.,* p. 62.

state, local); databases specializing in company information; published materials (directories, industry profiles, and articles); unpublished studies (government and articles); and private research services.

4. Keys to interviewing sources.

5. Organizing and managing information.

6. Reports that meet the need.

7. Managing ongoing competitive-intelligence projects.

8. Company policy and competitor investigations.

Flexible Products/Services Designs Are Required to Meet the Tailored or Specialized Needs of Business Customers and Consumers

Over the last 100 years, the industrial economy has been characterized by "inflexible" design: To achieve economies of scale in industrial terms has required the massive use of capital and energy to establish factories with assembly lines that could stamp out products quickly and in a standard way. The mass economy as we have come to know it in the United States is based on not only mass-consumer tastes but on mass production as well. The two processes have gone hand in hand to elevate a definition of productivity based on the principle "the more, the better." The underlying technologies of the industrial economy, such as machine tools, assembly-line technologies, electrical and mechanical motors, conveyors, and machines have increased the cost of plant conversions, product differentiation, and tailoring of services. For example, the auto makers in Detroit have been slow to downsize their cars not only for marketing reasons, but perhaps more importantly, because of the long lead times and substantial costs involved in the conversion of manufacturing processes geared to producing large cars. Moreover, as consumer tastes have shifted over the last 15 years from large cars to small cars to large cars and back again, the automakers' slowness to respond to market shifts has been due in part to inflexible manufacturing systems and massive "sunk costs" in existing plants, machinery, and know-how.

In contrast, for the Japanese and Western European competitors, the operative definition of productivity has been to do more with less by investing in flexible systems of manufacturing that employ computer-assisted design and production processes, and making heavy use of industrial robots. Thus, competitive manufacturing in the information economy has meant the increasing use of computer and communications technologies in the factory to produce more tailored and flexible products at a lower cost enabling the manufacturer to meet more differentiated consumer needs. Moreover, flexible manufacturing systems have also contributed to the movement toward improving the quality of products and goods. Paul Hawken has characterized this shift as a change in the ratio between the "mass" and "information" contained in goods and services:

> *Mass means the energy, materials and embodied (energy and labor) resources to produce a product or perform a service. While the mass economy was characterized by economies of scale, by many goods being produced and consumed by many people, the informative economy is characterized by people producing smaller numbers of goods that contain more information. What is this information? It is design, utility, craft, durability, and knowledge added to mass. It is the quality and intelligence that make a product more useful and functional, longer-lasting, easier to repair, lighter, stronger, and less consumptive of energy.* [20]

The emphasis on quality control, flexible manufacturing processes, and product differentiation in the 1980s has been paralleled by a decided shift in consumer tastes towards individualized products and services of high quality. For example, within the United States, as the "baby boom" generation of the post World War II period has matured in the 1970s and 1980s, consumer markets have gone through massive shifts in this generation's tastes in housing, consumer goods, cars, food, recreation, clothing, financial, and other services.[21] Since there are 68 million people represented in this generation, constituting nearly one-third of the

---

[20] Paul Hawken, *The Next Economy*, New York: Holt, 1983, p. 9.
[21] Geoffrey Colvin, "What the Baby-Boomers Will Buy Next," *Fortune*, October 15, 1984, pp. 28–34.

U.S. population, the purchasing tastes and needs of these people coupled with their relative affluence have and will continue to define the requirements of consumer markets. Moreover, as the baby-boom generation matures into their thirties and forties—the peak purchasing years—their values, reflected in the demand for individual services and high quality goods, will require flexible design and distribution of products and services.

The Business Environment Is Becoming More Information-Intensive

Until now we've used the terms *information resources* and *information assets* without defining them. Before proceeding we need to remedy that. By *information resources* we mean:

1. Individuals having information-related skills
2. Information-technology hardware and software
3. Information facilities such as libraries, computer centers, communications centers, and information centers
4. Information handling and processing suppliers

By *information assets* we mean:

1. The formal data, document, and literature holdings of the company
2. The know-how it possesses both in the form of intellectual properties like patents and copyrights, and in the form of individual expertise
3. The business intelligence it possesses on its competitors, its business environment, and its political, economic, and social environments

It is hardly surprising that doing business in an information economy requires companies to be more information-intensive. This means that they must spend a larger and larger share of their capital and investment dollars on information resources. What is often not clearly perceived however, are the reasons for this underlying shift in the mix of resources.

The most obvious reason why businesses are more information-intensive is due to the evolution of communications and computer technologies over the last 40 years. Clearly, these technologies have, as we noted in Chapters 1 and 2, facilitated the transition from the industrial to the information economy. All the same, new technologies alone are a necessary but insufficient explanation for this shift.

A second reason for the information intensity of modern business today is the fact that the basic nature of interactions in the information economy are quite different, as Daniel Bell indicated some 12 years ago, than the interactions in the industrial or preindustrial economies:

> . . . the design of pre-industrial society is a game against nature: its resources are drawn from extractive industries and it is subject to the laws of diminishing returns and low productivity; the design of industrial society is a game against fabricated nature which is centered on man-machine relationships and uses energy to transform the natural environment into a technical environment; the design of post-industrial society is a game between persons in which intellectual technology, based on information, rises alongside of machine technology. [22]

Thus, in the information economy, the interactions of people in sharing ideas, acquiring knowledge and information, and using their intellectual resources for competitive advantage, accelerates both the quantity and quality of these interactions. John Naisbitt has recognized that "This increases personal transactions geometrically, that is, all forms of interactive communication: telephone calls, checks written, memos, messages, letters, and more." [23]

In addition, the time-value of information also changes since communications and computer technologies do not limit human interactions by geographical space, but by "information space"; they expand the possibilities of interaction without reference to geographic and time limitations. Thus, the rate of change is accelerated as "information float" is reduced. *Information float* is the time and effort necessary for people to communicate over geographic distances. In "information space," as Yoneji Masuda, one of Japan's

---

[22] Daniel Bell, *The Coming of Post-Industrial Society*, New York: Basic Books, 1973, p. 116.
[23] John Naisbitt, *Megatrends*. New York: Warner, 1982, p. 19.

leading architects of the information economy, recognized some years ago, business is no longer contained by the limitations of geographic distance or the modes of physical transportation.[24]

Thus, the internal and external environments of business become more information-intensive. Externally, businesses must monitor and track a broader array of economic, marketplace, political, and social trends both domestically and internationally. These requirements lead, as mentioned earlier, to the evolution of management reforms like strategic planning and management, competitive intelligence systems and market research, which in turn demand more intense and sophisticated monitoring and analysis of the external business environment.

Internally, the demands for businesses to be flexible, entrepreneurial, quality-conscious, and sensitive to worker needs also lead to more information-intensive strategies such as quality circles, manufacturing resource systems, computer-assisted design and manufacturing, and office automation. As the composition of the internal workforce shifts from laborers to information and knowledge workers, the demands for efficient information use and communication also increase—necessitating new techniques for channelling human interactions and for controlling production or service-delivery processes. Moreover, as more and more companies have offices and plants worldwide that are managed from a distance, the use of information resources becomes integral to the coordination and management of human, financial, and capital resources.

One of the best examples of the increasing paperwork and information-intensiveness of business is the insurance industry. What has been fairly obvious and straightforward has been the early application of large mainframe computers to store active customer-policy data, help process claims, and compute premium and premium changes. What is less obvious, however, is the spread of PCs throughout the different departments to support many functions. Word processing, for example, has dramatically streamlined, simplified, and mechanized the processes of retyping policies, proposals, reports, and other related documents. Many

---

[24] See Yoneji Masuda, *The Information Society*, Toyko: Institute for the Information Society, 1980, pp. 72–74.

companies, such as Cotton States STATS (Solutions Through Advanced Technology Systems) Systems specialize in sharing with the insurance company general-purpose policy-administration software programs marketed through licensing agreements. Such ventures are intended to offer improved solutions to insurance interests based on more flexible and adaptable software packages, and extended services for consulting, education, and training. Cotton States believes that STATS, and systems communications more generally, are of vital importance to the future growth and development of the insurance industry.

Today, integration of technologies is beginning to play an important role in the way insurance companies cope with their information-management challenges. New developments in computer-assisted retrieval (CAR) of microfiche files have renewed interest in the micrographics area. By microfilming claim forms as soon as they come in, and by coupling those files with CAR technologies, very substantial labor and paper costs can be displaced.

We are more interested here in how the insurance industry is rethinking its identity. It is beginning to see itself not so much as in the insurance business, but as in the information business. By offering money-market and mutual funds, for example, this industry is offering nontraditional services and entering nontraditional markets. The key to these new product lines has, once again, been a shift in company thinking and a deliberate blurring of product boundaries.

Once the insurance industry realized that its computational algorithms for premium computation could be adapted to other kinds of return-on-investment calculations outside of the health field, it was only a short step to move into these new markets. This has not been an instance of an untapped data reservoir as much as it has been a case of an untapped know-how reservoir. Companies thinking about entering new markets should consider, in short, *both* their proprietary data assets and their proprietary know-how strengths.

Skillful Information Management and Use Are Growing Sources of Competitive Advantage

In an industrial economy, information management is largely a back-room function, carried out in the background of organizational life. Within the business enterprise, information management is a support function assisting in the management of paperwork, books and periodicals, payrolls, finances, telephones, copiers, print shops, mailrooms, and large centralized computers doing transaction processing to keep track of customers, receivables, payables, and inventories. In contrast to marketing, finance, R&D, and production, information management in the industrial economy is more of a cost center than a profit center. If a young person wants to be part of the senior management team in a company, the route to success has been through marketing, finance or production and not through the information-management function. The latter has been perceived either as a technician's domain (in the case of data processing or telecommunications) or as a staff function, rather than a management function as in the case of paperwork and records supervision, the library, and the print shop.

Today, in contrast, doing business in the information economy has required that information management move from the back room to the front office both figuratively and literally. In the literal sense, advances in computer and communications technologies have evolved to the point where their presence in the office, factory, and laboratory are both visible and required. As we mentioned in Chapter 2, this trend is both market and technologically driven as information technology cost-performance ratios continue to improve and new uses for small computers are found in these domains. The figurative move of information-management from a backroom support function to a concern of senior management is driven by the growing realization that information itself is a significant competitive weapon, not an overhead activity like maintaining a motorpool.

As we mentioned, for Sears the customer-service business has been significantly enhanced by using the information about who bought appliances to contact owners regularly by mail and telemarketing to renew service or maintenance agreements.[25] And as we called attention to already, for Owens-Corning Fiberglass Corporation, the home-insulation giant, information generated internally about the energy-efficiency of a wide variety of house

---

[25] See "Business Is Turning Data Into a Potent Strategic Weapon," *Business Week*, August 22, 1983, p. 92.

designs is being used in a computer program to come up with energy-efficiency ratings for new designs. Owens, in turn, uses this information by offering builders free evaluations of their designs if they agree to buy all of their insulation from the manufacturer and meet a minimum standard of energy-efficiency. Moreover, through its advertising campaign to consumers, Owens is trying to persuade consumers to demand more insulation from builders.[26]

Although financial services companies and airlines were pioneers in using customer or account-related information for competitive advantage, today even traditional industries are beginning to move in this direction. For example, the farm-equipment maker Deere leads many of the heavy-equipment manufacturers in managing its in-house information to keep the cost of production low. By cataloging the characteristics of the 300,000 parts it uses, from tiny screws to hydraulic pumps for farm tractors, Deere has been able to produce families of parts more efficiently. Deere has also enabled engineers to design new equipment more quickly and cheaply by allowing them to search the database for parts with similar characteristics before they design new parts.[27]

These and similar innovations in the management and use of internal company information and external information about customers and competitors are symptomatic of the evolution of information management as a strategic-management function in the information economy. Whether one is in a declining industry or a mature industry, or whether one's business is domestic or international, it will become increasingly more difficult for senior management and planners in corporations not to treat information as a competitive resource alongside human, financial, and technological resources.

In the Information Economy the Boundaries of the Business Enterprise Are Extended

For many years, the operative model of the enterprise used by business schools to teach the management of information systems

---

[26] *Ibid.*, p. 92.
[27] *Ibid.*, p. 92.

Figure 3–5. Traditional view of company.

has been the triangle (see Figure 3-5), which defines a top-down hierarchy and a series of decision-making levels from strategic planning to management decision making to operations. In the 1960s and 1970s, this organizational model was the context in which computer-based information systems were developed. At the lowest level were the transaction-based systems such as payroll, inventory, accounting, and customer-billing systems, which in turn formed the informational foundation for management information systems (MIS) providing aggregated statistical reprints to managers and decision-support systems (DSS), which were conceived as problem-oriented software programs designed to help the planner optimize his solution to inventory control, materials management, or budgeting. To a great extent, these MIS, DSS and transaction-based systems took advantage of third-generation mainframe computers and required extensive systems-development staff over long periods to actually implement working systems.

Thus, the MIS function's view of the corporation was significantly influenced by the narrow range in which automated information systems could be developed. The MIS view perceived the corporation as a tight, hierarchial structure whose decision-making requirements were relatively stable and routinized over time, and whose information needs were largely limited to transaction-based systems and the management reports that could be derived from their files. This view was reinforced by the relatively expensive software and hardware technologies which were predominantly mainframe dependent.

It was not until the late 1970s and early 1980s that this view of the corporation began gradually to shift. It did so for three major reasons. First, corporations in a turbulent economic environment were no longer able to confine their needs for strategic information for management decision-making to the internal MIS systems. As we noted earlier, as the boundaries of business markets shifted and became unstable, a corresponding need arose for more systematic information about the swiftly changing *external* business environment which most computer-based information systems could not satisfy. Second, the move by many corporations to develop strategic planning and management systems, as well as to pursue explicit competitive strategies, required a broader range of information sources and needs than most MIS departments could satisfy. And, third, by the late 1970s and early 1980s, the information-processing industry began to offer new technologies such as personal computers, video discs, videotex, and so forth, which not only permitted more corporate users to employ information technology in their jobs—separate from the MIS department's priorities—but also provided new opportunities to use computers and communication networks to *extend* the reach of the corporation to its suppliers, dealers, and customers. Moreover, computer vendors such as IBM began to urge large and medium-sized corporations to become value-added dealers (VADs) for personal computers and small business systems to their own dealers, agents, and customers as a way of selling lower-cost technology in the volumes necessary to support aggressive growth by the computer company, and to tie major corporations to a vendor in a new way—not just as *users* of software and hardware, but as *dealers* trying to add value through software and specialized services to sell a vendor's computer hardware.

As Figure 3-6 suggests, this shift in thinking about the competitive use of information resources and technology has in turn led to the evolution of the notion of the *extended enterprise*. Strategic business planning today must incorporate the environment in which the business operates into its internal management needs. Thus, this business strategy forms the context in which the strategic use of information resources and technology is defined, not

Figure 3–6. The extended enterprise.

only to address internal information needs, but more importantly, to address informational interactions with suppliers, dealers, and even customers.

For example, health-insurance companies have established business units to market hardware and software services (using personal computers) to physicians' and dentists' offices. In doing so, a company can lower the cost of transactions between the physician's office and the health-insurance company's data center, and can also gain a competitive advantage by supporting the physician's staff in processing information internal to their office; thus raising the *entry costs* for health-insurance competitors and at the same time raising the *switching costs* for the physician (since once his office automates its records on a particular health insurer's software and hardware, switching to another company's services is very costly.)

Similarly, a manufacturing company can tie its suppliers, through an intelligent terminal, to the company's inventory and manufacturing information system, lowering the cost of business transactions and tieing the supplier more closely to the company's business strategy.

Thus, in designing competitive business strategies today, a company must add an *information-management strategy*. A competitive information-management strategy must, in turn, not only be integrated with the other areas of business strategy, but must also be accounted for in evaluations of the major forces driving industry competition, as we will discuss in the next chapter.

In the Information Economy, A Company's Information-Management and Human Resource-Management Strategies Must Be Closely Tied

In Chapter 1, we noted that working smarter and not harder is an important criteria of business success in the information economy. In developing an effective corporate strategy, it is no longer sufficient to proceed as if a company's human resource-management strategy and its information-management strategy are distinct and separate. The business environment for the effective use of information resources and new technologies is directly influenced by the learning capabilities, attitudes, and educational backgrounds of workers and managers alike. Since most workers in the economy are knowledge workers rather than service technicians, farmhands, or laborers, it becomes clear that maximizing the intelligence, creativity, and decision-making capacities of these workers will require paying careful attention to attracting and retaining these workers, compensating them at competitive rates, assessing and appropriately rewarding their performance, and focusing on their social and psychological needs, not simply their physical needs.

Moreover, individual companies will adopt different mixes of human resources and information-management strategies depending on their strategic objectives, style of management, competitive environments, and type of products or services. Firms in declining industries may adopt human resource and information-management strategies aimed at cost leadership. In this case, the firm's information-management strategy may emphasize aggressive use of office and factory automation, and its human resource-management strategy may emphasize providing workers with retraining programs, relocation policies for plant closings, and reward systems tied to productivity improvement. In contrast, for entrepreneurial firms in emerging industries, the information-management strategy will seek to promote creative use of information and technology and adopt human resource policies promoting new ideas for R&D, more aggressive marketing and customer analysis, and flexibility in the design and use of information systems to support a nonroutinized, dynamic internal business environment.

In each case, the intent of corporate strategy should be to promote the appropriate mix of human resource and information-management strategies that maximize intelligent use of information and brainpower to achieve corporate objectives, whether the objective be cost leadership, product differentiation, new market entry, or any mix of these. As we will point out in Chapter 8, it is not coincidental that the quest for quality improvement and business excellence today emphasize proactive human resource management. Human intellectual resources are the strategic resources of the information economy, and can be enhanced by the skillful use of information resources and the products and services of the information-processing industry, or can be constrained and even frustrated by careless or inappropriate corporate information-management strategies. Long-term productivity improvement in the information economy can only occur when corporate strategies are attuned to optimizing intellectual resources through appropriate strategies for managing information resources and new technologies.

Dinosaurs or Adapters?

Glenn Meyers believes there are just two breeds in the information age: dinosaurs and adapters. He emphasizes the "small is better" strategy as a way of insuring that ideas are churned up from the bottom, and in staying in closer touch with the needs of the marketplace. "It is clear," he says, "that the emerging industries of the information age are keeping a close watch on where they'll be tomorrow and are not skittish when it comes to adapting. The current state of the world economic system makes it painfully apparent: if you're unwilling to evolve, then prepare for extinction."[28]

---

[28] Glenn Meyers, "Changing of the Guard: Information Age Restructuring the World of Business," *Colorado Business*, V7, July 1982, pp. 18–26, 51-53.

SUMMARY

The purpose of this chapter has been to identify and define the impacts of the information economy and the information-processing industry on the development of corporate and overall business strategy. We have identified eight major characteristics of the business environment in the emerging economy which provide a context in which specific corporate strategies must be articulated. As we noted, these characteristics affect not only the ability of a company to maximize short-term profit or shareholder wealth, but also affect the long-term growth of corporate wealth, that is, the competitive conditions for survival and the quality of a company's human, financial, technological, and information assets. Moreover, the extent to which senior managers can accurately read the changing business environment will be significantly influenced by their assumptions about the economic and business environment in which they find themselves. In this regard, we have emphasized that defining corporate strategy as if one exists in an industrial versus an information economy not only represents a misreading of the current and future business environment, but more importantly, jeopardizes the long-term conditions under which productivity improvement and competitive advantage can be achieved.

CHAPTER **4**

NEW STRATEGIES FOR GAINING COMPETITIVE ADVANTAGE

If corporate strategy provides the identity and basis for the creation of corporate wealth, the business-unit strategy provides the direction for relating the company's lines of business to specific competitive industry environments. As Michael Porter has suggested:

> *The essence of formulating competitive strategy is relating a company to its environment. Although the relevant environment is very broad, encompassing social as well as economic forces, the key aspect of the firm's environment is the industry or industries in which it competes. Industry structure has a strong influence in determining the competitive rules of the game as well as the strategies potentially available to the firm.* [1]

[1] Michael E. Porter, *Competitive Strategy,* New York: Free Press, 1980, p. 3.

83

As we noted in Chapter 3, the business-unit strategy specifies: (1) the scope of that business in a way that links the strategy of the business to that of the company as a whole, and (2) the basis on which the business unit will achieve and maintain a competitive advantage. At this level of business strategy, the impacts of the information economy and information-processing industry on decision making are concerned less with overall economic and business trends and more with the specific relationship between the business unit's products and services, and the role of information resources and technology in providing the business unit with a competitive edge in its current and potential markets.

In this chapter, we will focus on the emerging role of information resources and technology in providing a source of competitive advantage for business units. Also, we will identify seven ways in which companies are integrating information-resource strategies as part of their business-unit strategies. In Chapters 5, 6, and 7, we will discuss how the growing use of information resources as sources of competitive advantage significantly alters the firm's *functional* strategies in managing, organizing and using information resources and technology in support of strategic business units.

COMPETITIVE ADVANTAGE AND THE ROLE OF INFORMATION RESOURCES

Legal Protection

Information resources have always played a role in shaping the competitive strategies of business. Copyright, patent, and trademark laws all protect some form of information developed by an individual. Such laws are directly related to the acceptance of the English philosopher John Locke's notion that a primary function of government is the protection of property, and that some ideas are property and therefore must be managed according to proprietary concepts. On these two principles rest the legal sanctions enacted by the state to enforce copyright, patent, and trademark protections for individuals and firms involved in industry and commerce. Over the last 400 years of Western development, these laws and the supporting decisions of state and federal courts have gone a long way in refining proprietary-information practices in business, and have provided some of the ground rules by which businesses compete in the free-enterprise system.

The Learning Curve

A second way that information resources have influenced competitive practices in business can be found in the concepts of experience or "know-how." Intuitively, businesses have recognized for many years the value of cumulative training on the job by managers and workers as an important basis of competitive advantage. That is, the tendency for unit costs to decline as a business unit gains cumulative experience in producing a product has been observed. In addition, as Michael Porter points out, the effects of experience on learning curves can influence not only manufacturing, but also distribution, marketing, and other business functions:

> *Costs decline because workers improve their methods and become more efficient (the classic learning curve), layout improves, specialized equipment and processes are developed, better performance is coaxed from equipment, product design changes make manufacturing easier, techniques for measurement and control of operations improve, and so on. Experience is just a name for certain kinds of technological change and may apply not only to production but also to distribution, logistics and other functions. As is the case with scale economies cost declines with experience relate not to the entire firm, but arise from the individual operations or functions that make up the firm.[2]*

Moreover, since the effects of learning curves are experienced by people, the way people are managed, motivated, compensated, and treated has historically strongly influenced the capability of individual business units or functional operations to take advantage of the technical know-how or learning contained in the brains of individual employees and managers.

[2] *Ibid.*, pp. 11–12.

Business Intelligence

A third way that information resources have long played a role in commercial enterprise is concerned with the management and use of business intelligence. While the development and use of intelligence has long been a part of Western political and military history, it is easy to forget that the growth of international commerce after the Middle Ages was strongly influenced by the need for acquiring and using information about the actions of governments and businesses in international trade. The emergence of international trading and banking houses, joint ventures, and holding companies to exploit the wealth of the New World and other colonial holdings created a strong need for accurate information about distant places, persons, and institutions.

> *One of Europe's first international banking houses was founded in the late fourteenth century by the South German House of Fugger . . . . To keep the numerous branches of their far-flung operations current on important matters, the Fuggers of Augsburg developed one of the first manuscript newsletters. Filled with columns of political and commercial information that would influence the bank's important financial decisions, it was a private commercial intelligence report that equaled and probably exceeded the scope and accuracy of comparable diplomatic intelligence reports. Available to selected outsiders, particularly those with important political connections, the Fugger newsletters were widely imitated by other emerging international trading houses, and to some extent became the prototypes of public newspapers.* [3]

In addition to the Fuggers, the Rothschilds in the eighteenth and nineteenth centuries developed an international trading and banking empire based on the skillful use of insider information, as the following example aptly illustrates:

> *In promoting their employers' financial interests from headquarters in Frankfurt-am-Main, London, Paris, Vienna and Naples, Rothchilds agents were often able to gain vital intelligence before governments did. In 1815, while Europe awaited news of the Battle of Waterloo, Nathan Rothschild in London already knew that the British had been*

---

[3] William L. Sammon, M. A. Kurland, and R. Spitalnic, *Business Competitor Intelligence*, New York: Wiley, 1984, p. 29.

victorious. In order to make a financial killing, he then depressed the market by selling British Government securities; those who watched his every move in the market did likewise, concluding that Waterloo had been lost by the British and their allies. At the proper moment he bought back in the low, and when the news was finally generally known, the value of government securities soared. [4]

Although the communications capabilities of the Fuggers and Rothschilds were very slow and often inadequate by today's standards, they set an important precedent. The significant increases in international trade and commerce that have followed have in large measure depended on the ability of trading companies to structure organizational arrangements to accommodate the collection and use of competitive information. Moreover, the strong desire of some businesses to gather intelligence on their competitors in both legitimate and illegitimate ways has often resulted in industrial espionage, which in turn has resulted in the evolution of the private investigative industry to thwart or discover espionage activities. The startling arrest and indictment of executives from Mitsubishi and Hitachi (two leading Japanese electronics corporations) by the FBI in July 1982 on the accusation (supported by videotape evidence) that they conspired to steal and transport to Japan trade secrets belonging to IBM, was a clear reminder of the undercurrents of industrial espionage present in commerce and trade today, and the lengths to which some businesses will go to seek proprietary competitor information at great risk to themselves.

More prosaicly, successful executives have long recognized the need to collect business intelligence whether the information is gathered at trade shows, country-club parties, or informal lunches. However haphazard the process has been, the need for securing intelligence on competitors, government actions and plans, and even consumer trends and tastes has emerged as an important, if not always visible, aspect of business management.

The Global Village: Telecommunications Networks

A fourth way information resources have influenced competitive practices in business has evolved over the last 150 years through

---

[4] *Ibid.,* p. 30.

the development of international and national telecommunications systems. In the early 1800s in England, the potential opportunity for improving business and diplomatic communications across the British Empire resulted in the major capital investments for laying transoceanic and transcontinental telegraphic cables over the next 50 to 60 years. Companies such as Cable and Wireless, Ltd. helped to literally wire the major capitals of the world by forming regional and national companies to invest the resources necessary to lay and maintain telegraphic cables and wires worldwide.[5] Moreover, as inventions such as the telephone came on the scene, the commercial and governmental infrastructure for the expansion of worldwide telecommunications largely evolved out of the holding companies, joint ventures, and national companies formed during the era of the telegraph.

Therefore, as the demands of industry and commerce for instantaneous phone communications and improved mail, facsimile, and radio communications increased, so did the evolution of the telecommunications industry, as suggested in Chapters 1 and 2. Today, it is difficult to imagine an era when the conduct of business was not influenced by the technological capabilities and regulatory and commercial practices of the telecommunications industry.

Paperwork Control

A fifth way in which information resources have historically shaped business practices arises from the evolution of the tools and techniques used to manage paperwork and records in the office and plant.

Again, it is difficult to imagine that the typewriter, tabulating machine, and microfilm were invented less than a century ago. Since their invention, these tools have continued to shape and influence both the organization and layout of the modern office, as well as the procedures and practices used in developing correspondence, organizing files, distributing mail, and retaining records. In addition, these basic procedures for managing paperwork in general have influenced the organization of inventory control, distribution,

[5] See Hugh Barty-King, *Girdle Round the Earth*, London: Heinemann, 1979.

and even financial management, accounting systems, and practices in business. Despite the extensive progress in computers and telecommunications technologies in recent years, and their widespread application in business, the modern office remains a paper-intensive environment driven by the necessity of developing and maintaining efficient procedures and systems for collecting, storing, disseminating, and disposing of correspondence, mail, files, and records on employees, customers, products, and services. Moreover, just as in the telecommunications industry, the office-equipment industry of the early twentieth century provided the organizational basis for the evolution of the leading corporations in the computer industry, such as IBM and NCR.

REDEFINING THE ROLE OF INFORMATION RESOURCES

If business practices have historically been significantly shaped and influenced by information resources, what factors in the 1980s have led to a sharp redefinition of the roles of information resources in shaping business-unit strategies and competitive advantage?

Four factors account for the rising significance of information resources to competitive advantage. The first was articulated in Chapter 1. The information economy's maturity has caused a major shift to occur in the nature of work—from physical labor to intellectual labor. This basic shift has in turn affected the way business is carried out in both the service and manufacturing sectors. Second, the evolution of the information-processing industry has provided an increasingly diverse array of technological innovations, which in turn have provided opportunities for the design of new products and services, and the transformation of old ones. The third factor contributing to the emerging importance of information resources to business resides in the increasing complexity and uncertainty of regional, national, and international markets. As the boundaries between service and manufacturing, and between national and international markets become increasingly blurred, and as the pace of change continues to accelerate, the pressures on businesses to scan external environments for strategic planning, management, production, and marketing techniques continue to increase.

Finally, the impacts of information resources on businesses prior to the 1970s and 1980s tended to be quite even across business markets and sectors. Successful firms in a particular industry all used telecommunications and computers for basically the same applications. While there might be variations in their use of business intelligence or technical know-how, the adjustments of competitors in relatively stable markets to specific competitive advantages were relatively smooth and nonthreatening. Today, as we will suggest in this chapter, the innumerable options open to individual businesses in exploiting information resources and new technologies, coupled with increasingly complex and turbulent business environments, affect every aspect of competitive strategy.

Lawrence and Dyer, in a fascinating study entitled *Renewing American Industry,* suggest that businesses today must not only *adapt* their internal environments to changes in external environments, but must also continually engage in readaptation. They point out that "a form of organizational adaptation in which the organization and its relevant environment interact and evolve toward exchanges that are more acceptable to the internal and external stakeholders as evidenced by continuing high levels of innovation, efficiency and member involvement"[6] is crucial to the success of today's businesses.

Businesses will engage in organizational learning where they will define strategies that effectively link their internal arrangements with conditions, events, and changes in the external environments or markets. As Figure 4-1 suggests, Lawrence and Dyer have developed a conceptual model whereby the degree of complexity and uncertainty in the "relevant" environment of an organization (that is, its relations with customers, competitors, suppliers, unions, and government) will impact the business's strategies and use of organizational resources including information resources.[7] Moreover, the relative availability of organizational resources will influence the response to information complexity, which will in turn determine whether or not a firm is very good at

---

[6] New York: Free Press, 1983, p. 295.
[7] *Ibid.,* p. 269.

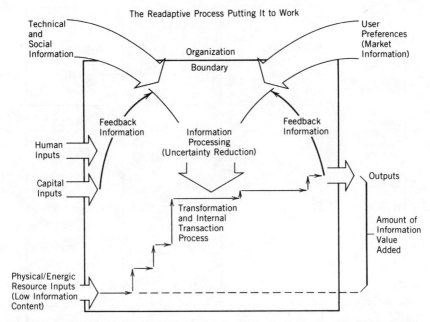

Figure 4–1. The information resource transformation process of an organization. Reprinted with permission of The Free Press, a Division of Macmillan, Inc. from *Renewing American Industry* by Paul R. Lawrence and David Dyer. Copyright© 1983 by The Free Press. See note 7.

readaptation. Over time, as Lawrence and Dyer demonstrate, various industry sectors will migrate (see Figure 4–2) from different positions, either toward or away from the area of highest readaptation (see Cell 5).[8] As they do so, organizational strategies involving the management of internal resources in relation to the characteristics of the domain of information complexity, will also shift and either improve or worsen the opportunities for readaptation.

INFORMATION-RESOURCE STRATEGIES FOR GAINING COMPETITIVE ADVANTAGE

As we discussed in the previous chapters, the impact of information resources and technology on business corporate strategy lies

[8] *Ibid.*, p. 240.

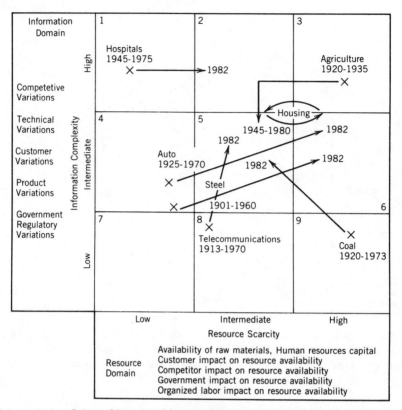

Figure 4–2. Selected historical locus of seven essential industries. Reprinted with permission of The Free Press, a Division of Macmillan, Inc. from *Renewing American Industry* by Paul R. Lawrence and David Dyer. Copyright© 1983 by The Free Press. See note 8.

in three areas: (1) the characteristics of the economy, (2) the evolution of the information-processing industry, and (3) trends in specific industries. At the strategic business unit level, the impacts of information resources on business strategy lie in two areas: (1) the effects of critical competitive forces, and (2) the selection and implementation of a firm's specific business strategy.

In his classic work entitled *Competitive Strategy,* Michael Porter of the Harvard Business School defines, as Figure 4–3 suggests, the key forces driving industry competition.[9] These five forces act

[9] Porter, *Competitive Strategy,* pp. 3–33.

Key Competitive Forces	Implications for Business Strategy
Potential entrants	Barriers to entry
	Economies of scale
	Switching costs
	Capital requests
	Access to distribution channels
	Product differentation
	Proprietary product technology
	Learning or experience curve
	Government policy
	Expected retaliation
	Structure of prices of entry and costs of entry
Rivalry among existing competitors	Competition
	Price
	Product
	Marketing and advertising
	Distribution and services
Substitute products	Limits on returns
	Limits on prices
Bargaining power of buyers	Force prices down
	Higher quality
	More services
	Encourage competition
Bargaining power of suppliers	Raise prices
	Reduce quality
	Reduce services
	Squeeze profitability out of industry

Figure 4–3. Impact of Competitive Forces.

collectively to determine the intensity of industry competition and its profitability. The strongest force or forces to affect a business unit significantly channel and define that unit's business strategy.

An effective competitive strategy will require a firm to take a defendable position against the five competitive forces and will demand both offensive and defensive actions.[10] Each strategic

[10] *Ibid.*, p. 29.

business unit may adopt a unique combination of offensive and defensive moves to successfully defend and/or exploit its competitive position. In the context of the management and use of information resources, a strategic business unit may adopt one or a combination of seven basic strategies to pursue its business objectives of cost leadership, product differentiation, or focus in specific market niches. In Figure 4–4, we have defined a grid on which a company might select a generic information-resource strategy to pursue one or a combination of business objectives. In using this grid to characterize the actions of specific companies or in developing a specific business unit's strategy, we must avoid the temptation to associate the identification of information resource

Information Resource Strategy	Generic Business Objectives		
	Cost Leadership	Product Differentiation	Focus
Using information resources strategically inside the firm			
Using information resources in new and creative ways			
Using information resources to offer a new product or service			
Using information resources to market and distribute a product or service			
Using information resources in manufacturing			
Getting into the information-management business as a by-product of what you do			
Engaging in a collaborative information-management venture			

Figure 4–4. Information Resources Strategy Selection by Business Objectives.

and business strategies with business success in the short or long term. Indeed, the jury is still out on the degree to which companies that have adopted innovative information-resource strategies for competitive advantage are completely successful in accomplishing their specific business objectives. However, one point is clear: Specific strategic business units that fail to seriously consider the impacts of information-resource strategies on business objectives may incur considerable risk of failure. Such a narrow view today is akin to ignoring the management of human resources, or the relevance of financial and capital resources, to business success.

Using Information Resources Strategically Inside the Company

The first strategy that a company might adopt in using information resources for competitive advantage is to maximize the use of the information resources already contained in the firm. In Chapter 3 we noted that in an industrial economy, information management is largely a back-room function, carried out in the background of organizational life. The information-management function is fragmented into a series of cost centers such as the mail room, copier center, word-processing group, telephone operation, and data-processing department. Being cost centers, these subunits are accounted for as part of the *overhead* expenses of doing business, and therefore, their contribution or lack thereof to the profitability of a business unit's product line is rarely identified. In turn, since information management is not perceived as a traditional resource-management function akin to financial management, personnel management, or to the classic business functions of marketing or production, the nature of the information-management function in the firm is often seen exclusively in cost-reduction terms rather than in profit-center terms. Thus, the objective of top management toward the data-processing department, copier center, or telecommunications unit focuses almost entirely on keeping the cost of operations to a minimum.

Until the late 1970s and early 1980s, the primary attention that the information management function received from top management was based on the perception that as cost centers, the managers of data-processing departments, telephone sections, library, file and records groups, word-processing and copier centers must hold the increasing cost of doing business to a minimum. Their role was not directed at finding ways of contributing to the business strategy of the firm, but rather was confined to the narrow objective of holding the line on the "support" services they operated. It was up to other managers in the business—in marketing, in production, sales, and so forth—to define and pursue the competitive strategies of the firm.

As the information economy matures, this narrow and confining view of the information-management function is increasingly being cast off by firms as they perceive the value of information resources inside their business units as sources of competitive advantage. Adopting the Porter view of the generic business strategies of cost leadership and product differentiation, Gregory Parsons of the Harvard Business School has provided an interesting perspective on the ways companies can and do view the use of information resources and new technologies to achieve business strategies in specific functional areas of the business (see Table 4–1).[11] According to Professor Parsons, nearly every function of a firm can be enhanced in the long term by some use of new information technologies. The real issue revolves around determining the most appropriate applications to automate, given the scarcity of financial, personnel, and capital resources and the demands of timing and scheduling:

> *Clearly, a firm should use IT (Information Technology) to support, reinforce, or enlarge its business strategy. In general, firms pursuing an overall cost leadership strategy should use IT to reduce costs either by improving the productivity of labor or by improving the utilization of other resources, such as machinery and inventory. Firms following a differentiation strategy should use IT either to directly add unique features to the product or service or to contribute to quality, service or image through the functional areas. Although a firm may benefit from IT application that is not consistent with its competitive strategy, it will enjoy much greater strategic benefits from an IT application that is consistent with and supportive of its competitive strategy.[12]*

[11] Gregory L. Parsons, "Information Technology: A New Competitive Weapon," *Sloan Management Review,* Fall 1983, p. 12.
[12] *Ibid.,* p. 11.

TABLE 4–1.   Information-Technology Applications that Support Generic Strategies of Firms

	Low Cost	Product Differentiation
Product design and development	Product engineering systems Project control systems	R&D Databases Professional work stations Electronic mail CAD Custom-engineering systems Integrated systems for manufacturing
Operations	Process engineering systems Process-control systems Labor-control systems Inventory management systems Procurement systems Quality-monitoring systems	CAM Quality-assurance systems Systems for suppliers Quality-monitoring systems
Marketing	Streamlined distribution systems Centralized control systems Econometric modeling systems	Sophisticated marketing systems Market databases Graphic display systems Telemarketing sytems Competition-analysis systems Modeling systems Service-orientated distribution systems

TABLE 4–1 *(Continued)*

	Low Cost	Product Differentiation
Sales	Sales-control systems Advertising-monitoring systems Systems to consolidate sales functions Strict incentive monitoring systems	Differential pricing systems Office field-communication systems Customer/sales support systems Dealer support systems Customer-order entry systems
Administration	Cost-control systems Quantitative planning and budgeting systems Office automation for staff reduction	Office automation to integrate functions Environment-scanning and nonquantitative planning systems Teleconferencing systems

Source: See note 11. Reprinted from "Information Technology: A New Competitive Weapon" by Gregory L. Parsons, *Sloan Management Review,* Fall 1983, p. 12, by permission of the publisher. Copyright © 1983 by the Sloan Management Review Association. All rights reserved.

Thus, depending on a particular firm's business strategies, information resources already available to the firm can be used to facilitate product designs and development, improve the quality or flexibility of operations and production, streamline or reorient marketing approaches, assist in monitoring sales or improving customer satisfaction, provide greater control over costs, and enhance the information resources used by all employees in the office or factory. Thus, information assets and technologies can be used more strategically inside the firm, to support whatever business objectives the firm or its individual business units pursue. In doing so, however, top managers of these firms must expand their view of the information-management function from being predominantly a supportive back-room function, to being a strategic management function in the enterprise.

Using Information Resources in New and Creative Ways

It is one thing to use information resources more strategically inside the firm for cost leadership or product differentiation. It is another matter to find new and creative ways to use information resources in pursuing business strategies. Increasingly, leading firms are using existing information resources in new ways—that is, reinventing and adding value to investments already made.

For example, in California, Mobil is marketing gasoline by installing point-of-sale terminals at the gas pumps which can be used with the automated-teller machines of two leading banks. Sears Roebuck and J. C. Penney are using videodisks and personal computers to automate their customer-order catalogs, and extending the use of their walk-in services by offering the same catalog information to customers in their homes. Textile companies in South and North Carolina are arming their salesmen with videodisk players so that they can effectively demonstrate to potential customers the color and style variations of lines of products the companies offer. Airlines, car-rental firms, and hotel firms are teaming up to offer new bonus programs for frequent travelers through automated systems that track bonus points and disburse awards.

What all of these examples have in common is the use by companies of existing information resources or technologies in new and creative ways. This trend is supported by an equally strong tendency to permit entrepreneurs within companies to acquire resources and organize internal units to experiment with and pilot test new uses of information resources to market, sell, and distribute products and services. Hence, new units are being formed both within and without traditional MIS or data-processing departments to do electronic banking, telemarketing, videotex, and home retailing, point-of-sales development, and information retailing and wholesaling. Their objectives are usually to research and pilot test new and creative ways of extending the services and products of the company by building on existing information resources about customers, buyers, or suppliers and extending through information technologies the services offered in new or existing markets.

For example, the Buick division of General Motors has organized a "marketing through technology" department to develop a new information system called EPIC to aid in the marketing of their automobiles.[13] EPIC is being used by Buick in dealer showrooms, in public areas such as hotels and shopping malls, and in homes via videotex services. In dealer showrooms, the EPIC system uses personal computers in kiosks which allow a salesman in a showroom to respond to customer questions about the availability of various models, colors, options, prices, and financing terms for Buick cars. If a customer is interested in a particular model, the salesman can use EPIC to determine the nearest dealership that has the car, and if the customer is comparison shopping with other makes of cars in mind, the salesman can, through EPIC, use another videotex service called CompuServe to get data on most makes and models of cars to compare with the Buick model under consideration.

Thus, EPIC provides better and more accurate information about the Buick product line to salesmen and customers alike, as well as integrating the use of a car-locator system for inventory control and an external-information service for comparison shopping. The long-term mission of the marketing through technology department is to determine the profitability of using new technologies to extend the reach of information resources in creative directions to enhance the sales effectiveness, inventory control, and productivity of the dealer workforce.

One of the most strikingly creative ways of using "old" *information* with "new" information technology we've encountered, is provided by Robert C. Waggoner. As reported in *Business Week,* Waggoner bought one-third of an antiquated newspaper-clipping company, Burrelle's Information Services, Inc. As *Business Week* reported:

> It [Burrelle's] was on a slow track to nowhere. Sales were growing at a sluggish pace, profits were modest—and Burrelle's was still cutting and pasting much the way it did when it was founded in 1888. But Waggoner changed all that. The hustling Harvard MBA pushed Burrelle's as a growth company. It now [through a computer system]

[13] "The 'Chief Information Officer's Role," *EDP Analyzer,* November 1984, Vol. 22, No. 11, pp. 1, 2.

monitors 16,000 newspapers, magazines, and trade journals for 40,000 categories, from company and product names to political issues. Customers say they've come to regard fast access to clips as a necessity.[14]

Using Information Resources to Offer a New Product or Service

A third strategy for using information resources strategically is based not on the capability of finding new uses for known information, but on using information resources in offering a new product or service. In this case, information resources are embedded in the new service or product in such a way as to appear indistinguishable from the nature of the product or service itself. In recent years, many examples of companies inventing new products or services where information resources play the pivotal or key role have begun to appear.

In 1977, Merrill Lynch first announced its new cash management account (CMA) which was an information resource product that permitted the integration of four services to investors: (1) automatic investment of cash and dividends in a Merrill-managed money-market account, (2) credit through a standard-margin account, (3) cash withdrawal by check or debit card, and (4) investment advice in managing and diversifying the account. Although each of the services standing alone were not innovative, the integration of these services in a single product—the CMA—provided an unprecedented competitive advantage for Merrill Lynch.

The CMA was supported by a complex network of databases, voice-data communications networks, and software programs. It was sold through Merrill's brokers to investors with minimum balances of $20,000. Although the growth of the CMA has slowed in recent years, Merrill Lynch was able to amass more than 450,000 accounts and $20 billion in assets before serious competition appeared in 1982 from other investment houses (for example, Dean Witter), banks, and financial-services companies.

Moreover, since the CMA concept's invention, banks and

[14] *Business Week*, "An Unlikely Gold Mine: Newspaper Clippings," March 4, 1985, p. 114.

financial service companies have used their financial-information resources and computer and communication technology to manufacture whole new types of financial products "on the fly."

Wiseman and MacMillan provide an interesting example of the development of a CD fund by a large investment fund:

> At 6 A.M., leaders at a brokerage house called London to order sheafs of CD's from foreign banks, which often pay higher rates than their U.S. counterparts. By 11 A.M. they had accumulated $50 million of the paper. The next step in the fund-creation process depended on an information system that took the prices and rates, juggled them according to the firm's objectives and constraints embodied in its computer program, and arrived at management fees and commissions. Thirty-six hours after the start of this production run (job-shop style, to be sure), brokers were ready to start selling the fund.[15]

The creation of new financial products on a real-time basis has brought the principles of "flexible manufacturing" to the financial services industry. Portfolio-management systems of companies such as Shearson/American Express, Citicorp, Bank of America, and others offer new opportunities to tailor complex combinations of investment services to businesses or consumers with diverse assets and investment outlooks.

Similarly, in the express-delivery industry, the merger of transportation (air, land) and communications services (facsimile and imaging machines), has resulted in the creation of new competitive products. During the early 1980s, Federal Express began planning and developing a new delivery service called "Zap Mail," which depended on the availability of improved imaging technology and mobilizing its fleet of 10,000 delivery vans. In its initial phase, Federal Express offered a two-hour delivery, enabling customers to send high-quality duplicates of documents and diagrams to recipients thousands of miles away in the United States.

Customers call Federal Express for a Zap Mail pickup. A Federal Express courier picks up the document and takes it to the nearest Federal Express Imager I machine. The machine electronically

---

[15] Charles Wiseman and Ian C. MacMillian, "Creating Competitive Weapons from Information Systems," *The Journal of Business Strategy,* Fall 1984, Vol. 5, No. 2, p. 44.

transmits the document to the Federal Express facility closest to the recipient, where a high-quality duplicate is placed in a Zap Mail envelope and delivered by courier within two hours. The price when the service was initiated was $35.

In May 1985, Federal Express extended this basic service by leasing 3000 Imager II machines to some of its heaviest users. With the Imager II, customers can transmit and receive documents from Federal Express, eliminating the need for pickup, and, in some cases, ending the need for delivery.

The Imager technology and the fleet of Federal Express vans are designed to eliminate problems that have plagued businesses using previously available facsimile transmission services. Those problems included poor quality, slow transmissions, and lack of compatible machines to send and receive documents. By the late 1980s, Federal Express expects at least 30 percent of its revenue to come from Zap Mail.

Federal Express's approach to Zap Mail, which relies on the delivery of hard copies, is not without criticism in the competitive market by those who argue that long term growth and profits in this market will be in high-speed data-transmission services using computers and word processors such as MCI Communications Corporation's MCI Mail.

In MCI Mail, for example, a message can be typed into a computer that has access to the MCI system. The message may be sent through MCI to the recipient's computer, or printed at a station near the recipient for hand delivery by a local courier. The service is less expensive than Zap Mail, however, it is harder to use and cannot send charts and graphs. It's application has been for customers who wish to send *one* message to hundreds or thousands of recipients. For example, a manufacturer who wants to send a single message to dealers can type the message into a computer in which a list of dealers' names and addresses has already been stored. With a few key strokes, the manufacturer can send the message to hundreds of recipients at a cost of only a few dollars for each recipient.

The competition for market share between Zap Mail and MCI Mail represents a clear use of information resources for competitive advantage. Moreover, what is at stake in this competition is not just product differentiation, but cost leadership. In addition, both Federal Express and MCI Communications Corporation are using information technologies to tie their customers directly to their product offerings by making available on-premise software and hardware for the customer to interact with the network. Similarly, financial-service companies and banks are moving beyond the design of new products such as CMAs and portfolio-management systems by offering these services to customers who are directly tied to the seller's databases and communications links by terminals and personal computers. Innovation in the design of new information-based products and services spills over into their marketing and distribution.

Using Information Resources to Market and Distribute a New Product or Service

A fourth strategy for using information resources to competitive advantage involves using these resources to market and help distribute a product or service. Although electronic marketing will not replace more traditional forms of marketing in the near future, it does provide new types of tradeoffs in the expected benefits and costs of direct marketing. Shopping malls and retail outlets will continue to be an important part of retailing and shopping in the United States. However, communications and computer technologies will be used increasingly in homes, offices, and many public places (including shopping malls) to permit more widespread shopping for many goods and services.

Direct marketing is another term for selling without stores. The Direct Marketing Association defines direct marketing as "an interactive system of marketing which uses one or more advertising media to effect a measurable response and/or transaction at any location."[16] While direct marketing is often thought of as just direct mail, it also includes the use of radio, TV, telephone, print ads, coupons, store catalogs, package inserts, bill stuffers, and even match book covers. Compared to newspaper, magazine, radio, and TV advertising, direct marketing is interactive. Moreover, in its electronic forms, direct marketing can establish direct links with

[16] Lawrence Strauss, *Electronic Marketing.* White Plains, NY: Knowledge Industry Publications, 1983, p. 39.

	Network TV	Spot TV	Space Ads	Direct Mail	Tele–marketing
Access to the mass market	10	5	5	5	2
Cost per inquiry	3	5	5	8	9
Cost per order	2	5	4	8	9
Access to special markets	1	3	6	8	10
Pre–sell	1	5	5	6	10
Follow–up	1	2	2	5	10
Synergism with other media	5	5	5	5	10
Personal contact with customer	1	2	3	6	10
10 = maximum					1 = least

Figure 4–5. The Direct Marketing Matrix. *Source:* See note 17. Reprinted from *Telemarketing®* magazine, Volume 2/No.10, dated April 1984, published by Technology Marketing Corporation, 17 Park Street, Norwalk, CT 06851, USA. Copyright © 1984 Technology Marketing Corporation, all rights reserved.

customers 24 hours a day from practically anywhere in the nation. In addition, direct telemarketing compares favorably with other forms of more conventional marketing as Figure 4–5 suggests.[17] While telemarketing does not compete with television for mass-market appeal, in every other feature it either equals or surpasses TV, space ads, and direct mail letters when these are used alone:

> *It [telemarketing] works in combination with virtually all media. Telemarketing can improve results of a direct mail campaign, space ads—and even TV. It is cost effective, particularly with higher priced products, it is extremely comparable with other marketing strategies; it is the only sales method that is designed for pre-sell, sell and follow-up efforts.*[18] *(Emphasis added.)*

As the oldest form of electronic marketing, telemarketing has been used to sell virtually all types of products and services. In

[17] Edward Blank, "Telemarketing: The Key Element of the Direct Marketing Matrix," *Telemarketing,* April 1984, Vol. 2, No. 10, p. 48.
[18] *Ibid.,* p. 48.

recent years, firms have combined telemarketing strategies with personal computers and videodisks to provide new forms of direct marketing. Among the top 30 direct marketing firms in the United States, it is difficult to identify any which have not begun to develop computers and communications technology based on marketing strategies. Sears Roebuck and J. C. Penney are pilot testing new home videotex services with IBM and AT&T, to offer two-way home-shopping services known as videotex. Moreover, most major retailers are developing ways of using videodisks and personal computers to automate their catalogs. Cosmetics firms such as Avon and Elizabeth Arden are offering computer-based make-up analysis to provide customers with more individualized cosmetic recommendations. Personal and property-based insurance companies are offering customers in malls the option of using a videotex kiosk as a means of finding the most cost-effective insurance policies for their needs. Upscale retailers such as L. L. Bean in Freeport, Maine, use computers to combine sophisticated systems for order handling, tracking customers and inventory, sampling mailing lists, and performing complex modeling exercises of direct marketing strategies. Finally, real-estate brokers are using videodisks and personal computers not only to automate listing services, but also to provide video images of the properties and houses that prospective buyers can screen instead of going on time-consuming weekend house hunting expeditions.

In addition to these forms of electronic direct marketing, most major retailers are linking with banks and credit-card companies to develop point-of-sale systems that provide customer convenience as well as increase the company's ability to track inventories on a daily rather than weekly or monthly basis. As the lines between the physical store and electronic store continue to blur, it will be difficult in the future to design effective product and service marketing strategies without considering the tradeoffs of costs and benefits inherent in all forms of electronic and traditional marketing.

Using Information Resources in Manufacturing

A fifth strategy for using information resources to competitive advantage is to manage the information resources within the manufacturing process more effectively. During the last 15 years, a dramatic change has occurred in both Japan and the United States, concerning the role of manufacturing as a competitive weapon. Throughout the 1970s and early 1980s, manufacturing productivity declined in the United States, while it rose significantly in countries like Japan and West Germany. While the exact causes of the changes in productivity have yet to be defined, it is clear that a change occurred in the significance given to quality control and process manufacturing among Japanese and West German businesses in contrast to U.S. manufacturers. Indeed, a growing debate evolved in the business community concerning how to adopt quality-control and manufacturing improvements used in Japan, West Germany, and other advanced economies into American manufacturing.

Throughout this period, two types of quality-improvement strategies have been adopted. The first type is very technology intensive and is aimed at improving the design, production, and control of products throughout the manufacturing process through the *use* of computers and communication technology. As Figure 4–6 indicates, manufacturing management is very dependent on the information-resource strategies used to control the

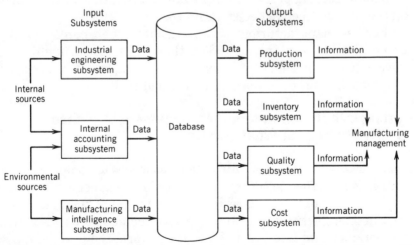

Figure 4–6. Model of a manufacturing information system. *Source:* See note 19. From *Management Information Systems* by Raymond McLeod, Jr. Copyright© 1983 Science Research Associates, Inc. Reprinted by permission of the publisher.

production, inventory, quality control, and cost control functions.[19] These functions are in turn influenced by three support functions: (1) the industrial-engineering function, which influences the design of products, (2) the internal job-scheduling and production-control system, and (3) the manufacturing-intelligence function which monitors the use of labor and suppliers. For all of these functions to work effectively, a great deal of information management is required. In recent years this need has resulted in the development of highly automated systems such as MRP—manufacturing resources planning, and CAD/CAM—computer assisted design/computer assisted manufacturing.

The second type of quality-improvement strategy, in contrast to the first, is very people-intensive and is aimed at improving the way workers are motivated, the way they work together as teams to solve problems and make operational decisions, and the way they interact with and use new technologies. A variety of techniques and policies have evolved to assist the worker in being a more informed decision maker and participant in the production process. These include quality-control circles, job sharing, and improved education and training on the job. All of these strategies have had as an integral component providing a closer link between the manufacturing process and the information that workers need to make more effective decisions on the job.

Thus, as manufacturing has increasingly been perceived as a competitive weapon in the 1980s, the objectives of quality improvement and productivity have required improved information resources, human resources, and technical strategies.

Getting into the Information-Management Business as a By-Product of What You Do

A sixth strategy for using information resources to competitive advantage is for a firm to enter the information management business as a byproduct of what it does in its main line(s) of business. Many firms in manufacturing and services have accumulated a great deal of experience and internal skills that can form the basis of a new

---

[19] Raymond McLeod, Jr., *Management Information Systems*, Chicago, IL: Science Research Associates, 1983, p. 447.

service. In some cases, capitalizing on this corporate know-how and experience may result in a new consulting service, or in other cases, it may result in a new information service. In the first case, many large corporations such as Dupont and General Electric have over the years accumulated considerable experience and know-how in specific areas, such as health and safety management services or facilities management, which they in turn have marketed outside the company as a value-added service. In the second case, companies such as Policy Management Systems Corporation (a software-service company to the property and casualty-insurance market), or Dun & Bradstreet (a credit-reporting service company), have over the years acquired information resources about their customer bases which they in turn can market as new information services.

William R. King of the University of Pittsburg gives us the example of Foremost-McKesson, which used innovative information systems to gain a competitive edge in a noninformation business. In their case, he found, it was necessary to make major changes in the structure of drug wholesaling and to get into new information businesses such as the processing of insurance payments related to drug purchases in order to survive.[20]

Another approach to entering the information-management business as a byproduct of what a firm does is to capitalize on the physical resources a company may have. For many years, companies in manufacturing or services with underutilized capacity in computer operations have offered external time-sharing and computer services. Today, railroads are using their rights-of-way to establish major fiber optic communications networks and marketing these services to other companies.

A third approach to entering the information-management business as a byproduct of one's main business line is to enhance the information value of one's products. In this case, manufacturing companies can enter the information business by engaging in "systems selling" as opposed to product selling. Selling solutions to customer problems requires a great deal of enhanced expertise and information management to respond to diverse customer

---

[20] William R. King, "Information as a Strategic Resource," (editor's comment), *Management Information Systems Quarterly,* (i), 1983.

problems. In some cases, companies have organized specific service units to offer specialized expertise and technical help for a price. For example, fertilizer companies have offered farmers specialized software programs to assist in analyzing crop characteristics and fertilizer needs for more than 15 years. Moreover, some aerospace firms have provided computer services and industry management consulting and software design on a for-profit basis, while other large corporations have engaged in marketing communications network-management services based on their internally developed expertise in this area.

The routes to the information management business that firms can take are quite diverse. More than anything else, what is required is a realization of the firm's real value in information investments, both in people and in databases that can be treated as physical assets and be capitalized. All that is needed is an entrepreneurial spirit to look beyond the borders of one's traditional business lines for new opportunities.

Engaging in a Collaborative Information-Management Venture

The seventh basic strategy for using information resources for competitive advantage is to engage in a collaborative information-management venture. In the information economy, business has become too demanding and fast paced for a company to mount a significant presence in the marketplace across all its business lines. Increasingly, more emphasis is being placed on leveraging in a cooperative way the resources of two or more firms, to provide entry or a presence in selected markets. In a 1984 study by the consulting firm of Coopers and Lybrand, which examined 38 collaborative ventures, interviews with participating executives revealed, as Table 4–2 indicates, that the sharing of complementary strengths and sharing of resources were the two leading reasons for collaborative ventures, although some executives clearly believed that joining a "winning team" and sharing the risks of development or large capital investments were also factors.[21] Underlying the reasons for collaboration

---

[21] Coopers & Lybrand (with Yankelovich, Skelly and White, Inc.), *Collaborative Ventures: A Programatic Approach to Business Expansion in the Eighties,* New York: Coopers and Lybrand, 1983.

TABLE 4–2.   Reasons for Collaborative Ventures

Reason	Number of Times Mentioned
Complementary strengths	35
Shared resources	21
Joining a winning team	19
Sharing a risk	17

Source: See note 21. Reprinted with permission of Coopers & Lybrand© 1984 Coopers & Lybrand (U.S.A.).

were the convergence of technological innovations which blurred boundaries between markets and industries, as well as the pace of international competition which required companies to form new alliances.

While collaborative ventures have traditionally been used in the manufacturing sector primarily due to larger capital requirements, more recent trends (see Table 4-3) indicate the growth of ventures among firms in the information-processing industry as well as among traditional service or manufacturing firms who wish to enter this industry.[22] Moreover, although research and development ventures such as the Austin-based Microelectronic and Computer Technology Corporation, where 15 major U.S.

TABLE 4–3.   Use of Collaborative Ventures by Industry Sector

Manufacturing	34%
Information/communications	21%
Transportation	9%
Natural resources	8%
Financial services	7%
Retail	7%
Construction	6%
Other	8%

Source: See note 22. Reprinted with permission of Coopers & Lybrand© 1984 Coopers & Lybrand (U.S.A.).

[22] Coopers & Lybrand, *Collaborative Ventures: An Emerging Phenomenon in the Information Industry.* New York: Coopers and Lybrand, 1984, p. 3.

Type	Purpose	Example
Equity investment	Ensure supplier viability Establish an informal working relationship and exchange of technology	GM acquisition of Electronic Data Services
Research and development ventures	Share costs and results of basic research and development	Microelectronics & Computer Technology Corporation
Cooperative ventures	Undertake a specific enterprise which does not entail creation of a separate operating company	Communications Satellite Corporation and Holiday Inns
Operating ventures	Establish a stand-alone operating company—a "new business"	Satellite Business Systems (IBM and Aetna Insurance Company)

Figure 4–7. Types of Collaborative Ventures.

computer firms are partners, have been among the more visible collaborative ventures, the more common ventures occur among firms seeking an equity investment in another company, firms undertaking specific lines of business which do not entail creation of a new company, or firms joining together to form a stand-alone company for the purpose of entering a new market.

Figure 4–7 provides some examples of these types of collaborative ventures. In type one—equity investment—a collaborative venture often results in outright ownership or majority shareholding of a company. In many cases, the acquired company is allowed a great deal of latitude in conducting its business, at the discretion of the parent company. The IBM acquisition of Rolm and the GM acquisition of Electronic Data Services Inc. both fall into these latter types of cases. In still other cases, a company may set up its own subsidiary to enter a new business and then acquire a majority interest in an outside company as well. For example, in 1982 Ford Motor Company created Ford Aerospace

Satellite Corporation as a subsidiary to operate satellites and lease space in them to companies for voice and data transmission. Then, in 1984, Ford agreed to buy 80 percent of San Diego's Starnet Corporation to increase its customer base and expertise in the voice data communications field.

In type two—research and development venture—two or more companies will agree to share the costs and results of basic research and development. On August 12, 1982, the Microelectronics and Computer Technology Corporation was incorporated following the concern of Gordon Bell at Digital Equipment Corporation about the Japanese "fifth-generation" computer project. MCC's intent is to share R&D personnel and resources from a number of computer companies to evolve strategic initiatives in the knowledge management and expert systems field; in part to meet the Japanese challenge, and in part to accelerate R&D into new technical areas demanding high levels of scientific and technical know-how.

In type three, two companies may share their involvement in a new service without need of forming a third independent business unit. In the fall of 1984, Communications Satellite Corporation and Holiday Inns, Inc. approved a joint venture to offer television programming and teleconferencing by satellite to the hotel chain's 1500 U.S. facilities. The agreement was between Comsat's Comsat General Unit and Holiday Inns' HI-NET Communications subsidiary.

In a type four venture, two companies will agree to form an independent business unit. In the early 1980s, IBM and Aetna Insurance Company created a new company called Satellite Business Systems to enter the market for satellite-based data-transmission services for large corporations.

While there are many examples today of the traditional and emerging firms entering into joint ventures, it is important to note that, as the information economy and information-processing industry continue to evolve, the need for collaborative ventures will continue to accelerate. Moreover, collaborative ventures in the information-management business will be used as both offensive and defensive weapons in the marketplace, to hold off increased competition or entry on the one hand, and to explore and focus on new market niches on the other. Also, as the information-processing industry emerges as the world's leading business, the boundaries for collaborative ventures will extend far beyond national economies. An example is AT&T's recent joint venture with Italy's Olivetti.

SUMMARY

The purpose of this chapter has been to focus on the emerging role of information resources and assets in providing strategic business units with a source of competitive advantage, and to identify seven ways that companies can pursue those competitive advantages through information resources strategies. While information resources historically have always played a role in shaping the competitive strategies of business, there is and will continue to be a growing role for information resources in the shaping of business strategies in the years ahead, due to the evolution of the information economy, and the dynamic growth and dominance of the information-processing industry in world competition. Moreover, as more and more traditional and emerging manufacturing and service firms seek business success in the global information economy, the need for continued adaptation and readaption to changing opportunities in the external business environment will in turn result in major modifications in the internal structures and functions of business units. As we noted in Chapter 3, the functional strategies that firms adopt for managing information resources will have to be in tune with, and appropriately support, redefinitions of corporate and strategic business unit strategies—a subject which we will develop in Chapters 5 and 6.

CHAPTER 5

STRATEGIC INFORMATION MANAGEMENT

As corporate and business-unit strategies change in response to shifts in industry structures, marketplace trends, and technological innovations, the demands on functional strategies increase as well. A basic objective of a business firm's strategic management should be to link corporate, business unit, and functional strategies together to eliminate, or at least minimize, conflicts in the implementation of strategies across business units and functional lines in the firm. No matter how many lines of business a firm may have, or how centralized or decentralized the firm's organizational structure may be, the requirement to evolve functional strategies that are compatible with business unit strategies and across diverse lines of responsibility remains.

Therefore, as the uses of information resources and technology have emerged as growing sources of competitive advantage for more and more businesses, the demands placed on the functional strategies for information management within business have also changed and expanded.

As we suggested in Chapter 3, doing business in the information economy has led to a clear shift in the information-management function from being a back-room, support function within the firm to its emergence as an integral strategic-management function to be included in the business' overall management approach. Moreover, since information-management activities are so pervasive within the firm, the significance of managing information resources as corporate assets has extended well beyond the specific groups or departments normally considered to be responsible for information management (for example, the MIS department, telecommunications groups, corporate library, records managers, and the like), to the marketing, strategic planning, manufacturing, and distribution functions as well. Indeed, as we will explain in this chapter as well as in Chapters 6 and 7, the demand for managing information resources for competitive advantage has come as often from functional managers and business-unit executives, as from the information-systems managers and technical groups. The latter have often been more preoccupied with the management of technologies than the evolution of information management as a strategic function within the firm.

In this chapter, we will focus on the historical evolution of the information-management function as a prelude to defining an analytical framework for understanding strategic information management in business today. We will also discuss the steps involved in formulating an information-management strategy to support corporate and business unit strategies. In Chapters 6 and 7, we will extend our view of strategic information management to incorporate the changes occurring in the organizational structures to support this function, as well as in the techniques used to plan, budget, and account for information resources as valued assets to the firm.

THE EVOLUTION OF THE STRATEGIC INFORMATION-MANAGEMENT FUNCTION[1]

A great deal of confusion exists today over the appropriate role and scope of the information-management function in business

[1] This section is adapted from Donald A. Marchand, "Information Management: Strategies and Tools in Transition," *Information Management Review,* Vol. 1, No. 1, Summer 1985, pp. 27–34. Copyright© 1985. Reprinted with permission of Aspen Systems corporation.

organizations. For many years, "information management" was equated with physical paperwork handling and records management. As such, the information-management function was considered a necessary evil which was conducted in the background of organizational life. During the last 20 years, however, information management has been significantly influenced and shaped by innovations in computer and communications technologies. The rapidly changing products and services of the information and communications industries have served as a major external stimulus to business organizations in rethinking and adapting their concepts and policies for information management to each new "generation" of data processing, communications, and office-automation technologies.

The historical evolution of information management is dramatically different from the evolution of personnel or financial management. Unlike the evolution of the personnel and financial-management functions, where no comparable technological forces have prompted radical rethinking of the basic concepts and policies underlying these support functions, the information-management function is constantly adapting to the marketing strategies and product innovations of the communications and information industries. Thus, both the tools and strategies of information management are in constant transition, and they play a major role in influencing the objectives, scope, and organizational significance of the information-management function.

It is no wonder that managers in many businesses today are unsettled regarding the current status and future evolution of the information-management function. In many cases, neither their previous work experience nor their educational training provides them with meaningful guideposts to comprehend the direction of the evolution of the strategic information-management function. The purpose of this chapter is to provide a map of the transitions which the information-management function has gone through in the last 40 years, and to clarify both the present status and expected future direction which this management-support function is likely to take. Five stages in the evolution of the information-management function are presented. Within each stage, particular attention is placed on explaining the precipitating forces, management strategies, organizational location, and technological influences which have shaped the information-management function.

Stage One: Paperwork Management: The Physical Control of Information

The first stage in the development of the information-management function began in the late 19th century and lasted until the late 1950s.[2] During this period, the typical American company moved from being a geographically localized entity, with one or a few product lines in which the span of control was smaller and communications between levels of management were simpler, to an organization with diverse product lines, geographically dispersed offices, and production plants in which the span of control widened and communications became slower and more complex. Moreover, after the Great Depression, government, at both the federal and state levels, went through tremendous growth, increasing in size and adding to its regulatory powers over business.

Business growth and diversification, coupled with the increased size and regulatory powers of government, led to a significant expansion in the volume of paperwork generated and maintained. With space costs continually rising and the costs of paperwork processing (equipment, supplies, and personnel) soaring, it became clear that the costs of creating and maintaining correspondence, reports, and records was a major expenditure of every business. Therefore, controls had to be placed over paperwork much in the same way that controls had been placed over manufacturing functions. The basic aim of these controls was to increase procedural efficiency in processing paperwork, and to control the physical volume of paper that a company retained.

To meet these objectives, companies instituted a variety of techniques to guide the process by which paper in its many forms was handled, processed, and disposed of in the organization, such as records and reports programs, mail management, directives management, and correspondence management. In addition, a great deal of attention was placed on office design and layout to increase the efficiency of communications between organizational units, and decrease the time required to move stacks of records and reports from one office to another for processing and review.

[2] J. L. Kish and J. Morris, "Paperwork Management in Transition," *AMA Management Bulletin,* No. 56, New York: American Management Association, 1964, pp. 3–15.

As these management techniques developed, organizational responsibilities were created and personnel assigned to oversee the paperwork and administrative management process. By and large, these personnel tended to be at the supervisory or lower middle management levels of the business. In small companies, office managers, administrative assistants, and executive secretaries assumed these responsibilities. In larger firms, specialized positions were created for correspondence-reports managers, mailroom supervisors, and records managers.

Assignment to these supervisory positions, in most cases, did not lead to promotions to senior management levels. For the most part, a young person desiring to be a senior vice-president or chief executive officer of a business did not seek opportunities for advancement in the information-management support function, but rather through career promotions in the finance, marketing, or personnel functions of the firm. Furthermore, coordination within the paperwork-management functions tended to be fragmented. No particular managerial logic dictated where these responsibilities were assigned.

In this stage of its evolution, the information-management function was a lower level, support-oriented activity which occurred in the background of organizational life. The costs of paperwork management were therefore not directly identified, but considered to be part of the overhead expense of doing business. As a support service, paperwork management was removed from the business-planning activities of the firm.

Stage Two: Management of Corporate Automated Technology

The second stage in the development of the information-management function occurred in the 1960s and 1970s, and was characterized by the separate evolution and application of electronic data processing, telecommunications, and office-automation technologies in American business. The primary strategic objective of the information-management function was enhanced technical efficiency and physical control of the new technologies and resources which became available. In the 1960s, second and third generation computers provided new opportunities for automating routine, repetitive applications. The main focus of the electronic data processing (EDP) function was on internal, transaction-based information which formed the basis for the development of MIS in the 1970s. Moreover, during the 1960s and 1970s, advancements in word-processing technology and electronic-duplicating machines provided the basis for restructuring paperwork-processing and text-processing functions around the new technologies. Finally, enhancements in voice-communications equipment and the emergence of data communications, which linked together computers and users in remote locations, provided additional opportunities for the evolution of the telecommunications function in the firm.

As businesses began incorporating more and more technologies, new organizational forms emerged which had as their primary objectives the use of new technologies and the supervision of technical personnel needed to operate these new information-handling tools. Centralized data-processing departments were created to tend to the new computers, while telecommunications coordinators and managers focused on the voice communications needs of the firm. Similarly, word-processing and duplication centers were developed to maximize the economies of scale derived from supporting at one central location the duplicating and text-processing needs of diverse operating units in the organization.

Despite these organizational innovations, the management control over new technology was usually determined by the individual manager or group that acquired the technology first. In many cases, the dominant mode of management was to acquire a new computer and then figure out how it would be used and who could use it. (Unfortunately, the same is true in some companies today.) Moreover, technical personnel overseeing the use of new technologies for automated management of information rarely, if ever, relied on the policies and practices developed by those who managed manual, paperwork-oriented functions. Automated management of information was perceived as both different from and ultimately supplanting the manual management of information. Furthermore, unlike the paperwork-management stage where users had direct control over the media and tools of information processing, second-stage technical personnel acted as intermediaries between the needs of users, and the manner by which these needs were defined and interpreted in applying new technologies. Thus, it is not surprising that, during this stage, significant communications gaps appeared between the users of information and the suppliers and handlers of information technology in organizations.

During Stage Two, the organizational status of the new technical-management activities were usually confined to middle-management levels in most businesses, with one exception. The corporate EDP function moved during the 1960s and early 1970s from being a middle-management concern to more of a senior-management concern as data-processing management emerged as MIS management. Increasingly, large businesses appointed vice-presidents for information services or MIS, as expenditures and the size of the EDP departments continued to grow. In contrast, the managers of telecommunications, word processing, and duplication units were confined to largely middle-management or office-management positions. Thus, during the second stage of development, the information-management function continued to be fragmented and uncoordinated.

Stage Three: Management of Information Resources

The third and current stage in the evolution of the information-management function has been precipitated by the increased convergence, both technical and functional, of data processing, office automation, and communications technologies. In contrast to the second stage, where vertical management of these technologies was required, the 1970s and early 1980s have been characterized by the emergence of technical tools and concepts which increasingly break down the distinctions between data processing and word processing, between voice and data communications, and between centralized and personal use of computing resources in organizations. The advent of distributed data processing which uses mini and micro computers, local-area and long-distance networks which integrate voice and data communications, multifunction workstations which incorporate electronic messaging and document production as well as electronic time management, and, finally, personal computers, has been important in a number of respects. These technologies have served to redefine the use of information technology, to narrow previous gaps between users and suppliers of information technology, and to change the relationship between those who manage manual versus automated information systems in the organization.

Consequently, four significant and related changes have occurred. First, many business organizations have replaced the vertical management control over data processing, office automation, and communications technologies with integrated organizational management of these technologies for strategic planning and operations. Second, as organizations become more dependent on internal use of information technology, more attention is placed on incorporating information-technology planning into the strategic business plans of the firm. Third, the requirements to design multifunctional office automation networks have necessitated more interdisciplinary use of data-processing, communications, office management, and paperwork-management personnel. And lastly, in many businesses, increased investments in the firm's information assets—all of the data, documents, and literature stored in electronic or paper form—have required more involvement of top management personnel in overseeing the use of information technology in the firm.

With these changes, the strategic objectives for the information-management function have shifted away from an exclusive focus on physical control of paperwork, and the supporting electronic technologies, toward treating information *itself* as one of a firm's key assets which can be managed like other strategic assets such as personnel, materials, or capital investments. This shift has implied applying resource-management techniques (like planning, costing, budgeting, and evaluating) to the information resources of the firm, and assigning the position for information-resources management responsibilities to more senior levels within the organization.

The ultimate result of these trends has been to recognize more explicitly the significance of treating information management as a resource-management function at the same level of importance to the firm as marketing, financial management, and personnel management. In addition, it has also created a movement to integrate concerns over the effective management of information resources and technology within the strategic business-planning function of the organization.

These organizational changes have been incorporated under the umbrella of the *information resources management* (IRM) concept.[3] At the center of this concept is the concern that some order must be established within the previously uncoordinated, and at times, chaotic use of new technologies. Simultaneously, information resources management represents the recognition among senior executives that information itself must be explicitly taken into account both as an operational necessity, and as an integral part of the overall strategic business planning of the firm.

Stage Four: Business-Competitor Analysis and Intelligence

We are just now beginning to see signs of the emergence of the fourth stage in the evolution of the strategic information-management function. As international trade competition intensifies (evidenced by the tough postures being taken by the United States and Japan beginning in the spring of 1985), firms realize that they must move from a relatively passive to a much more proactive strategy of using information, not just as an input to R&D, product development, market development, and so forth, but also as a means of finding out what the competition is doing.

Of course government intelligence agencies have known for years that "interesting statistics" do not win wars. Rather, what the opposing general ate for breakfast on the morning of the battle, and how much sleep he got the night before, are in the end, more, or at least equally critical variables as are details on order of battle, troop strength, and so on. This is the stuff of which spy thriller novels and films are made. But industrial espionage is not new either. Indeed, from time to time episodes of it spill onto the front pages. What is "new" is that the corporate intelligence function (or, in classic military terms, the G2 function) is undergoing a radical overhaul as firms begin to develop sophisticated information

[3] See F. W. Horton, Jr., *Information Resources Management*, Englewood Cliffs, NJ: Prentice-Hall, 1985; and W. R. Synnott and W. H. Gruber, *Information Resource Management*, New York: Wiley, 1981.

systems and databases that systematically track what the competition is up to. Early-warning trip wires such as the rise and fall of key stocks of an acquisition takeover candidate or a competitor are almost, nowadays, a trivial example of the lengths to which corporate giants are going to develop sophisticated business-competitor analysis and intelligence capabilities.

What makes these capabilities work, however, is careful attention to information details—the prosaic tasks of making databases that can talk with one another (using integrated corporate-information architectures), tying internal and external data resources together, and so on. That is where a solid information-management underpinning comes in. Without it, firms are thrown back to ad hoc, disjointed, and fragmented approaches to collecting, storing, retrieving, analyzing, and using information on competitors for bottom-line results.

In short, the fourth stage of evolution will see the melding together of passive information with active intelligence. Coupled with the use of computer models such as software packages already available in the forecasting field, at this level of development the corporate-information manager is transformed into a corporate G2, and becomes an accepted and invaluable member of the corporate general staff.

Step Five: Strategic Information Management

As the fifth and topmost level of evolution, the information-management function finally implicitly recognizes that knowledge itself supplements data and information as the key resource. What this means is that by this juncture the firm has succeeded in harnessing both the internal and external domains of knowledge that it requires for effective competitor intelligence and effective support of the traditional management functions (marketing, manufacturing, and so forth). Thus, a premium is placed on electronic communications in lieu of manual forms (although we subscribe to the general view that paperwork and manual systems will always have their place).

Some people call this stage "knowledge management." That term, and the one we are using here, connote approximately the same kernel idea—that managing knowledge itself becomes a basic part of the general management philosophy in the firm, and is adopted by all levels of management.

In stressing that knowledge itself becomes the key strategic resource, we don't mean to suggest that data and information have no place; obviously they do. Rather, we suggest that by this stage of evolution the firm has learned successfully not just how to transform data into information, but to transform information into knowledge. In short, far more information in the databases and information systems is factual, accurate, complete, correct, and represents what is sometimes called "settled" opinion.

At this stage, it can be argued that the firm truly becomes "intelligent" and strives to increase its IQ in a very conscious way, through an active education and training program. We'll talk about this in Chapter 8.

STRATEGIC INFORMATION MANAGEMENT: AN ANALYTICAL FRAMEWORK

For many executives today, understanding the evolution of the information-management function can be compared to walking through a cluttered landscape. While it is easy to recognize that information management can no longer be exclusively confined to paperwork management, it is more difficult to perceive any clear guideposts when new technologies are constantly being offered to executives as cures for their personal or organizational information problems. In many instances, managers are tempted to put the cart before the horse in seeking answers to information-management problems. They frequently invest in new tools and techniques *before* considering how their businesses should be organized to manage information resources, and what contributions the information-management function can make to corporate growth and profitability. As a result, the evolution of the information-management function in business often seems to lag behind the tools and techniques available to deal with informational problems. The outcome is often inappropriate use of new technologies, wasted expenditures, and lost opportunities.

To reverse this trend, a conceptual view of strategic information management is required which is large enough to incorporate the concerns with people, technologies, and information resources embedded in current and past approaches to information management, and which clarifies the range of business objectives, organizational responsibilities, and internal and external environmental demands to be pursued in this functional area to support business unit and corporate strategies.

In examining the evolution of information management, two dimensions for analyzing this functional area stand out. The first is the movement of information management from predominantly a support function in the era of paperwork management to a business-management function in the current period of information resources management. The second dimension emphasizes the shift in business objectives from the earlier period when administrative or technical efficiency were the dominant objectives of the information-management function, to the current period, which emphasizes concern with organizational effectiveness such as competitive advantage or overall business performance. Thus, in reviewing the historical development of information management, there is a clear trend in the direction of making this function more *management-intensive.*

In addition, as we mentioned in Chapter 3, the demands on businesses to exist in more complex and dynamic national and international markets require a serious consideration of strategic management and competitor analysis. Each of these activities, in turn, demands that business management be more *information-intensive.* That is, it must comprise increasingly fine-tuned analysis of industries, markets, competitors, customers, suppliers, government-regulatory behavior, and socioeconomic trends. These information requirements go beyond the need to manage information resources and technology inside the firm, and extend to the management of human and intellectual resources involved in performing these critical functions for the firm. Along the two dimensions noted earlier, the trends toward competitor analysis and intelligence, and overall strategic management, are directly oriented to the management concerns of improving overall business performance.

As Figure 5-1 suggests, understanding strategic information management today requires a broader view of business objectives

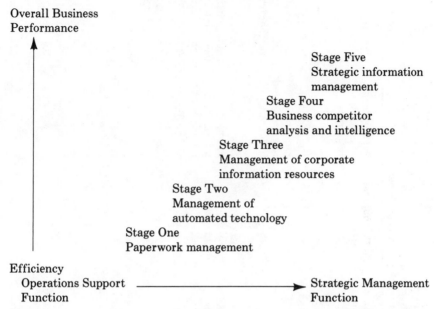

Figure 5–1.   Five Stages in the Development of Strategic Information Management.

and functional responsibilities than has emerged directly from the history of internal MIS or information systems departments. This is not to say that these historical components of strategic information management are not important today. Indeed, from a functional perspective, a business organization should, as Figure 5-2 suggests, view each of the requirements for managing paperwork, automated technology, information content, as critical. These must be viewed as *cumulative,* not sequential, building blocks or stages in evolving a strategic information-management approach. Each of the intellectual disciplines and technical approaches represented in the five stages of strategic information management work towards improving the overall business performance of an enterprise.

In Figure 5–2, we provide an expanded view of the five stages of strategic information-management development along six major dimensions. Our intent here is to provide a map of the development of the strategic information-management function with which specific companies can evaluate their activities in this area. We must caution that the firm cannot rest at early stages of

Growth Stage	Primary Focus	Media vs Content	Organizational Status	Internal vs External View	Tool Dependent vs People Dependent	Business Objective(s) Served
Strategic Information management	Corporate strategy and direction	Focus on content of decision support for strategic use	Top-management strategic function	External and internal focus	Management of human resources	Overall business performance
Business competitor analysis and intelligence	Business-unit strategy and direction	Focus on quality of intelligence analysis and information use	Top-management staff function	External focus primarily	Emphasis on human resources, and information	Competitive advantage for the business units and the firm
Management of corporate-information resources	Management of information resources	Focus on cost-effective management of information technologies and manual and automated information	Top management support function	Internal focus primarily; some external focus	Business management of information resources and and systems	Cost-effective management and use of information resources and technologies
Management of corporate automated technologies	Management of information technologies	Management of technical attributes	Middle-management function	Internal focus	Management of technical resources and technical personnel	Technical efficiency
Paperwork management	Management of paper-based resources and media	Management of physical attributes	Supervisory, clerical and support function	Internal focus	Management of physical resources	Procedural efficiency

Figure 5–2. Strategic Information Management: An Analytical Framework.

strategic information-management development. In order to satisfy (in most businesses) the full range of information requirements necessary to support every business-unit strategy in the firm, the enterprise must progress to the final stage. Indeed, each step of the way represents a package of cumulative strengths and constraints which managers in a firm must be aware of in selecting the most appropriate *mix* of specific information-management strategies and functions for their enterprise. Informed choices at this level can go a long way toward avoiding unnecessary and unproductive conflicts and contradictions in the information-management strategies of business units of the firm.

Let us proceed now to utilize the analytical framework in Figure 5-2 to clarify and amplify each of the five stages of information management evolutionary growth.

Stage One: Paperwork Management

As we said earlier, the primary focus of paperwork management has historically been to establish a system of procedural and physical controls over the paper-based resources and media in the firm, whether they were records, correspondence, mail, directives, or manuals. Drawing on the evolution of "scientific management" and Taylorism in the 1940s and 1950s, the intent of paperwork management was to increase the physical control work units had over paper-based forms, correspondence, and records to increase procedural efficiency.

Although attention to paperwork management has by now been overshadowed by the evolution of management concerns with automated management of technology and data, nevertheless, paperwork management continues as a supervisory and clerical support function in most businesses today. Moreover, despite the impact of computers and communications technologies on the workplace, paperwork management and the related concerns with work-flow analysis and work simplification remain useful, if not very visible, approaches to improving the productivity of office procedures and information flow.[4]

Not many enterprises are still at Stage 1 in their evolutionary

[4] See, for example, Monroe S. Kuttner, *Managing the Paperwork Pipeline*, New York: Wiley, 1978.

growth, but a few are. What is interesting is that some apparently are content to stay at this stage. For example, in an information-management survey of 120 European companies undertaken by one of the authors in 1982, perhaps less than 5 percent of the firms contacted believed that automation, for the most part, "is a waste of time." A managing director of a leading British retailer of ready-to-wear clothing, for example, had this to say:

> *Late in the afternoon of each day I get on the telephone with all of my store managers and buyers. Within minutes we know exactly how sales have been going, and what to do about inventory levels. More-over, our buyers are the best money can hire, and their decisions at the shows are what we stand by. We have no competition, to speak of. So sophisticated information technologies, for the most part, are a waste of money, we believe.*

One might point out that even in this kind of company there are telephones, small computer-based inventory-control systems, and probably personnel-payroll and other financial control systems. But this company undeniably believes it has all the "brains" it needs.

One might also try to argue that this company's competition has not yet, at least, gotten tough. Perhaps this retailer exercises so much marketplace power that it doesn't have to worry about do-mestic competition. But what of its potential international or multinational competitors?

In short, we believe it may be too early to tell whether some industries and some firms can legitimately remain secure and profitable at Stage 1, or whether their decision to stay at that level is an aberration—an accident of historical marketplace secu-rity—rather than one of careful premeditation. Obviously control over the paperwork in this or any company *is* critical. Sales, ship-ments in, inter-store transfers, and all the rest of the transactions have to be organized, tallied, and processed very quickly for the daily phone call technique to work—whether manual or auto-mated techniques are used.

Stage Two: Management of Corporate Automated Technologies

The pursuit of technical efficiency in the operation of the complex technologies operating in the office, plant, and laboratory will continue to require skillful management of these technologies, and the technical personnel needed to operate and maintain the tools. Like paperwork management, this activity will largely be concerned with managing the technical attributes of the tools (that is, their performance, throughput, meantime between breakdowns, and so forth), and not with the management of the use and intellectual content of the information and knowledge. In addition, the management of automated technology will focus on internal operations of technologies and largely remain a middle-management and professional-staff function. Although this stage of information-management development will continue to expand as more complex technologies are introduced in business enterprises, if the firm chooses to remain at this stage of growth, it implicitly regards information as primarily a support function to the business units of the organization.

As far as we can see, most firms and industries are currently at Stage Two in the evolutionary development of the information-management function. That is, unlike our rather secure British retailer in the preceding discussion, firms at this stage are moving to readily embrace the whole range of mainframes, minis, micros, networks, and all the rest. But they are doing so *not* because they see how the technologies are able to produce better information for strategic decision making, but because they want to:

Displace relatively expensive labor with relatively cheaper machines

Streamline cumbersome operations, procedures, and systems

Simplify complex processes so that workers can more easily be trained and retrained to do a greater variety of jobs

Mechanize manual operations.

It might be argued that the enterprise could well rest at this plateau, since cost savings are usually quite significant. Few companies are yet convinced that the information in their databases and manual files is *really* worth exploiting. We challenge that contention, of course—that is what this book is all about.

Stage Two companies often have or plan to organizationally and functionally integrate data processing and telecommunications. Many have formal multi-year plans forecasting their technology needs and costs. Most often the MIS/DP title is still retained for the chief official in the area, or perhaps has been changed to vice-president for information systems or services.

Quite often Stage Two companies have encountered unanticipated difficulties because of organizational and operational problems: Integrating the technologies often demands new structures and functions that many firms are not prepared to assume.

Stage Three: Management of Corporate Information Resources

The third stage of information-management development reflects a decided shift in objectives and focus from primarily a support function to a management function in the business, and from primarily a focus on efficiency to a focus on effectiveness. As we noted earlier in this chapter, a major reason for the shift by businesses to the management of information resources today is the realization that the dictates of technical management, as previously discussed, will not suffice. If the use of the converging technologies of computers and communications is to be effective, much more emphasis will need to be placed on *business* management of information resources *and* information assets, as well as on the organizational structures and management personnel who will define and direct the use of these assets and resources in the firm. Moreover, the pressures for change in adopting a more management-oriented view of this domain are arising from senior management and business-unit managers who are beginning to recognize the enormous potential for profitability and productivity embedded in the emerging products and services of the information-processing industry.

The largest banks are probably a good example of an industry that is moving into Stage Three, management of corporate information resources. In the April 15, 1985 issue of *Business Week,* these main points were made:

1. Bank of America's (B of A's) primary functional product lines are being more closely linked using information systems (that is, every time the bank approves a mortgage, a new loan-processing computer system will automatically generate a report about the buyer to the B of A branch office closest to the mortgaged property).

2. More money is being spent to enhance and upgrade information-resource capital investments (for instance, Citicorp says it will spend $5 billion on new technologies as well as on the maintenance of its old systems).

3. New top level corporate-information officials are being established (B of A has created an executive vice-president and placed him in charge of B of A's new systems development).

4. Corporate subsidiaries and geographically dispersed sales offices, plants, and other facilities are being linked together. (B of A's 950 California branches, previously treated as independent units, are being networked together using telecommunications. Twenty different systems are being integrated into a single, flexible network.)

5. Banks are using corporate information resources to track a total relationship with a client. (They are able to pull up an electronic file on a customer's current account balances, loans outstanding, foreign exchange positions, and so on.)[5]

Stage Four: Business-Competitor Analysis and Intelligence

The fourth stage of strategic information-management development is oriented to the business objective of gaining competitive advantage in business unit and corporate strategy and not exclusively to cost-effective management of information resources and technologies. Its primary focus is on business-unit strategy and direction, and on integrating the business unit's external and internal environments. As a management function, this stage is decidedly dependent on the quality of the intelligence analysis and information collection and processing performed by managers and staff rather than on the use of information tools.[6] While the latter play an increasingly important support role in competitor analysis, the major responsibility of management is the skillful management of the staff persons and strategic information managers actually doing competitor intelligence. Moreover, responsibility

---

[5] "Bank of America Rushes into the Information Age," *Business Week,* April 15, 1985, p. 110.

[6] See William L. Sammon, Mark A. Kurland, and Robert Spitalnic, eds., *Business Competitor Intelligence,* New York: Wiley, 1984.

for this activity rests primarily with corporate and business-unit managers and only secondarily with the managers of information resources and technologies.

Stage Five: Strategic Information Management

The highest level of development is primarily focused on the setting of corporate strategy and direction, and emphasizes the quality of decision making and information use which is required to attain the objective of improving overall business performance and effectiveness. At this stage the firm is dependent on capable management of human resources, and is occupied in setting and implementing corporate and business strategies. Strategic management involves not only a heavy dependence on the quality of information resources collected from the internal and external environment of the firm, but also sets the overall organizational context in which the various functional strategies can operate.[7]

Moreover, the strategic management focus also provides *linkage* to the functional strategies of the business such as finance, human resources, manufacturing, marketing, product development, and R&D. Thus, to maximize overall business performance, strategic management requires not only the effective use of information resources and technology, but also demands that information management strategies be effectively integrated into, and supportive of, the other functional and business strategies of the firm.

So much for a look at the growth stages. How do we move up the growth ladder? Does a company have to pass through each stage iteratively, or can it leap over the intermediate stages? The answer lies in a deeper understanding of just what is meant by the *strategic value of information management*.

ASSESSING THE STRATEGIC VALUE OF INFORMATION MANAGEMENT

In evaluating the strategic value of information management in a business, there are several analytical steps suggested by the

---

[7] See Arnoldo C. Hax and Nicolas S. Majluf, *Strategic Management*, Englewood Cliffs, N.J.: Prentice-Hall, 1984.

previous discussion. These can help information management play a strategic role in enhancing business effectiveness and competitive advantage, rather than be valued only for its technological wizardry or getting bogged down with intellectual preoccupations. Here is an evaluation procedure that we believe is helpful.[8]

Identify the Information Resources and Uses of Information Technology in the Firm

The point of departure in developing an information strategy is to identify how information resources and technologies are being used in the firm. How do they support the business units of the firm? What technologies, whether mechanical or electronic, are being employed? And what resources (human, financial) are being expended for various functional support systems or for supporting and driving business unit strategies?

It is not enough to merely request that the MIS department or office managers report on their information management activities, since a large proportion of information use is performed within business units or in other corporate functions such as marketing, R&D, and even manufacturing. To evolve a deeper understanding of the role of information resources in the firm, it is necessary to identify the relative contributions of manual and automated information resources and supporting technologies to the valued activities of the business, as we will suggest in Chapter 7.

Identify the Relevant Information Resources in Other Related Industries or Under Development in the Information Processing Industry

As we emphasized in Chapter 2, no manufacturing or service business can afford to ignore how trends in the information processing

[8] It is noteworthy that Michael Porter's recent research on competitive advantage does not specifically address the role of information management, although his general analysis is clearly applicable to this domain. See Michael E. Porter, *Competitive Advantage*, New York: Free Press, 1985, especially Chapter 5, "Technology and Competitive Advantage," pp. 164–200. Following the publication of the latter book, Porter has clearly sought to explicitly correct this omission in his earlier writings. See Michael E. Porter and Victor E. Millar, "How information gives you competitive advantage," *Harvard Business Review*, Vol. 63, No. 4, (July–August, 1985), pp. 149–160.

industry are affecting traditional business strategies or information management practices. New technological and information-based products and services are constantly evolving which pose distinct opportunities or threats to a firm's functional and business-unit strategies.

In addition, a firm must examine the strategic information management practices and developments in related industries and in the markets in which it competes. It must analyze its information management strategies and make plans based on its analyses so that lost opportunities and lagging behind in exploiting information resources of potential importance to its strategic marketplace standing, may be avoided. Moreover, this comparative evaluation should apply to all valued information management practices in the firm, whether they support new products and services, or internal functions such as finance and accounting, marketing, manufacturing, or human resource management. Thus, no area of the firm's information management practices—whether manual or automated, product-oriented or process-oriented, structured or unstructured—should escape periodic review as an actual or potential contributor to business performance or competitive advantage.

Determine the Directions in Which Changes Will Occur

Not all changes in the technological products and services of the information processing industry, or in the use of these products or services by actual or potential competitors will be of equal importance or even relevance. Assessing the likely direction of change in these two dimensions and their potential impacts on buyers, suppliers, internal operations, business units, and barriers to entry will provide important insights about the scope and timing of changes in a firm's own information-management strategies.

Determine Which Information Management Strategies Influence Competitive Advantage or Industry Structure

As we noted in Chapter 4, an effective competitive strategy requires a firm to take a defendable and sustainable position in its industry and markets. To do so, the firm will require a strategy that incorporates both offensive and defensive actions. To position itself appropriately, a firm must develop a clear view of how information-management strategies do or do not affect its critical sources of competitive advantage and, in the larger context, its markets and industry structure. Without this critical information, a firm cannot sustain its position in industries or markets where information-management strategies of competitors are critical to success. As we noted in Chapter 4, the increasingly widespread effects of information-resource strategies on emerging and traditional as well as manufacturing and service industries, means that firms that do not understand the value of their information-management practices relative to their businesses will be at a significant disadvantage and risk future losses. Furthermore, whether a firm decides to be a leader or follower in evolving its information-management strategies is not directly relevant to the need to know where it stands in this area in its industry and markets. The latter information and business insight is necessary before any decision can be made about the appropriateness of being an industry leader versus a follower in this critical domain.

Evaluate the Firm's Relative Capabilities and the Costs of Making Improvements

Every business must have a realistic picture of its relative strengths and weaknesses in managing and using information resources and technology. Whether the firm is oriented to cost leadership, product differentiation, or some mix of both, the executives in that firm will need to evaluate the costs of improving their information management strategies along several key dimensions:

Opportunity costs

Financial costs

Risk tradeoffs

Timing costs

Attitudinal and motivational costs

Costs of upgrading existing resources (people, equipment, and data)

Uncertainty costs

Each of these costs considerations and the corresponding actual or potential benefits must be assessed directly in the context of the firm's business performance and sources of competitive advantage. This means that financial costs alone should not be the dominant dimension against which information management strategies are evaluated. A business may squander its information resources as effectively if it is "penny wise and pound foolish" as if it is profligate in its expenditures on dazzling technologies or new automated databases.

Select an Information Management Strategy that Reinforces a Firm's Overall Business Performance and Competitive Advantage

An information management strategy must reinforce the overall business or competitive strategy a firm is seeking to sustain or achieve. Those aspects of a firm's information-management strategy that help it to sustain its lead in the marketplace, or at least to attain a defendable position, will be most important. In addition, a firm may also attain an important cost advantage or improve its other sources of competitive advantage through its information-management strategy. In these instances, the firm's information-management strategy can play a key role, if not the dominant role, in sustaining successful business performance.

Make Sure the Information Management Strategies of Business Units and Functions Are Closely Linked

As we suggested earlier in this chapter, the evolution of information-management suggests an uneasy relationship between this function and business units. Often, a company's senior management and business unit managers will exhibit a love/hate relationship with the information-resources function. In part this is often due to the poor history of performance in the automated information systems area and in part to the growing recognition that the new technologies and resources in this area hold the keys to a firm's long-term success—if only they can be effectively managed. The latter concern is often the underlying reason for providing a more visible corporate role for the information-management function, as well as for urging a stronger management orientation in this functional area. Moreover, it is a reason for placing much more attention on the *interrelationships* between this functional area and business units. As we will discuss in more detail in Chapter 6, the need for evolving effective interrelationships between business units and the information management function is at the center of important shifts that firms have been making in organizational structures, functions, and management and technical competencies for information managers and staff.

SUMMARY

The purpose of this chapter has been to provide an introductory view of the historical evolution of the information-management function as a prelude to defining a conceptual framework for understanding strategic information management in business today. We have also provided the major steps in evaluating the strategic value of the information management function in the context of improving overall business performance and competitive advantage. In the next two chapters, we will extend our conceptual framework for strategic information management to incorporate changes occurring in the organizational aspects of this function as well as in the techniques used to plan, budget for, and evaluate the performance of information resources as valued assets to the firm.

CHAPTER **6**

NEW STRUCTURES AND FUNCTIONS FOR CORPORATE INFORMATION MANAGEMENT

Rethinking your business in the information economy, formulating new strategies for gaining competitive advantage, and raising the level of awareness of people throughout your company to the notion that information itself can and should be looked upon as a strategic corporate asset, are all necessary first steps. But they still aren't enough. The company must put its convictions into operation, and turn them into the reality of an intelligent organization. To do that it must make both structural and procedural changes. In this chapter we deal with structures and functions.

The material in this chapter is subdivided into three parts:

1. Why and how the industrial and information ages demand different organizational approaches—in short, the larger focus

2. Why and how the nature of work itself is being changed by the technologies

3. Why roles (of managers, functional departments, and end-users, and so forth), in the various work environments (office, factory or laboratory), are changing, and how they should be reconstituted.

We begin in the first part with a consideration of the broad, basic factors that have traditionally been taken into account when organizing. We then quickly move into comparing and contrasting the fundamental aspects of the highly centralized corporate giants of the smokestack era and the highly decentralized firms of today. There are, as we shall see, very significant differences in both production and distribution flows, as well as information flows, between industrial and information-era firms. We also consider in this first part "environmental changes" such as information overload that are impacting today's companies.

BASIC ORGANIZATIONAL ALTERNATIVES

Tricker reminds us that there are no panaceas in organizational design.[1] There are no correct solutions to the problem of determining appropriate configurations, degrees of centralization, or management styles. There are just some approaches that may give better results under some conditions. The search, he says, for the right balance between centralized control and decentralized autonomy, has fascinated philosophers for centuries. Two sets of forces pull at one another. On the side of centralization and the need for order are considerations of:

Scale economics

Coordination

Standardization

[1] R. I. Tricker, *Effective Information Management,* Oxford: Beaumont Executive Press, 1982.

Order

Optimization

While pulling in the opposite direction are considerations of:

Discretion

Evolved authority

Creativity

Trust

Participative motivation and commitment

If one of the underlying motives in an information economy is to raise the IQ of the enterprise, then it is imperative to reexamine traditional values implicit in industrial-age organizational structures. What are the choices, not just an enlightened choice of strategies, but of the management styles of the CEO and top decision makers—and the choices of structure as well? Tricker notes that while early clerical and computer methods tended to reinforce the classical command structure and hierarchical accountability, such approaches today can produce organizational inertia and an inability to adapt sufficiently fast to threats, and to seize upon unexpected opportunities. Traditional information systems can make organizations rigid and inflexible by filtering out the very signals that warn of necessary change.

Filtering Out Information: Less Is More

Dean Evelyn Daniel of the University of North Carolina points out that a dominant theme being advanced today by organizational theorists to describe how information-intensive enterprises are faced with an entirely new set of environmental factors, is the problem of how to keep information *out* of the organization.[2] This challenge is at least as important, if not more so, than bringing

[2] Evelyn Daniel, "Information Resources and Organizational Structure," *Journal of the American Society for Information Science,* 34(3): pp. 222–228; 1983. Copyright© 1983. Reprinted with permission of Aspen Systems Corporation.

information *into* the organization. She points out that new organizational designs are needed, both to handle the information overload in the enterprise, and to effectively play a gatekeeper role to keep unnecessary and irrelevant data from clogging the company's information systems and communications channels.

Like Tricker, Daniel reminds us that organization theory has evolved through a number of stages of inquiry. In the first third of this century, she says, the study of organization was generally dominated by the "scientific management" point of view. Frederick Taylor, Henri Fayol, and others dealt with such concepts as division of labor, work specialization, and line-staff relationships.

In the second third of the century, the study of organization was dominated by a set of interests and concerns often called *human relations.* Social psychology, behavioral science, organizational development, group dynamics, and the theories of leading thinkers of the day, like Leland Bradford, Rensis Likert, Christopher Argyris, Warren Bennis, and others, were given close attention.

Now in the last third of the century, she points out, we're under the increasing influence of the "general systems" paradigm school of organizational thought, which argues that no one organizational model can be best for all situations. This school believes that the model of the firm should be viewed in a classic systems theory context. That is, the firm receives stimuli (including, of course, information), called *inputs* in systems theory. It reacts to those stimuli by comparing them to internal value systems, goals, strategies, and plans. Then the firm transforms the results of that reaction-interaction process into *outputs,* which take the form of decision and actions.

To bring information more squarely into her line of thought, she refers to work by H. Mintzberg (published in 1979), who synthesized the major current approaches to organization analysis into a five-part model:[3]

1.　Workers at the operating core

2.　Middle-line managers

3.　Administrators at the strategic apex

[3] Henry Mintzberg, *The Structuring of Organizations,* Englewood Cliffs, NJ: Prentice-Hall, 1979, p. 20.

4. Analysts in the technostructure

5. Support staff

Robert Anthony's pyramidal triad (see Figure 3-5), much quoted in management and organizational theory, corresponds to Mintzberg's first three categories: Anthony's operational level is Mintzberg's first category; his tactical level is Mintzberg's second; and his strategic level is Mintzberg's third.

Daniel points out that information resources used in the operating core tend to be simple, concrete, and immediate. Information relates directly to the task at hand. The operating core of the organization has long been the target of automation efforts because of the relative ease of matching the repetitive patterned regularity of the work with data requirements.

She considers middle-line managers as the information transmitters and translators who must collect and summarize raw data about all aspects of the operating core and pass it up to the top administrators. The top level, she says, needs trend information, both from within and without the organization. Information resources for this group are much less predictable, in contrast to information resources passed in vertical flows from the operating core up through middle management to the strategic apex. Those are relatively simple and well understood, but the flow of information horizontally and laterally, as used in Mintzberg's last two categories (analysts of the technostructure and support staff), is much less understood.

Outmoded Industrial Age Structures

An information company president, Herbert Brinberg, points out that in addressing the place of the information function in today's organization, we tend to rely too much on traditional organizational concepts that were appropriate to the industrial age, but are not relevant now.[4] He points to the tendency to look upon infor-

---

[4] Herbert R. Brinberg, "Let's Put the Information Function in its Place—But Where Is It?" Presented to the Conference Board's Conference on "Executives in the Emerging Information Environment," New York: April 13, 1983. See also "Managing Information so Users Get What They Want—and Need," *Management Review*, February 1984, pp. 8–13, by the same author.

mation technologies as physical assets that should be managed the same way, for example, as materials and equipment inventories and capital assets were managed in the factory and plant. But the information environment in which the firm operates today is quite different from the industrial environment in which the same textile mill, steel factory, or automobile plant operated yesterday.

Before addressing the question of where the information function ought to be positioned, Brinberg finds it necessary to define more precisely what he believes the "information function" is, and what it is not. He stresses that it does *not* include any of the following:

Data processing

The corporate library

The records center

The corporate document file

Under the old organizational paradigm, those functions were driven by highly specialized technicians grouped around each of those activities, which were regarded as cost centers. Because nobody understood their jargon, the specialists tended to be in control of and to drive those functions.

However, Brinberg points out that today, with the pervasive spread of microcomputers through the office, factory, and laboratory, it is the *users* who must drive the new organizational paradigm governing the positioning of the information-management function.

Under the new paradigm, he asserts, the information function must be driven by those managers and professionals directly concerned with, and/or responsible for, implementation of corporate policies and strategies. It must also allow the user ready access across and through traditional departmental or functional boundaries or hierarchies. It must also eliminate the confusion caused by noncompatible hardware, systems, and data elements. Finally, it must shift the focus from mere comprehensiveness to relevance and selectivity, and make possible the segmentation and filtering of information to meet specific user needs, based on the responsibilities and functions of these users in the organization.

According to Brinberg, the information function must be based on four guiding principles:

1. Content must be integrated so that elements forming any one database are available for appropriate combination and manipulation with data elements from other databases; internal and external, text and numeric, with both hard and soft data.

2. Technology must be integrated so that machines and systems can talk to one another.

3. Information must be segmented so that it is not necessary to pick one's way through the universe of data.

4. Information must be filtered so that the user can selectively access specific, relevant information.

One of Brinberg's conclusions is that the proliferation of processing machines and communications technologies—operating on a wide array of information content, by means of a growing hierarchy of information management systems, and with the users the principal driving force—makes it impossible to place the information function neatly within the prescribed boundaries of traditional organizational charts, as was done in the past. Users and their individual information requirements do not reside in one place. Yet the very proliferation of machines, protocols, software packages, raw data, and databases, makes integration imperative.

Brinberg is therefore led to take the view that the necessity for integration dictates that there must be a single authority responsible for the integrity of the information function: It must be placed at the highest levels of the organization, reporting to the chief executive officer or the chief operating officer, depending on how these two executives divide up responsibilities for overall corporate direction. (See Figure 6-1.)[5]

Centralization versus Decentralization

No area stimulates more intense emotional debate among both theorists and practitioners than does the centralization-decentral-

[5] *Ibid.*, p. 3.

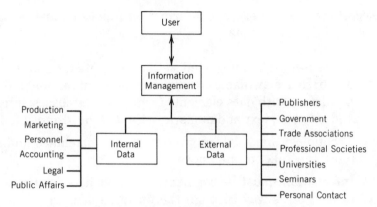

Figure 6–1. The information function as integrator-synthesizer. *Source:* see note 5. From "Lets Put the Information Function in its Place—But Where is it?" by Dr. Herbert Brinberg. Copyright© April 13, 1983. Reprinted with permission.

ization question. No one argues very much with the fundamental benefits of extending the power of the computer, and the power of the information resources the computer brings, to the end-user. The rub comes when devotees on both sides of this argument start debating the pros and cons of a quasianarchist information environment ("let a thousand flowers bloom"), in which end users are able to do virtually whatever they want, with virtually no central guidance or control. The converse would be a system whereby companies kept a tight reign over the hordes of machines and users that are spreading like Hydrilla plants on a Florida waterway.

Today, because competition with Japan and other foreign nations is intense, there is pressure to reduce layers of bosses and planners, get rid of red tape and paperwork, and reenergize the workforce. Many believe the term *decentralization* is imprecise because it really doesn't convey what is happening. Some call the phenomenon *cell mitosis.* The idea is to encourage "nodes" of intellectual foment, and, when an idea or product moves from the drawing board to the assembly line, not to turn the product-development team into a permanent, enshrined organizational unit. Rather, encourage its members to spin off to other nodes, and begin "networking" with other incipient islands of still more intellectual activity. Does this sound like the "age of aquarius?" It isn't really.

Tom Peters writing in the April 21, 1985 *New York Times*, gave this account of what happened in the British firm of Marks and Spencer:

> *Marcus Sieff, the recently retired chairman of Marks and Spencer, the huge British retailer, undertook his own "operation simplification" a decade ago. He took what he calls a year's "sabbatical" and hit the road. He debated, he cajoled, he ranted and raved, attempting to demonstrate to regional and store managers that they could maintain control with much less in the way of paper support. And he reduced the paperwork by 80 percent, or, by his count, 27 million pages a year. For example, he tossed out the 13 thick manuals store managers were supposed to use as guides, replacing them with two booklets, 12 pages each. In the process, he ended up eliminating 5,000 staff jobs (a hiring freeze of several years was required to work off the excess). At the end of the sabbatical year, he staged a major symbolic event. A bonfire, at which several tons of the reduced annual paperwork were put to the torch.*

Daniel J. Power at the University of Maryland investigated two alternative scenarios to contrast the consequences to organizational decision making of attempts to manage information.[6] One scenario was a tightly controlled, heavily centralized mode and style of operation; the other was a very loosely controlled, heavily decentralized mode and style.

In the first scenario, a person is chosen for the job of data administrator and given control over all information resources for the company, including access to historical files; creation and control of new information; overseeing integration among databases; procedures, standards, and guidelines development that would be used corporate-wide, and so forth. (See Figure 6-2.)[7]

In the second scenario, information-resources management is handled essentially by a committee. There is a nominal chief information officer (CIO) role, but the individual selected is a weak administrator, and is chosen precisely for his permissive, ivory-

---

[6] Daniel J. Power, "The Impact of Information Management on the Organization: Two Scenarios," *MIS Quarterly*, September 1983, pp. 13–20. Reprinted by permission of the *MIS Quarterly*, Volume 7, Number 3, September 1983. Copyright 1983 by the Society for Information Management and the Management Information Systems Research Center.

[7] *Ibid.*, p. 36.

	Variable Ranges	
Variables	Scenario One	Scenario Two
Data administrator	A strong administrator at executive VP level, with seperate budget	A weak administrator, committee coordination, many managers have DP budgets
Database management	High level of control, conceptual integration, data independence, e.g. relational database	Low level of control, redundancy, little integration of data, many databases
Data entry/output	Company wide procedures, on-line and sensory entry, graphics, work stations, projection TV	A variety of procedures, some on-line and some paper forms requiring batch entry, emphasis on reports, much staff intervention required
System control	Central control and standards, networking, data sharing in system	Separate, autonomous systems, no uniform procedures, no data sharing in computer system

Figure 6-2. Summary of Two Scenarios: Information Management Variables. *Source:* See note 6. Reprinted by permission of the *MIS Quarterly*, volume 3, number 3, September 1983. Copyright © 1983 by the Society for Information Management and the Management Information Systems Research Center.

tower, aloof philosophy—a "hands-off" posture toward departments and end-users.

Power sees Scenario One leading to the consequences identified in Figure 6-2. He believes the most dramatic changes occur under this alternative. In it, decision-making responsibilities and organizational design are radically changed. He saw Scenario Two, on the other hand, leading to the possibility of slower decision-making processes because more people and groups are involved in a collegial and participative mode. Moreover, under the second structure larger numbers of people are required, he believes, to support all three organizational levels—strategic, managerial, and operating—because of the greater intensity of information handling implicit in this style.

Power concludes that the benefits of the first scenario stem primarily from the refinement and targeting of information flows to decision makers in what he calls a "turbulent environment."

Benefits are primarily indirect, intangible, and difficult to document. He believes total costs would be higher under this approach, because of the added expense of developing the needed large integrated systems. Under the second scenario, such integrated systems would be minimal by contrast, and therefore presumably the costs would be correspondingly lower. It isn't clear, however, whether Power has taken into account the costs of everyone developing their own mini databases and mini information systems, which could be quite expensive in the aggregate.

Under the second scenario, Power emphasizes an improved organizational culture and climate. But he is not persuasive in taking a gigantic leap of faith that from this improved human climate will come an improvement of profits. There are warehouses full of research data, quite inconclusive, that in our view run counter to that kind of overly optimistic assessment.

Two other investigators, Haugan and Levin, in a survey of 16 Fortune 500 organizations' information-resources management (IRM) efforts undertaken in the 1983–1984 period, seemed to see a positive correlation between the move to IRM by the companies they surveyed, and the move to a more decentralized total operating company environment. At one point they say:

> *Another aspect frequently observed in the survey can best be summarized by the comment made by a senior manager—they were finally freed from the tyranny of the systems group. The move to IRM and decentralization solved problems of non-responsiveness or perceived non-responsiveness of the central dp organization to the users throughout the company. Had the dp organizations been listed and acted accordingly, some of the changes might not have been so drastic. A common approach was to reassign applications programmers to the organizations they had been supporting, and, in effect, to set up information centers.* [8]

We agree with the notion that a company's move to an information management environment, with greater emphasis on a

---

[8] Gregory T. Haugan and Ginger Levin, "Excellence in Information Management: A Survey of Selected *Fortune* 500 Activities," (unpublished paper available from the authors). Reprinted with permission.

decentralized mode of operation, can be ideally coupled with the formal introduction of a company IRM program. Our reasons are as follows:

1. Increased decision-support to decentralized managers and end-users is the very essence of the information resources-management philosophy. If the CEO makes that connection explicit, employees and managers will perceive a bonded relationship between IRM and an organizational climate and culture of maximized decentralized decision making.

2. Information is itself perhaps the crucial key to decentralization: If strengthened information flows, and stronger and more integrated corporate databases are put in place concomitantly with top management's move to decentralize, there is a greater likelihood of success.

3. Decision-support systems for middle and lower levels of management are now technologically feasible as the second generation of "smart" software packages reaches the market: As these packages begin to integrate both internal and external data resources in a single decision-support package, there will be greater acceptance of the IRM idea at the middle and lower levels, including, we believe, the acceptance of the counterbalancing need for strong centralized information-management policy guidance.

The last point is crucial. We see a common thread among corporations that seems to be pointing to a balanced centralized-decentralized strategy. That is, as companies experiment with delegating authority and responsibility further and further down to end-user levels, they are keeping a rather short leash on the situation. They are doing that by insisting that their CIO and central IRM departments keep a close watch on how the technology is being used. And they're not afraid to promote corporate information policies, and strong centralized information processing and information management standards and guidelines aggressively. In short, the more permissive and participative mode of decision making made possible by the micros that are transforming the nature of work at the end-user level has not caused these managers to abdicate their responsibility to ensure that technologies are being used effectively and efficiently.

Flattening Organizational Structures

John Naisbitt calls it "smashing the pyramid," and says that as we introduced more technology into society, the cold, impersonal nature of the bureaucratic hierarchy annoyed people more and more. "What we really wanted," Naisbitt contends, "was more personal interaction, more high-touch ballast in response to the further intrusion of technology into an already impersonal hierarchy." And with the failing of the vertical hierarchical pyramid comes the simultaneous rise of the horizontal networking together of work groups.

Naisbitt extols the virtues of the organizational structure at Intel, a leading company in the semiconductor industry. Its organizational attributes are listed as follows:

Workers have several bosses.

Responsibility and authority over certain support functions like purchasing and quality control are shared through a committee or council mechanism, rather than through single managers.

Partitions divide a communal workspace; there are no traditional compartmentalized office cubbyholes.

Informal attire is acceptable; white shirts and three-piece suits are out.

Authority at the top is shared. Naisbitt calls this a "triune of top executives, an 'outside man,' a long-range planner, and an inside administrator."

Problem solving and decision making are participative, involving all employees, not just formal management levels.

Challenge and even an occasional confrontation are seen as healthy, not as an intrusion on the prerogative authority figures.[9]

[9] John Naisbitt, "Megatrends: Ten New Directions Transforming Our Lives," New York: Warner, 1982, p. 222. From *Megatrends* © 1982 by John Naisbitt. Published by Warner Books. Reprinted with permission.

Naisbitt and the organizational school that has concentrated on "human factors" look at the flattening of structure primarily as a result of the need of small work groups and individual professionals to greatly enhance their communication capabilities. Another school of thought contends that the driving force behind this inverting of the organizational pyramid has been the onslaught of office automation. According to this line of reasoning, the technology integration is what is forcing the advent of new structural alternatives in the workplace. Among the nation's leading business and industry trade publications, *Business Week* has been particularly effective in recent years in advancing this second theory. In a series of special reports beginning in late 1982 and continuing into early 1983, *Business Week's* editors and writers began to talk of economic necessity and technological forces combining to squeeze down the ranks of middle managers—something we will call the hourglass syndrome.

The Hourglass Syndrome

Laterally networking to enhance communication between individuals is one thing. Squeezing down the ranks of middle management, so that the organizational profile looks like an hourglass, is something else. *Business Week* sees the following trends:

Corporate structure is changing to accommodate broader information gathering, and to let data flow from shop floor to executive suite without the editing, monitoring, and second-guessing that has been the middle manager's function.

Middle managers who do survive find their roles expanded and their functions changed. Generalists, not specialists, are needed as companies demand solutions to interdisciplinary problems.

Fewer business-school graduates are hired, and those who are find the ladder harder to climb. As corporate pyramids are flattened and the number of levels are reduced, more lateral moves and lowered expectations result.

Marketplace and manufacturing decisions are made by first-line managers whose power has been eroded by staff. Forepersons now serve in pivotal roles, managing better-educated, more demanding workers, and knitting maintenance, engineering, and personal managers into integrated operating teams.

Business education will focus less on analysis, financial maneuvers, and gamesmanship, and more on teaching manufacturing, marketing, and computer skills. For the next generation, retraining will become as important as initial training.

Displaced managers will need safety nets as their health and pension benefits are lost. Many will find it impossible to maintain their standards of living. Higher rates of drug and alcohol abuse and family problems reflect the psychological devastation of this group.

Middle managers, who have traditionally been politically conservative, may become radicalized under pressure, demanding welfare benefits they once only grudgingly conceded to the poor.

BusinessWeek mentions staff cuts of from 20 percent at Firestone and Crown Zellerbach, to 40 percent at Chrysler. These cuts were made to thin out the middle-management ranks.[10]

Temporary Organizational Structures: Project and Matrix Teams

Many companies are understandably reluctant to make permanent and irrevocable organizational changes that are far reaching and upsetting in terms of the organization's culture and established working relationships. Many are asking if there are not temporary, or transient organizational moves that they can make, while learning the full consequences of the changes involved. In short, are there ways to buy time?

Nearly 25 years ago Rensis Likert, then director of the Institute for Social Research, and professor of Psychology and Sociology at the University of Michigan, was widely honored for his "system four" theory of matrix organizational management, put forward in

[10] "A New Era for Management," *BusinessWeek*, Special Report, April 25, 1983, pp. 50–86.

such books as *New Patterns of Management.*[11] (See Figure 6-3.)[12] We are seeing today a kind of renaissance of Likert's work on the nature of highly effective work groups. This movement is exemplified by new books and articles recommending a more participative style of management, by the quality control circle (QCC) movement, and by our own discussion in this book of the need for a revitalized human resources management function that is more closely linked to the information resources management function.

Likert saw the following as the properties and performance characteristics of the ideal highly effective work group:

Members are skilled in all the various leadership and membership roles and functions required for interaction between leaders and members, and between members and other members.

A well-established and relaxed working relationship exists among all the group's members.

Members of the group are loyal to one another and to the leader.

There is a high degree of confidence and trust among the members of the group.

The integration of the values and goals of the group has been shaped by the group itself, not by others above them.

Harmonizing the values and goals of groups other than their own, to which they're linked.

Members are highly motivated and committed to achieving shared goals and objectives. This high motivation springs, in part, from the basic motive to achieve and maintain a sense of personal worth and importance.

We do not have the space here to go into detail about all of the elements of group dynamics and group theory. Suffice it to call attention to the work of early behaviorists like Rensis Likert, who gave us an alternative, decades ago, to coping with fluid and dynamic organizational work environments. Many contemporary

---

[11] Rensis Likert, *New Patterns of Management,* New York: McGraw-Hill, 1961. Copyright© 1961. Reprinted with permission of the publisher.

[12] *Ibid.,* p. 128.

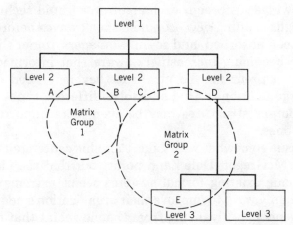

Figure 6–3. Likert "System Four" matrix organization. *Source:* see note 12. Reprinted with permission of the publisher.

observers of today's chaotic information-handling atmosphere seem to be calling for these approaches once again. The use of temporary work groups happens to coincide with the challenge of coming up with transitory as well as permanent structures that give the CEO, the CIO, and the department heads some breathing room.

A more contemporary writer, Zand, who is professor of Management at New York University, puts the organizational and work structure question rather succinctly:

> Let us assume that managers have a workable level of trust and therefore should reasonably be able to gain access to each other's relevant knowledge. Then the organization becomes the focus of concern. Does the organization help or hinder the flow and use of knowledge?

Zand underscores the increasingly turbulent environment in which managers operate. They are, he says, buffeted by unstable international relations among the major countries of the world, and by significant changes in military posture, and by governments alternatively constraining and subsidizing certain economic activities. Markets are increasingly unpredictable because of erratic swings in foreign exchange rates, rapid technological breakthroughs sending new economic shock waves before the old ones have been absorbed, and so on. Managers, under these conditions, are becoming increasingly aware that informed adaptability is at a premium. To attain it they may need different modes of organization to find and solve different types of problems. Temporary structures may be even more important than permanent ones.

Taking issue somewhat with Likert and his contemporaries like Bennis and McGregor, Dale Zand points out that the idea of totally displacing existing formal systems seems extreme to managers who simply want to improve their organization's adaptability and effectiveness.[13] Advancing from the viewpoint that different work requirements mandate different structural forms, Zand puts forth his "collateral mode" model, which he identifies as a supplemental organization coexisting with the usual, formal organization. Figure 6-4 shows the relationship Zand visualizes between the type of organization on the one hand, and the type of problem to be solved on the other.[14] Obviously, Zand feels that the organization itself can be a serious impediment to work and problem solving if the structure selected is rigid and inappropriate.

Very clearly Zand's idea is that the formal organization is in what he calls the authority-production mode, and the collateral organization is in the knowledge-problem mode. He concedes that this state of affairs may be reversed in some organizations such as research units and educational institutions.

Zand's research seems to bear out the idea that after using the collateral mode, the manager and his subordinates learn that the hierarchical organization can continue. "Disorder," he says, "does not take over. Directive behavior can still be used, but there is better understanding of how to integrate participation and group effort with formal organization through use of collateral mode. Perhaps most important, organization members learn concepts and methods which enable them to freely invent and use new modes for solving ill-structured problems."[15]

[13] Dale E. Zand, *Information, Organization, and Power: Effective Management in the Knowledge Society,* New York: McGraw-Hill, 1981. Reprinted with permission.

[14] *Ibid.,* p. 63.

[15] *Ibid.,* pp. 87–88.

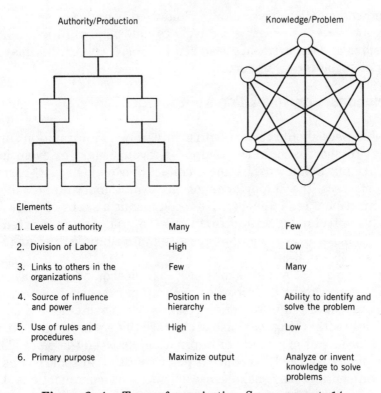

Elements		
	Authority/Production	Knowledge/Problem
1. Levels of authority	Many	Few
2. Division of Labor	High	Low
3. Links to others in the organizations	Few	Many
4. Source of influence and power	Position in the hierarchy	Ability to identify and solve the problem
5. Use of rules and procedures	High	Low
6. Primary purpose	Maximize output	Analyze or invent knowledge to solve problems

Figure 6–4.   Types of organization. *Source:* see note 14.

R. I. Tricker, a contemporary of Zand's writing on the European scene, agrees that there are no organizational panaceas, no correct single solutions to the problem of determining the most appropriate configuration, degrees of centralization, or management styles.[16] Like Zand and Likert, Tricker stresses the transient organization as a viable model for the future, because it is able to adapt constantly, yet with sufficient stability to achieve results. Matrix organizations, he says, in which task forces and project groups are formed to achieve specific purposes, are vital to the information-intensive firm in today's world. He even carries the idea a step further: Not only are internal units fluid with respect to their own boundaries, but larger units like subsidiaries, and

[16] R. I. Tricker, *Effective Information Management,* Oxford: Beaumont Executive Press, 1982.

even headquarters have equally fluid field boundaries as the corporation strives to react effectively to new opportunities. Whole divisions and departments assigned to subsidiary A today may be part of subsidiary B tomorrow.

Evolutionary or Revolutionary Approach?

At what pace should the enterprise integrate its information functions? In short, should the tempo be revolutionary or evolutionary? Arthur Schneyman, a key architect of Mobil Oil's IRM strategy, stresses the importance of an evolutionary approach to organizational realignments. He recommends a series of stages at which the technologies and functions are gradually integrated in order to move away from what he calls a "stovepipe" situation (See Figures 6-5 and 6-6.)[17]

Schneyman's stovepipe syndrome, so typical of industrial-age organizations, can be described as a situation in which isolated and compartmentalized information streams are moving up and down vertically within long-established channels. There is very little horizontal or lateral movement of information between the pipes. This early pioneer of the IRM concept points out that in some company environments it may make sense to put telecommunications and mainframe computer-center operations together as an integrated unit, particularly where the company is introducing a major new telecommunications network that is going to be used to move substantial volumes of data and voice traffic between its mainframe computer sites, to and through its communications switching centers. Or, in another instance, a company may be preparing to upgrade or enhance its mainframe equipment, and therefore will require a closer link with its telecommunications channels.

Schneyman also mentions that where the company is introducing office automation in a big way, it may make sense, as an evolutionary strategy, to create a corporate office-automation (OA) task force, in lieu of setting up a permanent new organization unit in or outside the central MIS/DP or IRM unit. Later, the company may

[17] Arthur H. Schneyman, "Organizing Information Resources," *Information Management Review,* Vol. 1, Issue 1, Summer 1986, pp. 35–46.

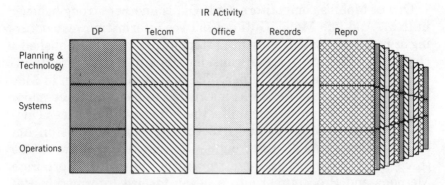

Figure 6–5. IR conventional organizations. *Source:* see note 17. Reprinted with permission of Aspen Systems Corporation. Copyright© 1986.

organizationally absorb the OA function on a permanent formal basis, after the equipment installation is completed and the new workflows are operating smoothly.

In short, Schneyman believes that there is no need to throw all of the information technologies and information-handling functions into the same organizational melting pot, suddenly, in one fell revolutionary swoop. In many, if not most organizations, he thinks such a course of action would be unnecessarily traumatic.

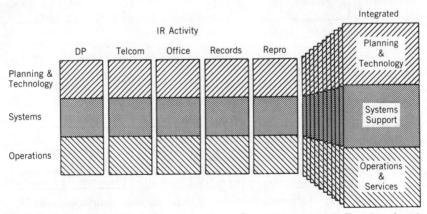

Figure 6–6. IR integrated organizations. *Source:* see note 17. Reprinted with permission of Aspen Systems Corporation. Copyright© 1986.

One of Mobil's competitors, Gulf Oil, is another strong believer in IRM. And like Mobil, Gulf doesn't see information restructuring as just a cost savings-oriented step. In 1982, Gulf established a corporate-wide task force to consider steps to restructure its information streams and holdings. The first step was taken in May of 1982, and the task force was instructed to focus on three major existing information service units: the Information Services Division, Corporate Methods and Procedures, and the Houston Accounting Center. As it turned out, Gulf decided to keep two of the three units autonomous, and transform the third (Corporate Methods and Procedures) into a newly formed Information Resources Department that would then serve as the key corporate core information-management policy group (See Figure 6-7.)[18]

Equally important, the task force recommended that liaison information-resources groups be established in each of Gulf's major organizations, to act as bridges between the information-

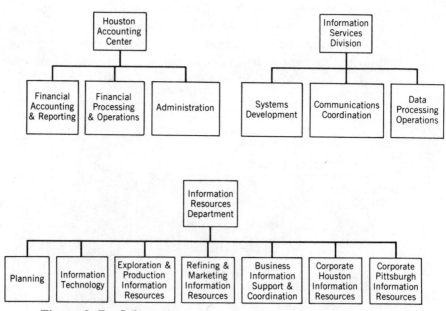

Figure 6–7.   Information resources organizations. *Source:* see note 18.

[18] "Turning Information Into Profits," *Gulf Oilmanac,* No. 5, 1983, p. 11.

service organizations (identified above), and individual users. Within the IRM department, an internal structure oriented to product lines was established.

INFORMATION WORK FUNCTIONS

In the first of the three parts in this chapter we looked at broad considerations of structure, including the flattening of traditional industrial work environments and the telescoping of organizational structures and environmental factors. These are the larger forces that are compelling changes. But theorists and practitioners alike admonish companies not to rush into automation without first reexamining their basic work processes and functions—because computers are transforming the nature of work itself. In this second part, we will look at how technologies are affecting the very basic way work itself is done.

Nearly everyone agrees that automating work flows without first making necessary fundamental changes and improvements is the wrong way to go about automation. You don't have to be a methods engineer to understand the logic of examining what can be consolidated, simplified, perhaps eliminated entirely, transferred, and so on, before investing in the machine.

Heijn, of the American Productivity Center in Houston, believes there are four major areas that should be carefully looked at.[19] First come the procedural issues. Here Heijn suggests a three-pronged attack: Define what work has to be done and how it can be performed; what skills are needed, and how they should be allocated; and what techniques can support production. Often existing products shouldn't continue to be produced; new ones would be better. Often needed skills are not backed up by position descriptions and functional statements. And too often the pooling of parallel and similar operations is not considered when installing telephone systems, copying facilities, and electronic filing systems.

[19] Herman J. Heijn, "Automate the Organization . . . or Organize the Automation?" Productivity Brief 14, June 1982, American Productivity Center, 123 North Post Oak Lane, Houston, TX 77024. Reprinted with permission of American Productivity Center, Houston, TX. Copyright© June 1982.

Heijn's second area relates to today's manual data-management systems, which he believes are prone to several weaknesses. Storing and filing of documents and records is an area that automation has long effectively addressed with impressive productivity, simplification, and streamlining results. Heijn's third area is related to decision support systems, which he says can provide direct input and feedback to managers faced with deciding among alternatives. And finally, the fourth area is communication support systems.

A detailed examination of work simplification, workflow analysis, and related subjects is clearly beyond our scope. There are many excellent case studies in this area and we list some of them in our bibliography. What is of more direct applicability to our scope and purpose is not to provide a detailed treatment of information work functions (we have already had something to say about the CEO and the new chief information office role), so much as to ask what existing roles will continue, albeit under different environments, and how will authorities and responsibilities be changed.

Office Automation: Opposing or Reinforcing the Middle Management Squeeze?

If top management is complaining that too many of their subordinates are paper pushers who do nothing more than make recommendations, and are incapable of making decisions, then will office automation exacerbate or reverse the middle-management squeeze? On the one hand it could be argued that the new workstation concept, combined with the enormously versatile software packages now available, could indeed help the middle manager to work a lot smarter than ever before, thus, perhaps, making him or her less dispensable. An equally persuasive argument is that all the electronic technologies do is give the middle managers a plaything—a new toy that will eventually be the nail in their coffins. Which is it? Or is it both?

BusinessWeek seems to be saying something like this: Used effectively, the middle manager's PC will help to make him or her more productive, help reduce the number of assistants required, and, if other necessary qualities and attributes are already there, can be a determining factor in whether he or she is retained or fired. But so far results are far from showing that the PC, per se, is the crucial factor in the equation. In short, if a manager already has formed "bad habits," and is already well on the way to his gold watch, the machines are likely to speed his or her demise. But if middle managers see the new capabilities as an adjunct to their problem-solving and decision-making prowess to be used circumspectly and judiciously, then chances are their position in the company will be solidified.

BusinessWeek editors writing in 1984 mention three case examples where technology has started to make structural changes:

[Hercules, Inc.] A sophisticated combination of work processing, electronic and voice mail, video-conferencing, and high speed communications has permitted Chairman Alexander F. Giacco to cut the levels of management between himself and Hercules plant foremen from a dozen to 'six or seven' says Ross O. Watson, vice-president for information resources at the Wilmington (Del.)-based chemical company.

[FMC Corp.] This Chicago-based producer of machinery and chemicals has installed a voice-mail system in one of its groups that allows salesmen and their regional and district sales managers to exchange messages and instructions at any time via telephone "mailboxes." The new system has vastly improved communications —and productivity, reports Lynn F. White, director of office automation. In fact, it enabled FMC to amalgamate sales districts and in many cases cut out a level of management. The reduction in the costs for long-distance calling alone paid for the group's voice-mail system.

[Citicorp.] This New York-based bank's North American Banking Group developed a sophisticated information system to improve customer service and make account and market information available to its corporate clients more quickly. The system has allowed the group to pare its staff—70% of whom were formerly clerical—from 2,650 three years ago to 2,150. And now 60% are professionals, says R. May Gould, head of the Customer Service Division. Furthermore, the bank has been able to move its customer-service operations closer to its clients, because information can be transmitted electronically rather than on paper. More than 90% of the company's people were based in New York five years ago, and now less than 50% are. [20]

[20] "Office Automation," *BusinessWeek*, Oct. 8, 1984, pp. 118–130 (special report).

In many ways, FMC's moves reinforce several other themes we've been advancing in this book. For one, a key architect in the structural changes mentioned above, and in others, is Dan W. Irwin who is director of Information Resources and reports directly to FMC president Raymond C. Tower. Irwin has been a pioneer in blazing the pathway for the chief information officer or CIO role in top Fortune 1000 companies. He sees his role as that of a facilitator; effectively applying information technologies to the task of increasing the returns of the corporation. FMC made a conscious decision to take the corporate information-management function out from under the controller or chief financial officer, and make it autonomous. In FMC, MIS, telecommunications, computing, and office automation all report to Irwin. According to Irwin, who was interviewed by *BusinessWeek*, "everyone will move in the same direction to boost productivity. No one company will be able to move out ahead. The real winners will be the ones that creatively apply technology to change the way business is done, to reach a competitive advantage."[21]

Structural Considerations in Harnessing External Information

Most companies by now have a pretty good grip on how to establish the kind of information-technology center initially espoused by IBM as a training focus for micro end-users. It is hard nowadays not to run into an information center wherein users are busily fingering the keyboards of an IBM PC, a MacIntosh, a Commodore, or some other popular brand; learning word processing packages, doing spreadsheet manipulations, or using a graphics or statistical package. But only the early wave of experimenters is as yet moving to establish appropriate organizational structures and capabilities to begin to harness the *external* knowledge resources now available from both commercial and government sources.

Berry and Cook were among the first to forecast the importance of an external-information-sources group within the

[21] *Ibid.*, p. 119.

company.[22] In their scheme, an "enterprise administrator" over-sees the various database administrators, the applications development groups, and an external knowledge-resource group. Taking a systems approach, these investigators suggest that there is more to accessing external information than just setting up a terminal somewhere in the back of the library, plugging it in, and writing a contract with a database vendor or distributor. Rather, they suggest that the first thing this unit must address is the need to develop some kind of model of the relationship of the enterprise to its external worlds—including customers, suppliers, the external knowledge resource group, shareholders, government entities, and even local communities. Then, once the model is constructed, they recommend that the information requirements for each of these functional relationships be specified in terms of content, volume, direction, and importance.

Berry and Cook's methodology for constructing and using the enterprise-to-the-external-world model is similar, they believe, to what the company's methods and procedures department may well have already developed for the enterprise's internal interrelationships. These models, in their view, not only serve as a representation of the goals and the current status of their achievement, but they can also provide the organization with the means for testing the impact of various hypothetical changes in requirements or organizational structure. Ultimately, they foresees the corporate information architecture integrating both the internal and the external resources into a single, overall model that embraces data elements, file structures, data bases, and flows that comprise the totality of the knowledge base of the company.

Another researcher, Robert Taylor of Syracuse University, underscores the need to identify, harmonize and integrate the incredibly diffused expert knowledge resources that are scattered all through a Fortune 1000 company.[23] There are important expert

---

[22] J. F. Berry and C. M. Cook, "Managing Knowledge as a Corporate Resource," U.S. Department of Commerce, National Technical Information Service, Report AD-A029 891, May 28, 1976, (available from NTIS, Springfield, VA 22161). Copyright© May 28, 1976. Reprinted with permission.

[23] Robert S. Taylor, *Value-Added Processes in Information Systems*, Ablex, Norwood, NJ: 1985.

knowledge resources in the general counsel's office, in the files of statistical offices, in consultant reports, in surveys of the company and its operations done by a wide variety of outsiders including government accountants and auditors, and so on. By no means is all of the corporation's "information resource" in its formal, automated data systems such as inventory control, personnel, and contract files. A great deal of it is in the files of staff offices, and in the files of consultants and experts all through the corporation. And, he emphasizes, much is in the *heads* of the lawyers, accountants, and engineers, that may never have seen the light of day on a piece of paper.

Taylor's thesis raises the whole question of how the enlightened corporation can even identify nonrecorded information and knowledge resources—which is really at the heart of how the whole expert system/knowledge-based system/AI develops.

Taylor, like Berry and Cook, foresee the day when there will be linked together a vast network of informal and formal expert systems, wherein the supporting knowledge base is a cluster of not so much formal domains of knowledge in a given subject field (covered in the open literature), but the collective experiential knowledge and wisdom of individual company experts. It is much like the idea of "brainscan" exit interviews of departing company professionals which ensure that, instead of taking all of their know-how with them, along with the gold watch upon retirement, they leave the legacy of all that they know about the company's business.

Islands of Specialization: IRM as the Unifying Framework

As we noted in Chapter 5, today's information-management function brings together the many specialized activities that historically have had their own professional bodies, expertise, technology, and unique management skills. But whereas yesterday these activities occupied separate islands in the information sea (Harvard's McFarlan calls them "islands in the information archipelago"), today their managerial, human, technological, and procedural interfaces and links are harmonized and unified under the IRM concept. Burk sees the scope of information-handling functions, information programs, and information resources at different levels.[24] (See Figure 6-8.)[25] He sees them as all part of the same management framework. Burk has advanced this scheme in the context of the office of the Auditor General's plans for auditing Canadian ministry information operations.

As a result of the Paperwork Reduction Act of 1980, U.S. federal agency departments have been:

1. Integrating their information technology under the IRM umbrella as a unifying framework

2. Clustering information-processing programs (that is, collection from, and dissemination to, the public) across internal departmental boundaries, at both departmental and lower level (bureau level)

3. Elevating the overall IRM function and its administration so as to pull up the management of information to higher levels than had formerly been the case

ROLE CHANGES: THE MIS/DP MANAGER

We now come to the third and last part of this chapter, which is to examine why roles in the office and other work environments (laboratory and factory) are changing, and how those roles should be reformulated. We begin with an examination of why and how the role of the MIS/DP manager is changing.

We've reviewed how structural, technological, and environmental impacts are changing the firm in the information economy, but what of the changes in the roles of the key executives? Surely no one—from CEO on down—can escape the consequences of the computer revolution. There is more to this change than sending the company president off to the Bahamas for a quick computer-literacy course, or corporate marketing officials taking a week-

[24] C. F. Burk, Jr., "Auditing The Management of Information Resources: A Challenge for the '80s," *Discussion Paper No. 39,* October, 1984, Office of the Auditor General, 240 Sparks Street, Ottawa, Ontario K1A 0G6, Canada.

[25] C. F. Burk, Jr., "Management of Departmental Information Resources: Report to the Executive Committee," Unpublished Report, March 25, 1980, Department of Energy, Mines and Resources, 580 Booth Street, Ottawa, Ontario, K140E4, Canada. Reprinted with permission.

Figure 6-8. General Distribution of Information Resources: Department of Energy, Mines and Resources (EMR). *Source:* See note 25.

Information Resources	DM's Office: SADM	DM's Office: Secretariat	P&E	S&T: ADM S&T	S&T: CANMET	S&T: GSC	S&T: SMB	S&T: EPB	S&T: CCRS	S&T: PCSP	S&T: Explosives	S&T: OERD	S&T: CCGD	MP: ADM MP	MP: AD	MP: RDD	MP: MMD	MP: ISD	En: ADM E	En: EC	En: FAS	En: ADM P	En: ADM CN	En: ADM EPA	Adm: ADM A	Adm: FS	Adm: PB	Adm: AS	Adm: CSC	Adm: OLB	Adm: Translation	Adm: InfoEMR	Totals
Sources:																																	
General inquiry centres					×	×	×	×	×		×									×							×					×	8
Sales & distribution centres					×	×	×	×	×		×									×												×	6
Libraries				×	×	×	×	×	×			×						×												×			6
Scientific & technical information centres		×			×	×	×	×	×	×	×				×						×			×		×	×	×	×	×		×	13
Record management centres	×	×	×		×	×	×	×	×	×	×				×				×	×	×	×	×		×	×	×	×	×	×	×	×	14
Services:																																	
Public relations					×	×	×		×						×			×		×								×				×	3
Publishing				×	×	×	×	×	×	×		×	×		×			×		×								×	×			×	8
Drafting & cartographic					×	×	×	×													×		×					×				×	7
Photographic						×	×		×	×																		×					3
Abstracting & indexing				×	×	×	×	×	×		×	×	×		×					×	×					×	×	×	×		×	×	8
Computing					×	×	×	×	×				×	×									×					×	×			×	3
Telecommunications		×	×	×	×	×	×	×	×		×		×		×					×	×	×						×	×				4
Copying & duplicating	×	×	×	×	×	×	×	×	×	×	×	×	×	×	×				×	×	×	×	×		×	×	×	×	×	×	×	×	25
Word processing		×	×	×	×	×	×	×	×	×		×	×	×	×			×			×	×	×			×	×	×	×		×	×	15
Mail & delivery					×	×	×	×	×						×													×	×			×	9
Systems:																																	
Scientific & technical data		×	×	×	×	×	×	×	×				×					×				×		×									7
Bibliographic data		×				×			×									×														×	3
Economic data									×																				×				2
Financial data																										×	×	×		×			3
Personnel data			×																								×	×		×			2
Materiel data		×																												×			1
Management information	×	×	×		×	×	×	×	×					×					×	×	×				×			×	×		×	×	6
Totals: Branch	2	4	2	3	12	14	14	10	13	4	4	3	5	2	6	0	0	4	2	4	5	3	3	2	1	3	4	9	7	2	2	7	
Sector	6		2	82										12					19						35								
Dept.																									156								

long "PCs for marketing staff" course. The very roles of every manager, professional, and employee throughout the organization are changing in ways that could not have been anticipated.

None of these role changes is more crucial to the firm trying to stay at the cutting edge of electronic-age changes than that of the MIS/DP manager. Since micros have spread to every nook and cranny in the office without the direct intervention of the central MIS/DP operations, end-users have been able to free themselves from what they perceive is the tyranny of the MIS/DP group. Old-line MIS/DP staff people don't know which way to turn. On the one side they are admonished by vendors to stand back and let the coming wave engulf the entire enterprise like a benevolent tidal wave. Vendor's point the finger at the computer-center head and say "you'd better not get in the way, or they'll run right over you like a great steamroller!"

On the other side, user departments, flushed from fresh purchases of personal computers by the hundreds (and even thousands in many firms), often begin straggling back into the computer center after a few weeks, demanding assistance with unanticipated hardware and software problems. They are "liberated," all right, but only to a degree. Like a child learning to ride a bicycle, they still need a parent to stand close by.

From above, the MIS/DP chief's own bosses are demanding that the MIS/DP staff "get with it," and strike a balance; retaining sufficient central control, and releasing the creativity and initiative of the new phalanxes of end-users. Top management doesn't have many answers, but they know they don't want to lose out to the company's competitors in the race to automate.

Jerome Klernan of John Diebold Associates has said that "the kings are falling right and left as the peasants come on in full revolt." Klernan makes MIS/DP people wince when he reminds them that when something goes wrong with a big purchase, they often become the "fall guys." Both those who use the ostrich approach (hoping the PC invasion will go away), and those who take the "information royalty" approach (aspiring to dominate the micro revolution) have failed.[26]

[26] Jerome Klernan, "Can MIS Royalty Survive the PC Revolution?" *MIS Week*, March 14, 1984, p. 46.

The MIS/DP manager's role is changing very significantly. Not only must he or she keep up with the operations of the mainframe central processing unit and all of the traditional mainframe applications, but he or she must now take on a whole new family of constituencies. These include many different classes of end-users with many different kinds of uses, not only for end-user hardware and software, but for telecommunications networks, accessing external information resources through on-line searches, up- and downloading data through the mainframe-micro links, and so forth. In short, the MIS/DP manager's life has become enormously complicated. Where mainframe applications are already old and rickety, many MIS/DP managers have their hands full just coping with enhancements, upgrades, and replacements. In such cases the CEO often brings in a chief information officer (CIO), who knows the company's overall business, and divides old authorities and responsibilities among two, three, four, or even more managers, where once only one—the MIS/DP manager— had the entire job.

To add insult to injury, many of the early wave of office automation gurus thought the creation of the CIO job, and the installation of an information-management function, was just a cover-up or, in the words of one, "a sinecure for aging computer center managers." Needless to say, that accusation didn't sit well with many old-timer MIS/DP managers, who see the OA community as a threat to their turf, particularly when many of these OA gurus insist that the OA chief bypass the computer and telecommunications departments and report directly to the CIO. We're finding, however, that top management is not usually convinced that this will work. Most companies are consolidating OA with computer and telecommunications operations and putting them under the CIO's IRM umbrella.

What is the answer for the MIS/DP manager? Much of the nature of the role changes faced by MIS/DP managers and their senior lieutenants can be effectively coped with through continuing education, increased visits to on-site installations where sought-after hardware and software is already in use, and more benchmark testing of competing hardware and software being considered for purchase. Also crucial is a broadening of perspective to understand how the new MIS and DP role fits into the larger context of the information management, information technology, and information policy concerns being faced by every enterprise in the information economy.

Should the MIS/DP Function Be "Anointed" as the IRM Function?

No single issue has caused more fire and smoke in corporate boardrooms than the question of whether or not the existing MIS/DP function should be automatically given the lead role in the company's new information resources management setup. On the one hand, old-line MIS/DP personnel believe they've earned the right to this mantle. They consider themselves the logical heir apparent. On the other hand, end-users are frequently adamant against such a move, fearing that the same old "big-systems" mentality will stifle the burgeoning PC end-user revolution.

John Diebold, a noted international automation and management authority, sees this organizational puzzle in six pieces, all of which are starting to come to a head.[27]

1. MIS/DP is highly organized, well developed, and generally reports to an officer level in large companies. But the CEO is challenging the MIS/DP chief to change the company's product distribution system; determine how information resources will help the company compete; and other very fundamental tasks.

2. By contrast, the office-automation function has typically reported at a lower level of responsibility, and reports in a very wide range of different ways. All too often, Diebold points out, OA's motivation has been almost exclusively cost savings. But the real focus, he is convinced, ought to be in terms of the improvement of productivity of professionals, whether they be managers, engineers, or scientists.

3. A third leg, the communications function, presents still another pattern. Like OA, communications has reported in many different ways, although more recently it tends to

---

[27] John Diebold, "Six Issues That Will Affect the Future of Information Management," *Data Management,* July 1984, p. 10–12. Copyright© July 1984.

report through the MIS/DP director. Mostly, Diebold says, it has been organized in a helter-skelter way, and has tended to focus on one source of supply: AT&T. Suddenly there is "option shock." A thorough consideration of these options usually far exceeds both the analytical ability of communications staffs at the technical detail level, as well as the managerial ability to keep on top of the situation.

4. Then there is the range of manufacturing systems like CAD/CAM. More and more, capital investments are being placed in this area, and increasingly the factory databases are being synchronized with the administrative-office and the R&D and engineering databases.

5. Diebold considers the emergence of the end-user as a fifth factor. This trend alone has forced the MIS/DP department into the role of a wholesaler, not just a retailer. This factor tends to pervade all of the other factors listed.

6. The sixth element in Diebold's puzzle is much the central theme of this book. This point is that information and information technologies are no longer just backroom support operations, but must be seen as strong forces affecting the competitiveness of the firm.

Diebold was among the first to point out that this last realization is giving the MIS people a run for their money, because they must suddenly participate with top management in substantive strategic decisions, whereas in the past they were seen by the front office just as data processors. He calls the phenomenon "incorporating the computer into the product." Some examples are: how an insurance company equips its agents, how a company changes it product-distribution channels in terms of what levels it jumps over, and so on. We dealt with these questions in Chapter 4.

James L. McKenney and F. Warren McFarlan point out that integrating the three major information technologies organizationally is much more than a matter of moving blocks around on an organizational chart. Data processing, telecommunications, and office automation have, historically, been managed in quite different ways. Nevertheless, these experts also see a gradual organizational integration of the technologies, for three compelling reasons:

1. Decisions in each area now involve large amounts of money and complex technical and cost evaluations.

2. The types of analytical skills, project-management skills, and staff needed to plan and implement applications are similar for each of the technologies.

3. Many systems call for the combination of these technologies into networks that handle computing, telecommunications, and office automation in an integrated way.[28]

In summary, we take the view that MIS/DP incumbents should *not* all be "anointed" to top IRM posts just because they happen to have control over the largest single information-technology capital investment and operating budget in the company. As more and more enterprises come to know and understand the value of accessing external databases and tapping into on-line resources, the need for a CIO who understands how these vast, externally available knowledge resources, as well as expert knowledge resources available internally, can be applied to solve the company's bottom-line problems, becomes apparent. This is far more than a "change-the-magnetic tapes" decision. Information resources managers' jobs, in short, should be based not just on the job titles and occupational specializations of applicants, but upon their willingness and ability to grasp the significance of how their companies can and should be using their information assets to chart and change the course of business.

Role Changes: The Functional Users

When we say *functional users* here we are referring to the finance department, for example, or the marketing department, R&D, engineering, and so on. These are the primary line and staff groups (including corporate staff), that carry out the basic production and distribution tasks. These tasks are becoming increasingly dependent on reliable and timely information and technology, and the manner in which these information resources are being

---

[28] James L. McKenney, and Warren McFarlan, "The Information Archipelago—Maps and Bridges," Chapter 8 in *Catching Up with the Computer Revolution*, New York: Wiley, 1983.

harnessed and mobilized is changing the roles of users radically. Why is this the case?

First, the roles of users are changing because information in corporate databases can now be downloaded by virtually every employee, and manipulated in a thousand ways. Departmental functional managers must face up to a number of information policy issues thereby precipitated, to which they were formerly immune.

Under the traditional centralized DP-shop environment, each user functional department was in charge of the corporate data within the sphere of its respective functional cognizance. The problems of theft and security, misuse and abuse of data, inadvertent disclosure, quality erosion, and so forth, were minimal because access was severely limited. But now access problems and abuses are rampant. Working with the CIO, functional managers must now develop corporate-information policies that address such questions as what data can be used by which groups, and under what conditions, what actions constitute a punishable offense because of data abuse and misuse, and so forth. Such a policy must also deal with security and protective measures down to the micro level.

Second, the work of functional managers is itself undergoing substantial changes due to the introduction of information technologies. The use of electronic spreadsheets is a simple example. Moving up the scale of complexity, the need for auditors to take special training to keep abreast of how to follow the "electronic-audit trail" is an example of an impact of medium complexity. Somewhat less than 20 percent of the audit and accounting curricula at major universities have even a single course on computer auditing. Further up the complexity scale, the corporate long-range planning and economic-forecasting departments now have very complex and sophisticated computer models available to do their work. There is great competition among software vendors to improve the first and deliver the second generation of this product line. Each major software trade show has dozens, if not hundreds, of new computer modeling products displayed by participating vendors.

Third, functional managers, particularly those in corporate-headquarters staffs, are being buffeted by the increasing availability of legions of external on-line databases, both commercial and governmental, that can and should be used in their work. (We will later touch on the computer and information literacy-sharpening skills needed in greater detail.)

In short, even the MBA just out of business school who moves directly into the company's controller's shop, and who has spent a very substantial number of hours as an undergraduate and graduate student poring over the keyboard of a CRT, is by no means fully equipped to meet the demands of his new job. While doctors can walk out of medical school and into their offices, ready to use a stethoscope, and law students can prepare a will after the first year of law school, the marketing assistant and production-control supervisor on the plant floor are faced with a long and arduous apprenticeship that involves learning electronic information processing and management skills that can only be acquired on the job.

Role Changes: Service and Support Groups

One must wonder if inventory managers, plant operations personnel and administrative support employees are not a little miffed at all the attention their professional information worker colleagues are getting. Vendors, consultants, and experts chorus uniformly in the pages of trade and professional journals how the marvelous new information technologies are going to transform the work of top and middle management, key scientific and engineering professionals, and end-users throughout the organization. But what of the drudgery of the rear-guard logistics troops? Will the support and service elements become the neglected, and even forgotten generation of the information age? Are their roles changing too? Should we not pay attention to those changes? Certainly their work is being affected. The company's top executive level, and its functional and technical managers and professionals may be getting the lion's share of attention, but the work of materials and equipment departments, property and contract management divisions, supervisors of company automotive and truck fleets, and the rest of the administrative and logistical support units, is just as much affected by the new technologies.

The flattening of managerial levels discussed earlier is making greater demands on the support group. For example, the expeditor of materials due in from suppliers must now contend with the demands of a whole new group of functional managers who may have on-line access to production schedules, inventory supply levels, purchasing data, contract data, and much more. Whereas in days past the expeditor could expect to interact primarily with closely related units, interpersonal and intergroup contact with individuals and units in all manner of organizational loci is a result of the current interoffice networking trend so important to Naisbitt's prognostications.

One consequence of this increased communications and intergroup interaction is pressure to improve the quality control of information for which the service and support staffs are held responsible. It is one thing for a single purchasing clerk, for example, to face the embarrassing result of discovery of erroneous information in the automated central-purchasing files when only he or she and a few peers in his or her own unit had access to the data. It is quite another matter when anyone from the CEO on down might well download and manipulate such information for purposes totally unknown to the purchasing-department employee. Unreliable data so used could have devastating results.

Another consequence is the integration of company support databases, spanning all across the above-mentioned functional areas, into tighter and more closely linked data subsets. This is occurring as companies move increasingly toward an overall corporate-information architecture that puts all the database pieces together into one integrated mosaic. This means that data and document linkage is dropping down to the data-element level, whereas at one time it was at the document-on-file level. All of these data linkages must be carefully described and oftentimes standardized. As data-element dictionaries and data directories come into being, data-element standardization programs are the glue that holds everything together.

In this increasingly formalized and structured database environment, even the employees on the lowest rung of the ladder in the service and support area may find themselves in the role of a data manager, held accountable for the integrity of large chunks of corporate data. Quality control, integrity, reliability, and credibility may be attributes for which such employees have never before been held responsible on a departmental, much less a corporate-wide basis.

Finally, on the bright side, there are tremendous opportunities for support employees to seize upon the rich information environment in which they now find themselves operating. They can innovate, by suggesting new approaches, techniques, models, processes, procedures, and so forth. One doesn't need to be a member of a quality-control circle to be able to make productivity, efficiency, and effectiveness improvements.

The Chief Information Officer (CIO) Role

We have already discussed generic role changes for three key groups: the MIS/DP group, departmental functional (end-user) groups, and service and support groups. We certainly have done more than just imply that an overall CIO seems to be an inevitable development in most, but not necessarily all, large organizations. There are some notable exceptions in cutting-edge companies, such as Hewlett-Packard, that we've discussed elsewhere. John Diebold has been a strong supporter of the CIO role, which he initially dubbed "director of corporate information" (DCI).

Whether one is discussing a company with a strong tradition of a highly centralized, tightly controlled style, or the opposite—a highly decentralized, laissez-faire modus operandi—someone or some group must play the role of pulling everything together from a corporate-wide standpoint. Where, for strategic or tactical reasons, a company strongly endorses the philosophy of "every men should be his or her own information manager," or leans to the other extreme (tight centralized control), there must be coordination of policy formulation on information and information technology requirements, uses, and enhancements. There must be management control of the myriad purchasing, design, development, testing, evaluation, and other tasks associated with hardware, software, and systems acquisitions. And there must be operating control over the efficient use of real economic resources (people, dollars, facilities, and materials) consumed in support of information activities.

John Diebold believes there should be a strong individual to ride herd over all of these elements. John Young at Hewlett-Packard (HP) believes in a more collegial, "IRM-by-committee" approach. In either event, we are convinced it is important to make sure that the component structural, policy, procedural, and audit-control functions are carried out by one person or one group. Diebold believes his top-down system, which is characterized by the use of a corporate team to structure corporate databases, is inherently preferable to HP's bottom-up approach, because it centralizes information management even though it sometimes fails to put together a team that really understands the business and its future opportunities. He also feels this approach has the advantages of management flexibility, allowing the company to reorganize itself in the future, for more collaborative decision-making.[29]

The concept of the CIO has also been picked up in government, beyond the Paperwork Reduction Act of 1980, which called for a senior official in every government agency who would be the information "czar." On January 20, 1984, J. Peter Grace, Chairman of the President's Private Sector Survey On Cost Control, commonly known as the Grace Committee, sent its *Information Gap in the Federal Government* report, Volume VII in the total series, to President Reagan. Its litany of findings mirrored those of the Commission on Federal Paperwork which labored in the same paperwork/information vineyards some ten years earlier. The Grace Committee Information Gap report found that government has too much information of the wrong kind, too little of the right kind, has too much inconsistent and incompatible and unverifiable data, acts too often on untimely data, and is unable to even identify and find the data it already has in its files when needed.

This report's investigators found a "structural void." That is, "no one (in government) is attempting to coordinate the selection and flow of management information. Without an assignment of responsibility, overcoming the roadblocks cited (above) is difficult." Figure 6-9 is the Grace Committee's answer: A CIO at every level of government, including the Executive Office of the President.

Mr. Grace would even take existing overall Federal IRM responsibility away from the Office of Management and Budget, where it currently resides pursuant to the Paperwork Reduction Act of 1980, and transfer the authorities to a new Office of Federal Management. A White House information manager would coordinate the whole shooting match for the president.[30]

[29] John Diebold, "IRM: New Directions in Management," Diebold Special Report, *InfoSystems,* October 1979, p. 41–42.

[30] "Information Gap in the Federal Government," Volume VII, President's Private Sector Survey on Cost Control, January 25, 1984 (available through the Department of Commerce, Washington, D.C.), Exhibit II-3.

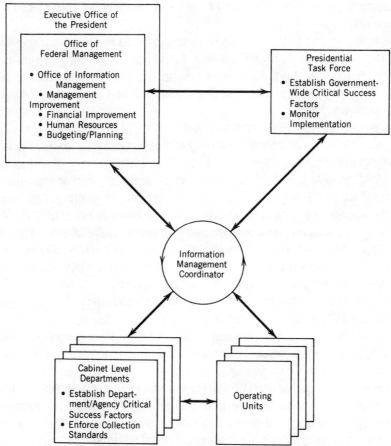

Figure 6–9. A structure to facilitate an information management process. *Source:* see note 29. Reprinted from *Infosystems*, October 1979. Copyright Hitchcock Publishing Company. Used with permission.

SUMMARY

Structural and functional considerations that must be taken into account today by the enterprise in the information economy are far more than a matter of division of labor, span of control, and centralization versus decentralization, as those "scientific management" principles were once applied by industrial engineers trying to plan an idealized workflow for a smokestack-era firm that needed little more than assembly lines, tool cribs, and blue collar workers who did what they were told.

Structure and function in the information age are heavily dependent on considerations of social dynamics that get deeply into communications, intergroup behavior, interpersonal behavior, motivation theory, and other psychological and sociological factors. One does not have to go back any further than the seminal work of the behavioral scientists of the 1940s and 1950s, to find research that is perhaps more relevant to helping to meet today's organizational challenges than it was to helping the smokestack-era firms at which it was initially directed.

Most experts seem to agree that an evolutionary rather than revolutionary approach—gradually consolidating and integrating information technologies and functions—is preferable. There is no unblinking IRM metronome that dictates the precise meter and pace of organizational realignments and role reformulations. Even the largest corporate giants, like Mobil and Gulf Oil, see the virtue of a gradual but deliberate program of bringing together the disparate organizational information pieces and fitting them carefully but incrementally into the total enterprise organizational and functional mosaic.

Above all else, it must be kept in mind that introducing information management is to introduce fundamental change itself into the organization. Once the CEO, the CIO, the department heads, and the senior professional and managerial staff understand that, their task is made easier. It would be nice if we could avoid organizational realignments altogether, but they are necessary. We should deal with them openly, for what they are, rather than ignore or defer them altogether.

CHAPTER 7

MANAGING AND PLANNING FOR INFORMATION PRODUCTIVITY

INTRODUCTION

Many corporations are so enamored with the power and versatility of micros, the intelligent workstation idea, local area networks, and so forth, that they find it very difficult to discipline themselves in purchasing, installing, and using these technologies. There is a kind of "everybody else is doing it" attitude around which prevents many companies from doing the necessary planning, managing, and controlling of this new equipment. "Let's just run out and buy up a batch of hardware and software, sit managers and professionals down in front of the screen," and, as in the Chinese proverb, "let their creativity blossom like a thousand flowers," they say.

Company reluctance to stifle creativity is exacerbated by the overwhelming crush of trade literature that daily floods into the offices of information managers, and down through the firm to the user level. Make no mistake, vendor marketing strategies nowadays are pitched directly to the end-user, deliberately by-passing central purchasing offices and central information-management offices. What better demand-pull strategy than to have the targeted company's end-users storm the doors of the central IRM and contract offices, demanding the latest dBase IV, V, or VI, or the sixth iteration of Symphony, or a new mainframe-to-micro downloading package?

Still, we believe in the rather old-fashioned idea that the corporation *must* utilize formal management and control machinery if the situation is not to degenerate into a kind of full-scale anarchy wherein end-users become so bloated with hardware and software they can neither fully understand, nor effectively use to achieve results. On the other hand, formalized structures and control systems should not be allowed to stand in the way of innovative and creative uses of the technology.

The material in this chapter is organized conveniently around the successive stages in what is often called the "information life cycle." See Figure 7-1. The notion here, simply put, is that information management, like manufacturing a product or developing a weapons system, follows a life cycle. That is, there is a logical succession of stages or steps, each dependent on the last. While there is some room for flexibility in completing stages simulta-

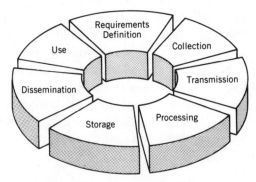

Figure 7–1. Information life cycle.

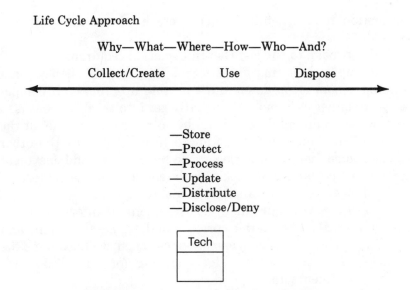

Life Cycle Approach

Why—What—Where—How—Who—And?

Collect/Create   Use   Dispose

—Store
—Protect
—Process
—Update
—Distribute
—Disclose/Deny

Tech

Figure 7–2.   Information Is a Resource!

neously rather in tandem, the process is still basically iterative.

As Figure 7-2 shows, the life-cycle analogy is also helpful in showing that there is a continuum along which different functions come into play at each step in the life cycle.

At the end of this chapter, we'll examine some of the specific management controls that are the glue that holds everything else together, but we'll begin here with the first step in the information life cycle—the idea of formulating an overall corporate information strategy. We have touched briefly on that subject already, but in a broader context. Now we'll shift to methodology. For example, we'll look at what an overall corporate information policy statement might look like, and what specific information policies might be candidates for incorporation therein.

Then we'll move on to the subject of linking the company's business plan with its information plans. It is in this context that the so-called "critical success factor" (CSF) idea finds fruitful expression. Once these planning linkages have been made, the company can finally get down to the serious business of articulating specific information requirements, and concrete hardware and software needs.

We don't mean to suggest that information requirements aren't a bottom-up, percolating process too. They are. We believe that planning is *both* a top-down and a bottom-up process. If companies go to either extreme, they usually get into trouble. That is, a top-down planning philosophy can be so rigid that nobody at the bottom of the ladder is even allowed to comment. At the other extreme, some managers' styles are so permissive and benevolent that overall corporate strategic goals get lost in the morass of low-level objectives. A balance is obviously needed.

To continue with our life-cycle treatment of information resources, we will look at how to price, and determine the value and cost of information products and services. Then, we'll examine the methodologies for costing and accounting for information resources investments and expenditures.

Some brief discussions of various kinds of technical management controls, such as data directories and data element dictionaries, information audits and evaluation studies, and information standards and guidelines, will complete the chapter.

One important undercurrent we will strive to get across is the need to integrate information-*technology* management and information-*content* management. And we'll try to pay special attention to helping CEOs and CIOs know what to expect by way of productivity-enhancement opportunities.

FORMULATING A CORPORATE INFORMATION STRATEGY

In Figure 7-3, Burk provides an overview of the process by which the stages of the information life cycle are linked to an organization's information plan.[1] What Burk's schematic portrayal clarifies well is the stepwise flow of this linkage.[2] His approach proceeds first with an analysis of the company's basic missions, goals,

---

[1] C. F. Burk, Jr., "Auditing the Management of Information Resources, A Challenge for the 1980's," Unpublished Discussion Paper No. 39, October, 1984.
[2] *Ibid.*, p. 11.

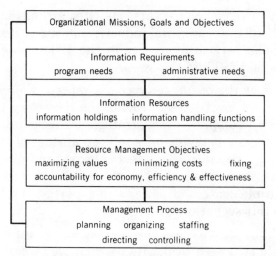

Figure 7–3. Basic elements and structure of the information resources management (IRM) concept. *Source:* see note 2. Reprinted with permission.

and objectives. Then, and only then, one can proceed to articulate information needs. Following that, we move on to the tools (resources) we will need. This process cannot be reversed. Buying the hardware and software before we know the uses to which they will be put virtually guarantees failure.

Burk's schema reminds us that just because we're buying *information* resources doesn't mean we can escape rigorous accountability for maximizing, conserving, and enhancing the value of those assets, just as we must for *any* kind of resource the enterprise acquires.

Now let us proceed to the formulation of a corporate-information policy. Janulaitis suggests that every organization has at least some of the characteristics of all three of the following generic visions of how to use their information assets and resources:

The first is the *strategic-technology-directed* strategy, where the company sees information resources as an integral part of the organization's unique strategy. This type of organization, Janulaitis points out, has an experience base that allows it to be involved with most leading-edge technology, and spends significantly more on information processing than its *nonstrategic-*

technology-directed competitors. He cites airlines in the 1960s, national hotel and car rental industries in the 1970s, and retail and financial service industries in the 1980s, as examples of industries that fall into this group.

Second comes the *business-directed* strategy, wherein information resources are used to provide the necessary information support for a company's key strategic business units, but this kind of company is trying only to keep abreast of the competition in using the information technologies, and usually cannot cope with introducing more than one new major technology at a time. Multiple centers of power and expertise compete for authority in this scenario.

In the third, or *manager-directed* strategy, information resources are still seen primarily as what we've called a "backroom operation," used in large-volume transaction applications like inventory control, personnel, payroll, and financial accounting. Almost always the information function is under the comptroller. Janulaitis estimates that 15 to 20 percent of all corporations are still following this strategy.[3]

In the end Janulaitis suggests that the company ought to develop a matrix that first identifies the company's major information and communications functions, then rates them as to maturity (low, average, high), and dependence (low, average, high), as well as absorption rate (that is, the ability to use them effectively). Then the company should plot its position relative to industry averages. Finishing that, the company can ask itself: "What are the directions, pace, and momentum of technological change within the industry and the organization? Are there opportunities for the company to gain a meaningful competitive advantage by leading in the industry's application of information resources? Is the company spending the right amount, too much, or too little in each information-resource area?"

Gad Selig puts the choice of an information strategy in more of a "corporate war games" context. He says that depending on the

---

[3] M. Victor Janulaitis, "Are the Risks Worth Taking?," *Computerworld,* In-Depth 13–22, August 13, 1984. Copyright© 1984 by CW Communications/Inc., Framingham, MA 01701. Reprinted from *Computerworld.*

overall business climate at any given time, the firm's information-planning strategy can and should assume one of several of the following macro-level strategies and substrategies:

1. Passive or Reactive Strategies:

    a. *Business-as-usual* substrategy. This approach tends to thrive in companies that are growing very fast and that are rapidly increasing their share of the market. Here, the information-resource activity has very low visibility—not only is it regarded as a relatively low-level service unit, but it is largely considered an after-the-fact service function.

    b. *Defensive* substrategy. Here the company has already been reduced to a defensive position and sees its information functions as basically supporting that objective. There is virtually no strategic business focus to the information function whatsoever.

    c. *Major contraction* substrategy. This approach is typically adopted by firms about to be, or already involved in divestiture or contraction, usually mature or declining businesses.

2. Proactive Strategies:

    a. *Modest improvement* substrategy. This scenario is seen in businesses where systems have become technologically obsolete and require maximum retooling with minimum investment.

    b. *Aggressive expansion* substrategy. Here are instances where shared systems and facilities as well as technology migration make sense, such as when the company is penetrating new markets for the first time.

    c. *Radical new direction* substrategy. This approach is close to that which we've been suggesting in this book, but not so much a "radical" adoption of strategy, as an absolutely necessary proactive strategy to cope with the "radically" changing information environment which we believe every company is facing. This substrategy consists of examining new opportunities and changing

organizational responsibilities and structures, to enhance information-resource penetration to the point of
adopting information-resource investments as a major
internal business strategy.[4]

R. I. Tricker reminds us that as companies move beyond transaction processing to the highly significant opportunities for
"facilitating" information throughout the organization, a multitude
of possibilities arise for rethinking both the structure of the organization and the style of management. Already, he says, technology is
far ahead of management's ability to recognize its organizational
and managerial implications. The developments that will emerge
over the next decade, he believes, are likely to increase the gap
between the technological potential, and senior management's ability to imagine its organizational implications and opportunities—
that is, unless there are significant changes in strategy formulation.

Tricker believes the challenge to senior management is no
longer one of using computing and telecommunications efficiently
and effectively. Rather, it is to appreciate the strategic significance of information systems, and to recognize that they bring
new opportunities for running the business, and new threats if
their implications are not understood well. The question is not so
much how managers want to use computers, but how they want to
run their businesses, considering that there are more options,
more issues, and more risks than many managers yet recognize.[5]

Linking Information Plans to Business Plans: Using Critical Success Factors

In an earlier era of centralized DP support to large-volume transaction applications like accounting, information-technology budgets were handled as an overhead component. Managers estimated a certain level of support in much the same way the

[4] Gad J. Selig, "Critical Success Factors for Multinational Information Resource Management Planning and Administration," *Managerial Planning*, March-April 1983, pp. 23–
27.
[5] R. I. Tricker, "How to Plan Information Strategy," *Management Today*, September
1982, pp. 62–65, 124–126.

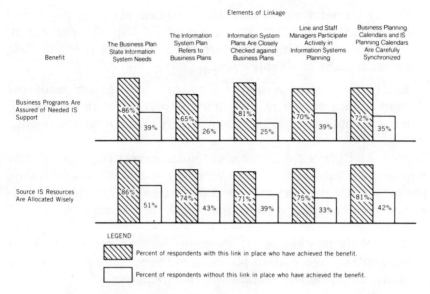

Figure 7–4. Impact of linkage on achievement of information systems planning benefits. *Source:* see note 6. Reprinted with permission from *Information Management*, Magazine, May 1983.

company estimated the space it would need to house offices and plants, or the extent of insurance coverage, or heating and lighting bills. Today everyone pretty much agrees that information-resource plans must be linked to overall business plans if they are really going to succeed. Simply dealing with the massive computer and communications investments as overhead won't do.

In the 1982–1983 timeframe, Cresap, McCormick & Paget, a leading management consulting firm, undertook a survey of 334 companies, about equally divided between large manufacturing and nonmanufacturing companies, to assess this information plan-business plan linkage (see Figure 7-4).[6]

Among the surveyed companies that explicitly incorporated information-system needs in their overall business plans:

[6] Eric Knutsen, "Impact of Linkage on Achievement of Information Systems Planning Benefits," Cresap, McCormick & Paget, as reported in *Information Management*, Vol. 17, No. 5, May 1983, p. 28.

Eighty-six percent said that "their business plans are assured of needed information-resources support"; only 39 percent of those who did *not* include information-resources needs in their business plans made this claim.

Eighty-six percent also said that their information resources were "allocated wisely"; but only 51 percent of those who did *not* spell out information-resource needs made that statement.

Cresap, McCormick & Paget also found, interestingly, that information planners seem to have more difficulty in understanding the overall business direction and requirements of their own companies than in coping with technological uncertainty:

Twenty-six percent of all company respondents cited as the number one information planning problem "lack of knowledge of overall business direction and requirements."

By contrast, only 11 percent ranked "uncertainty about the future of technology" as the number one problem.

Another leading management consulting firm, Peat, Marwick, Mitchell & Company (PMM), has also explored the problem of how to link information-resource plans with business plans. Gene Altschuler, database specialist with PMM, proposes that many companies would do well to establish a three-tiered information planning and control structure that links business strategy with automation strategy.[7]

At the top tier, Altschuler believes an overall systems architecture is needed to administer the data-administration functions at the macro level. This expert believes that this basic element of an integrated information planning and control structure fills the role of a functional user interface; looking down the road at what has to be done, and planning the relationships of major systems to other major systems. Without this macro-level link, Altschuler says, companies find that a programmer is setting corporate policy with a coding pencil.

[7] Paul Gillin, "Exec Urges Plan to Align DP, Business Strategies," *Computerworld*, October 24, 1983, p. 14. Copyright© 1983 by CW Communications/Inc., Framingham, MA 01701. Reprinted from *Computerworld*.

Altschuler's second major area of information planning and control is the automation planning and control function, which handles the more technical requirements of the DP installation. Here would be included high-level enterprise modeling of basic business needs, establishing operational plans for automation, planning communications facilities, quality assurance, data administration in the more classic sense, and project management control.

Finally, at the lowest level of his hierarchical pyramid model is the research and development function. This is the group that looks at new mainframe and peripheral devices, systems and applications software, and fourth generation technologies, for possible use.

Unlike many of his peers, Altschuler strongly believes in planning and controls that do *not* provide for end-user's control of their own data. He thinks that course could be disastrous. And he believes planning and control must be clearly separated from the more technical functions.

John Diebold, whose works we've referred to already, believes the essence of linking information-resources planning to overall corporate business plans lies in using a "critical success factors" (CSF) methodology. He asserts that information-resource services can (or should) no longer be viewed as support functions provided by former "machine accountants." In a 1984 MIS and telecommunications budget survey undertaken by his company, the Diebold Group, the following CSFs were identified:

The role of information technology in contemporary business reflects an enormous change in its function as a business resource. Most organizations consider the proper use of information technology to be absolutely essential to business success. This usage incorporates not only the support of internal operations and decision making, but also the extension to the marketplace of many products and services that would not be possible without the information technology.

The idea of a *chief information officer* (CIO) as found within the survey companies is more than just another periodic reorganization of the MIS function. The growing awareness is that information is a critical resource to be managed on a corporate level and employed to gain profitable advantage in the market-place.

The integration of information technology as a key resource during business-strategy planning is an idea that is gaining growing acceptance in the business community. There are several instances in our survey of companies where business planning is either an integrated function with the information resource or is a coequal function reporting to the CIO.[8]

We suggest that a company start its linkage process with a simple list of questions:

1. Do you have an information plan of *any* kind?
2. Does your plan integrate information and information-technology needs with the company's overall business plan?
3. If you don't have an information plan, and/or if it isn't integrated with your business plan, why isn't it? (Here address questions such as lack of top-management support, lack of methodological know-how, ineffective resource prioritization, and the like.
4. If you do have a plan, and/or it is integrated with your business plan, how can it be strengthened? (Here address machinery for closer monitoring of the linkage, securing more involved participation from line and staff groups, the need for technical skills to look more professionally and analytically at the linkage, and so on).
5. Are consciousness-raising sessions needed to introduce departments to the basic linkage idea?
6. What about technical education and training for those professionals engaged in the planning processes?

Developing a Corporate Information Policy

John Diebold uses the spread of personal computers throughout the company as an example of why he believes information policies

---

[8] The Diebold Group, Inc., "The Chief Information Officer Concept: Report of Preliminary Research," December 1984, The Diebold Group, 475 Park Avenue South, New York, NY 10016. Reprinted with permission. Copyright© 1984 by The Diebold Group, Inc.

are necessary. In responding to a *Computerworld* interviewer's question in 1982, aimed at how to maintain central control over corporate resources in the face of strong decentralization pressures coming from the "PC revolution", he responded "your real question should have been not how to control decentralization, but what should the boundary lines be? Where do you want corporate policy to control some of these PCs and where do you not care, and let it go down into divisions?"[9]

Diebold offered some ground rules to help the company make that kind of boundary decision. One is that where corporate information is concerned, you must control the policies relevant to it. If information is relevant only to an individual job or department that does not involve corporate information, the policies concerning it will not be important to you. Obviously at some point you will want to introduce certain policies for procurement of equipment and software, but not where you feel this has to be locked into that corporate system.

Diebold believes there's too much of a rush to find *organizational* solutions to information-management problems, as opposed to *policy* solutions. That is why he believes policy statements can be a more responsive and flexible tool than moving blocks around on an organizational chart.

The Diebold Group believes that a comprehensive *corporate information policy* (CIP) statement should systematically, honestly, and thoroughly address five dimensions that tend to circumscribe the role of information resource in any organization: (1) strategic, (2) functional, (3) privacy and confidentiality, (4) fair practices (need to know), and (5) technical and procedural.

The strategic dimension addresses company information policies as they pertain, for example, to utilizing information to achieve company goals, produce new products, make new investments, and fund new markets.

The functional dimension addresses company information policies as they relate to the use of information to support key company functional decision-making and problem-solving processes such as marketing, financial portfolio management, inventory

---

[9] Catherine Marenghi, "John Diebold Talks About Information Management," *Computerworld*, In-Depth, ID/1-ID/25, November 22, 1982. Copyright© 1982 by CW Communications/Inc., Framingham, MA 01701. Reprinted from *Computerworld*.

management, payroll, personnel management, manufacturing, and so on.

The privacy and confidentiality dimension addresses policies as they pertain to measures taken to safeguard personal data on employees and company-sensitive data such as trade secrets, copyrights, patents, and so forth.

The fair-practices dimension addresses company policies relating to the "right to know" of groups inside and outside the company, where there is a balance between (1) the company's right to withhold certain data that might damage its interests or compromise the fiduciary role it has promised individuals on whom it holds personal data, and (2) the need to let different groups see and use information they need to do their jobs.

Finally, the technical and procedural dimension addresses company information-handling policies in the traditional support areas such as procurement and contracting, and property management—real, personal, and intellectual property; operating telecommunications networks, and so on.

Diebold lists the following as illustrative corporate-information policies:

1. *Information Is Not Free.* The company views data, information, and knowledge resources as valued but costly assets that must be managed.

2. *Manager and User Accountability.* The company intends to hold both managers and end-users accountable for the efficient and effective utilization of data and information resources entrusted to their care.

3. *Custodial Ownership.* The company expects that database administrators, data administrators, systems managers, information managers, and functional managers will be assigned to every one of the company's major information flows and holdings, and will be held responsible for insuring that they are accurate, complete, up-to-date, and so forth.

4. *Confidentiality and Privacy.* The company will take measures to protect against the deliberate or inadvertent disclosure, abuse, or misuse of information in its manual files and data banks, including both data on persons (for example, employees), and sensitive corporate trade information.

5. *Access and Need to Know.* The company will establish and use standards, criteria, and guidelines to govern access to each major kind of data holding it possesses, based on need to know and end purpose of use.

6. *Security.* There are a wide variety of physical, personnel, administrative and procedural measures, as well as technological ones, that the company will employ to safeguard its information technology centers, magnetic-tape libraries, files, and so forth.[10]

We could add to Diebold's list of corporate-information policies, but the above illustrations should get the company off on the right tract.

Orna and Hall see seven main purposes of a corporate information policy:

1. An information policy makes clear what the information function is, and defines the role of the information-management unit and its staff, and what services can be expected from it. It also defines where such services fit in and interact with other information-handling parts of the organization.

2. The policy statement provides an authoritative source of reference for the management of the organization of which the information service forms a part, and for the information manager. Acceptance of the policy by management can be taken as a reasonable guarantee of resources and commitment.

3. It provides a basis for monitoring progress and reviewing policy to meet changing situations.

4. It helps to ensure that information needs and information exploitation are taken into account in all policy decisions and in all forward planning.

5. It defines the role and standing of the information manager and provides him or her with a basis for initiatives

---

[10] The Diebold Research Program, "Administration of Information Resources, Part One: Information Policy," Software and Methodology Series, 187545, September 1980, (This report is for client use and may not be available to the public). Reprinted with permission. Copyright© 1980 by The Diebold Group, Inc.

which can be taken without constant reference to top management.

6. The combined effort by outside consultants and inside professionals means that what they propose has the double authority of: (1) someone who has experience with other systems and organizations, and whose work has been accepted by the commissioning organization as sound, and (2) someone who, as a member of the organization's staff, has the opportunity of day-to-day interaction with colleagues and of gaining their respect for his or her judgments. Interaction of the two means that the consultant's ideas are moderated by the manager's findings in practical day-to-day working, while the consultant can offer ideas from outside experience which can be evaluated for application to the present situation.

7. Interviewing users and collecting details for a policy provides the information function with an opportunity for public relations within the organization; for restating information thinking at a basic level. An example would be to focus attention on the benefits of an information center and encourage its use, thereby preventing duplication of effort and time wasting in the pursuit of information. It is a chance to demonstrate that information handling is a profession in its own right, and that it should be treated as such.[11]

These authors did their research in England in the British Construction Industry Training Board in 1979. This board was one of the earliest of the industrial training boards, set up under the British Industrial Training Act of 1964 to improve the provision for training of persons over compulsory school age in their chosen industries. The Board's thinking about the problems these people faced in gaining access to the information they needed to do their jobs as effectively as possible led to the Orna/Hall study.

[11] Elizabeth Orna and Geoffrey Hall, "Developing an Information Policy," Aslib Proceedings, 33(1), January 1981, pp. 15–22, Aslib, Information Huse, 26-27 Boswell Street, London, England.

PLANNING INFORMATION REQUIREMENTS

Planning is not the most exciting task managers like to undertake. Indeed, there is a school of thought that most planning is a waste of time. Especially, say professionals in the information-technology arena, because the area is so volatile due to continually changing products. Warren McFarlan, for example, in a paper dealing with the problems of planning information systems, had this to say:

> *As new products appear, as the laws change, as mergers and spinoffs take place, the priorities a company assigns to its various applications are likely to change as well. Some low-priority or new applications may become critically important, while others previously thought vital may diminish in significance. This volatility places a real premium on building a flexible framework within which such change can be managed in an orderly and consistent fashion. Hence, recognizing it is vital to planning an effective computer-based information system. Some executives choose to interpret this volatility as a pressure against planning. One installation manager stated that while his superiors required him to plan three years ahead, this single factor of technology uncertainty made it impossible for him to estimate realistically·more than one year in advance. He said he goes through the long-range planning process as an elegant ritual that makes his superiors happy, without any personal conviction that his output is meaningful.* [12]

Beyond the question of the volatile product environment, there is the question of whether or not, in the information area, one can ever hope to have all of the information one needs, in the right form, the right place, and so on. Many despair that trying to plan information needs is a hopeless exercise because managers will never be able to get all of the facts they should have. Most decisions have to be based on incomplete knowledge, either because the information is not available, or because it would cost too much in time and money to get it. It is not necessary to have all the facts

---

[12] Warren McFarlan, "Problems in Planning the Information System," *Harvard Business Review,* March-April 1971, pp. 75–89. Reprinted by permission of the Harvard Business Review. Copyright© 1971 by the President and Fellows of Harvard College; all rights reserved.

to make a sound decision, but it is necessary to know what information is lacking. This enables one to judge how much of a risk the decision involves, as well as the degree of precision and rigidity that the proposed course of action can afford.

Trevor J. Bentley points out that there is nothing more treacherous, "or alas, more common, than the attempt to make precise decisions on the basis of coarse and incomplete information."[13] Bentley's point of departure in the information-planning process is shown in Figure 7-5. Once some decisions are reached as to the leftmost and rightmost of his two Venn diagrams, respectively the information needed and information available, then where the two circles overlap is the area of "satisfactory information."

At this point, the company is supposed to either acquire from the outside, or produce on the inside, the needed information. Moreover, Bentley sees as just as important eliminating the information not required, on the grounds that it will inevitably clog communications channels.

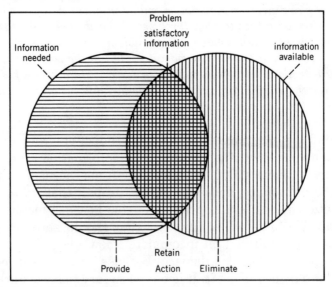

Figure 7–5. Defining management's information needs. *Source:* see note 13.

[13] Trevor J. Bentley, "Defining Management's Information Needs," *Management Services,* March 1979, pp. 4–7. Reproduced by kind permission of *Management Services*.

Before we get too far ahead of ourselves, however, we should specify the objectives of the information-requirements determination process in the first place:

To acquire most economically the minimum amount of data needed to accomplish the company's goals and objectives.

To assure that the required data is acquired on time, and that it is serving its intended purpose and is shared to the maximum extent practicable between departments to achieve many purposes, not just single purposes.

To prevent the acquisition of duplicate or overlapping data where using existing information flows and holdings could preclude the recollection of duplicative data.

To safeguard against the deliberate or inadvertent misuse of data for purposes unrelated to that for which it was collected, where the prior express permission of the respondent(s) (for example, a company employee, supplier, or customer) from whom the data was collected in the first place, was not obtained. This pertains primarily to data on individuals and on company copyrights, patents, and other sensitive information.

To link the company's information-requirement plans with overall corporate business plans (a subject we've already touched on generally but will go into in greater detail).

John Diebold points out that, unlike other resource categories like personnel, corporate-information needs have not traditionally been planned. Or, if they have been planned, requirements are not synchronized across departmental and functional boundaries within the total corporate umbrella. There are many unfortunate impacts of trying to deal with the information needs assessment challenge in a compartmentalized, department-by-department manner, instead of in an overall integrative context:

1. Economies in bulk information purchases are not realized. For example, different departments and divisions are acquiring the same or similar data, with little if any attention given to the possibility of pooling or sharing data for common use.

2. Incompatibility in hardware, software, information processing algorithms, and personnel training compound the problems of information analysis, interpretation, utilization, and dissemination. For example, information systems are designed along narrow-purpose, single-audience lines, rather than along multiple-purpose, wide-audience lines, thus proliferating a wide variety of systems in different programming languages, run on different hardware, and so forth.

3. Middle and top management do not comprehend total information costs; they are usually made aware of less than the total amounts, and in widely different management contexts.

4. Little leverage can be exerted over marginally effective information needs, because control over the information-requirements process is at the tail end of the process instead of at the front end. For example, a long and complicated survey that may cost hundreds of thousands of dollars to undertake, is never considered early in the company's normal planning context—rather, it takes on a life of its own, buried within a departmental program. By the time middle or top management learn of its existence, strong vested interests, both within the department and elsewhere—even outside the organization—make it almost impossible to back away from the survey without very serious moral, political, legal, contractual, or other problems.

5. Confidentiality, security, and privacy are not adequately considered. For example, the adequacy of security safeguards typically becomes an afterthought, and the problems hence become more serious, because appropriate data-security personnel are not brought into information planning and acquisitions early enough to point out deficiencies in company capabilities.

6. State-of-the-art technology is substantially suboptimized. For example, *database-management systems* (DBMS) have been around for a long time, but the single largest barrier to their successful implementation is that data definitions and controls have not been synchronized for the company as a

whole. As a result, data integrity is fragmented, uneven in quality and effectiveness, and data definitions are so disparate that the DBMS cannot be effectively employed.

Diebold's notion of an integrated company information plan is the result of a careful analysis and synthesis of information needs inherent in the basic decision-making and problem-solving processes of the corporation, including:

Overall strategic planning for new investments, new product lines, and new markets

Individual departmental plans for executing and evaluating performance in each functional area, including marketing, manufacturing, R&D, production control, and so forth

General-purpose statistical and research information needs of corporate headquarters, as well as long-range planning and other staff units

General-purpose reference materials as a whole, including books, technical and government reports, journal subscriptions, newsletters, on-line information services, the services of information brokers and so forth, including both recurring and ad hoc needs

Audit and compliance needs of internal auditors, inspectors, and similar groups; in this regard, there may be some redundancy in information requirements to insure adequate checks and balances

Information consulting assistance, which includes the help of a variety of specialists for temporary assistance in designing information systems, performing evaluations, doing feasibility studies, conducting surveys and other kinds of research tasks, and so forth[14]

So much for the "why" and the "what" of information requirements and planning. But just how do you actually implement them?

[14] The Diebold Research Program, "Administration of Information Resources, Part Two: Implementing Corporate Information Policy," Report 196S49, February 1981, The Diebold Group, 475 Park Avenue South, New York, NY 10016.

Albert L. Lederer points out that the question, "what information do you need in order to perform your job?" is easy to ask but difficult to answer.[15] First, workers are usually experts in their jobs but are not necessarily experts at describing their jobs. They are so deeply involved in their jobs that they find it difficult to articulate in sufficient detail the information they need in order to perform their work. Thus, Lederer contends, the question "what information do you need?" must be asked indirectly, not directly. He suggests a number of techniques for doing that.

First, *interviewing*. There is no special aspect of interviewing technique that is unique to assessing information requirements, as opposed to any other purpose. Good preparation, learning the language of the interviewee, giving advance notice, avoiding criticism, and so on, are the hallmarks of good interviewing technique. Like all interviewers, information analysts must learn these techniques.

Second, *paper simulation*. By this Lederer means a technique where the analyst imitates (simulates) the output of a hypothetical information system on paper (a computer is not yet used) and the user responds by working with the output as though it were the actual computer's output. As the user and analyst work through a scenario as a team, they modify and refine the output to better meet the user's precise information requirements. This technique gives a "hands-on" feeling to both the analyst and user, since they're dealing with inputs and reporting outputs.

Third, *brainstorming*. Once again, like the interview technique, there are no special rules to keep in mind here that are peculiar to the information arena. Brainstorming is a technique to encourage the free-wheeling discovery of new ideas and new approaches, through interaction between two or more people in a comfortable and constructive group setting where criticism is avoided and there are no "right" or "wrong" solutions.

Fourth, *protocol analysis*. Here Lederer is talking about allowing the user to "think out loud" while he is actually performing his tasks. The idea is that if he is asked to articulate what he is thinking about while he is doing his work, this is often preferable

[15] Albert L. Lederer, "Information Requirements Analysis," *Journal of Systems Management,* December 1981, pp. 15–19.

to asking him to think retrospectively about what he has done during the day, or to think about his information requirements purely in abstract terms.

Fifth, *direct observation*. Here the information analyst, like an industrial engineer, is actually observing what the information user does. Obviously this is useful in clerical and similar work, but doesn't work well in professional jobs involving primarily cognitive work. The value of direct observation is in its ability to derive information requirements from a current system. This can also be a detriment, however, because it can constrain the analyst to think only in terms of the current system.

Sixth, *questionnaires*. One research study cited by Lederer involved the use of questionnaires to help develop a computer-based information system where there were significant differences of opinion as to just what should be done. The questionnaire allowed the respondents to take more time to reflect on just what it was they wanted and expected the system to do. If interviewing or some of the other techniques had been used, the time element would have been different.

Seventh, *nominal group technique*. Here a group meets, typically for one-hour sessions, and considers a single specific task at each meeting, for example, the task of determining just how a new information service or telecommunications network might be used. The strength of this technique comes from the involvement and interaction of the group. A great deal of use is made of writing on large sheets of paper that are taped to walls, so all can see how the group as a whole is doing.

Eighth, *the delphi method*. This technique, essentially a statistical sampling of expert opinions, is particularly suited to gathering information from users who are not centrally located. It has been used extensively to obtain consensus among experts on tasks involving prediction of future events, and can be used as an information-gathering technique for information systems and services. More recently, people developing expert systems and knowledge-based systems, particularly those that require approaching in-house company experts rather than dealing with a relatively "settled" domain of knowledge in the literature, is an instance where the delphi method is very helpful.

Ninth, the *critical incident technique*. In this method the analyst uses questionnaires or interviews to determine user activities which had either outstandingly effective or outstandingly ineffective results. First the analyst gets a brief statement of aims from the users, then develops plans for collecting critical incident data, then collects the data, analyses it, and finally interprets it. The value of this technique lies primarily in separating the wheat from the chaff; that is, in separating critical needs for information from routine ones. It is thus close to the critical success factors method espoused by Rockart and others at MIT's Sloan School of Management.

To sum up, planning information requirements, in reality, is not so different from planning any other kind of organizational resource requirement. Nearly all of the same techniques and approaches are applicable. The main difference is in the novelty of the process. That is, companies that have never planned their information needs must go through a transitional period in formalizing the process. "People," as Lederer points out, "just don't often think of their information needs the way they do their other needs."[16]

CAPITALIZING INFORMATION ASSETS

Many experts now believe that by the end of the 1980s, every enlightened corporation will include information assets in its financial reports. In an internationally competitive environment, the challenge, according to David R. Vincent, will be to optimize the value of information.[17] By so doing, businesses will realize productivity gains and sustain their competitive edge. Vincent reminds us that the largest investment in many companies today is the creation and maintenance of information. Therefore, executive management and stockholder attention should (and, he feels, probably soon will), focus on the amounts spent on this investment, the return on

[16] *Ibid.*, p. 15.
[17] David R. Vincent, "Information as Corporate Asset," *Computerworld*, September 26, 1983, In-Depth, pp. 1–12. Copyright© 1983 by CW Communications/Inc., Framingham, MA 01701. Reprinted from *Computerworld*.

the investment, and the productivity gains to be made both in current operating reporting periods and in the future.

It has been estimated by Vincent that in organizations such as banks and insurance companies, as much as 25 percent of the organization's payroll expense is invested in creating and maintaining information needed to continue normal business operations. Therefore, it would not be unusual to see a major corporation with a total payroll of $100 million per month investing $300 million annually in information. This total does not include information systems, which may run another $2 million per month, bringing the annual total up to $324 million. Out of this total, only 7 percent represents the portion that has traditionally been considered DP. Where is the significant investment reported and analyzed?

The recognition of information and knowledge as true corporate assets has a basis in current economic and accounting theory. An asset classically has three essential characteristics:

1. It embodies a probable future benefit that involves a capacity, singly or in combination with other assets, to contribute directly or indirectly to future net cash flows.

2. A particular enterprise can obtain the benefit and control another enterprise's access to it.

3. The transaction giving rise to the enterprise's right to control over the benefit has already occurred; that is, the enterprise has already made the investment, it is for exclusive use by the enterprise, and it is in usable form.

We've drawn an illustrative balance sheet of information assets and liabilities as Figure 7-6. Whether or not each information holding fits the tests accountants put it to in order to determine if it qualifies technically as a corporate asset, is only one of our challenges, however. There is also the question of how you value as an asset the know-how in people's heads. In short, not all of the corporation's information assets are recorded on paper or in computers. Much of this information is in the minds of internal company experts: professionals, managers, and employees. We might call these internal expert systems. Computing the value of know-how and "human capital" has long puzzled even philosophers.

Selected Assets		Selected Liabilities	
Patents (revenue-earning)	$ 364	Investments in patentable research	$ 20
Copyrights (revenue-earning)	120	Investments in copyrightable research	7
Trade secrets (revenue-earning)	68	Investments in trade secrets	6
Trademarks (revenue-earning)	20	Unusable and unimprovable data banks	65
R&D databases	150	Obsolete files and records	40
Manufacturing databases	380	Undisposed archives	10
Sales databases	24	Obsolete mainframes and minis	165
Mainframes and minis	1029	Unused micro investments	140
Bibliographic databases	160	Obsolete micro holdings	20
Archived data and files	60	Obsolete telecommunications networks	320
MIS Computer data	150	Obsolete printing equipment	140
Economic forecasting data	170	Obsolete photocopying equipment	20
Micros and workstations	950	Capitalized value of unusable information services	65
Telecommunications networks	1060	Capitalized value of annual operating expenses	
Data help by franchises and licenses	60	for antiquated information facilities	85
Unsold inventories of information		Capitalized value of lost knowledge to	
products and services	40	company when employees leave	650
Raw data acquisitions	180	Expert systems in development	220
Capitalized value of useable		Information systems in design and development	260
information services (annual)	75	Information services in design and development	180
Capitalized value of usable		All other liabilities	
information facilities (annual)	90		
Internal expert systems	65		
External expert systems	195		
Total	$	Total	$

Figure 7–6. The Information Resources Balance Sheet.

Tolly Kizilos, in an intriguing *Harvard Business Review* article, used Socratic dialogue to deal with the dilemma of capitalizing "human capital" in the context of productivity:

> *Little did Kratylus know, when he contracted in Corinth to buy some foot-operated potter's wheels for his workshop, that his capital investment would become the subject of a spirited discussion among four Athenians touching on such topics as olive harvesting, burial mound building, input-output measurement, and participative management. Formerly, 20 workers in Kratylus's operation turned out 200 urns a day; now, with the new pulley-equipped devices, 12 employees can do the job. What is productivity? How can you measure an individual's contribution toward a goal?*

And here is one part of the Socratic dialogue:

> *Kallias: Their productivity depends simply on their output, be it urns made, olives picked, marble slabs quarried, or what have you, divided by the cost of production, which is mostly wages.*
>
> *Nikias: You may think it's that simple, but I don't. Even a manual worker has a mind that he can use when he does his work. His productivity can be defined your way only if you rob him of his mind. If one does that by rigidly defining the input and the output, that is, if one dehumanizes him, then one can define his productivity accurately—so many urns per drachma of wages, so much earth moved to build a mound per load of bread, so many olives gathered per day's wage.*
>
> *One can go even further and define the productivity of those workers who work with their intellect that way—so many plays written, or songs composed, or theorems proved, or philosophical conclusions reached per drachma. But remember, the only way this can be done as if you set rigid, unalterable inputs and outputs. If a philosopher wrote a poem and an urnmaker proved a theorem of geometry, their productivity would be nothing.*
>
> *Ipponikos: In other words Kallias, you have to choose between having a precise definition of productivity and missing a lot of good work, or having at best a sloppy definition and allowing other, unanticipated but valuable work to be encouraged.*[18]

[24] Edward Roche, "Information Architecture," *Computerworld*, October 3, 1983, In-Depth, pp. 9–26. Copyright© 1983 by CW Communications/Inc., Framingham, MA 01701. Reprinted from *Computerworld*.

We believe that much the same situation arises when one tries to define and measure the value of corporate information assets. If we try to be too precise about the value of information assets, in a narrow, technical way (for example, just capitalizing the cost of physical records in the files, or just considering equipment and overhead when costing out data in computer data banks), like Kallias we may have a much easier job in measuring the asset. But as Nikias pointed out, and his colleague Ipponikos confirmed, in so doing we risk vastly suboptimizing the true worth of the asset.

Another researcher, Robert M. Gordon, agrees that it is not easy to estimate either the cost of information or its value. But it is obvious, he says, that information or the lack of it can be costly. The following is a corporate scenario Gordon puts forward to help illuminate the problem and how one might approach it. This episode differs from the Grecian scenario above, but the message is much the same.

Ralph Pattison is vice-president of engineering, and a director of Microtomics International, Inc., a high-technology company with some 13,000 employees, approximately 30 percent of whom are professional people. Gross revenues of the company in 1982, worldwide, were just over $800 million. Net earnings were not outstanding that year, but they were "adequate."

Six weeks ago Pattison emerged, brooding, from a meeting of the board of directors. At the meeting, George Whate, an outside member with a reputation for asking difficult questions, had asked two of them:

1. What is cost to Microtomics, and what is the resultant value, of information managed by the company's professional employees?

2. What are Microtomics's policies and practices governing the management of such information?

The immediate response of the company's officers on the board was to point to their records-management department. But Whate quickly indicated that that was not the kind of thing he was interested in. He wanted to know about the information contained in the collection of research reports, memoranda, journals, books, conference proceedings, and so forth. Pattison, asked to obtain answers to Whate's questions, was shocked to learn:

1. The company's approximately 4000 professional employees spent about 50,000 to 80,000 hours per week—30 to 50 percent of their time—managing information. This includes reading, editing, thinking about, searching for, collecting, organizing, storing, and retrieving information related to their work (as they perceive it).

2. The cost of, meaning the company's investment in, all of that activity was estimated to be from $700,000 to $1.2 million per week, based on salary, benefits, and overhead of about $60,000 per head for each professional employee.

3. Perhaps one-fourth to one-half of this information-management activity has to do with work-related "personal" information, that is, with matters deemed important by the individual doing the managing, but not necessarily a part of explicitly assigned duties. The company's investment in this activity was estimated to be from $200,000 to $600,000 per week— about $10 million to $30 million per year!

4. There *do* exist company policies and practices governing the management of information explicitly related to some assigned duties, for example, to the keeping of "engineering notebooks."

5. There do *not* exist any policies governing work-related "personal" information. For all practical purposes, such information belongs to the people who collect it. They are free to do with it whatever they please (not excluding regarding it as their private possession).[19]

Like Gordon, the lesson we derive from this episode is not so much who owns the data, or some philosophical insight into what constitutes "personal" data versus what is "corporate" data, but that management must be made aware that handling information,

[19] Robert M. Gordon, "Information as a Corporate Asset," *Management Technology*, June 1983, pp. 37–41.

when capitalized, can add up very substantially. Many of both the direct and indirect costs are hidden or buried in overhead or subsumed with other costs.

Pricing Information Products and Valuing Information Services

No topic is more complex than the one of finding useful ways to measure the value of information products (thereby leading to pricing policies), and of determining their costs. The costing task would appear, at first glance, to be simpler than the pricing and valuing task. But it turns out that, because information handling is so pervasive and difficult to get a handle on—on both the input as well as the output side of the equation—costing is not much easier. Here we can only hope to try to sensitize readers to some of the dimensions of the problem, and, we hope, to suggest some useful avenues to pursue. Research in the area is still very limited, and there is substantial disagreement at both the theoretical and the applied levels.

In the first place, there is the question of whether we can cost and price out information products and services as if they were ordinary commodities of commerce. They are not, at least not in the usual sense. Economists point out that unlike other goods, one doesn't really lose possession of an information good when one sells it or gives it away. Moreover, it usually does not depreciate or "deplete" like other goods do; oftentimes the more one uses data the more valuable it becomes.

On the other hand, in certain areas society has been pricing information commodities for a very long time, for example, books, periodical subscriptions, royalties for creative works, copyrights, patents, and so on. What these informational commodities have in common is that they involve original, creative contributions that are usually "one-of-a-kind," and are therefore, by definition, distinctive and not replicable except in the mechanical sense.

By contrast, as we move along the knowledge-information-data spectrum from the leftmost to the rightmost, the value and cost problems become more difficult. Computing the value of a single table of business or financial statistics in a report, or of a single on-line search of bibliographic database, is as difficult as estimating the ultimate total capitalized value of a new patent or copyright that may eventually lead to dozens of spinoff products the company can sell. Still, information and data products and services *must* be priced and costed just like knowledge goods.

Epstein and King point out that in designing an information system, some measure of information value is explicitly or implicitly used. But no entirely satisfactory measure has been developed that has general applicability. And the question of which measure should be applied in a given circumstance has not been adequately addressed. In a 1981 paper they write:

> *Most measures of the value of information apply to a unit that is at a low level of aggregation, e.g. the individual facing a specific choice. If this is the sort of information value concept that must be used in designing an information system, the designer is left either to design systems idiosyncratically for individuals, or to aggregate information values across individuals in order to construct a single measure that best reflects that organization's information values. The former is extremely costly and the latter presents conceptual and practical problems such as those suggested by Arrow and Gymn & King. If it were possible to ascertain the appropriate level of aggregation on the domain ranging from the individual to the entire organization, it would greatly simplify and facilitate information system design. For instance, if a single department or managerial level could be shown to have values and needs for information that were relatively homogenous and significantly different from the values and needs of other groups, the appropriate design level for the system would require little further specification.* [20]

This approach, these authors point out, has come to be referred to as the "contingency view" of information-systems design. And in their own study they found that managers in three different functional areas and at two different hierarchical levels in the firms studied did not exhibit significant differences in their value models. Their conclusion: General information-systems design

---

[20] Barry J. Epstein and William R. King, "An Experimental Study of the Value of Information," *OMEGA, The International Journal of Management Science*, Vol. 10, No. 3, 1982, pp. 249–258.

does not require provisioning information in significantly different ways to different groups of managers, because users tend to value the same information in approximately the same way. Epstein and King do not assert that their limited investigations are definitive. They suggest that further study is required before these issues can be better understood.

On the cost side of the equation, Chick points out an analogous set of factors to value estimating that compound the problem of costing out information goods and services:

1. *Terminology Problems.*   There is confusion between the terms "value" and "cost" as well as with other related but nonsynonymous terms such as *expense, asset, commodity, resource,* and many others. Terminology problems in the information-resources management arena seem to be magnified when the concepts of information as a commodity, resource, or asset are introduced.

2. *Limitations of Traditional Cost-Accounting Systems.*   Today's accepted accounting methodologies do not accumulate and present financial information about information costs. A possible exception are accounting systems designed for organizations that are in the business of producing information (often for sale).

3. *The Often Intangible Nature of Information.*   This can cause a cost-allocation problem. The concept of managing information as a commodity has many valid points. However, information has some unique characteristics, such as (1) electronic representation which cannot be seen by the naked eye, (2) potential simultaneous uses of the same information by many, even while it still resides in storage (inventory), and (3) unknowns involved in the number of times information may be used and by how many users.

4. *A Lack of Consensus on the Notion of Information Value.* Besides attaining consensus, there is an evident need for more research in developing approaches for assigning monetary measures to represent information value for use as a management tool. Many people perceive information value

from their own personal perspectives. Few, if any, have attempted to synthesize these perspectives for use as management tools in making various decisions about information.[21]

Chick reminds us that reducing the cost of information production, while a worthy objective, does not necessarily increase the value of the information produced. Moreover, he also points out that there are a wide variety of long-accepted accounting methodologies that the information manager ought to consider in trying to discover information costs, including direct cost finding, cost estimating, auditing and spot checks, formal accrual accounting systems, cost accounting systems, and so on.

King Research, Inc., a Rockville, Maryland firm specializing in the problems of information economics, takes a fairly straightforward approach to dealing with the price-costing problem. They suggest that with some exceptions, information goods and services do indeed exhibit many if not most of the same attributes as more conventional goods and services. For example, as price increases, demand decreases. Therefore, a price demand curve can be graphed. Also, demand curves can shift because of changes in consumer income, advertising, performance of a competing product, introduction into the market of a substitute, changes in consumer taste, and so forth. King Research suggests that companies perform a pricing experiment, analyze a time series of price versus demand over time, and then compare the price and demand of two similar products.

1. Costs of generating data (that is, data collection and data production)

2. Costs of processing information (direct costs of initial processing, prerun costs in printing, and so forth)

3. Costs of reproducing and distributing information and handling requests (direct costs associated with reproduction, distribution, and the like)

4. Indirect costs such as rent, overhead, and administration (related to (2) and (3) above)

[21] Morey Chick, "Information Value and Cost Measures for Use as Management Tools," *Information Executive,* The Institute for Information Management, Vol. 1, No. 2, 1984, pp. 46–56.

Once costs are determined, alternate pricing policies can be tested. These include:

Marginal cost pricing (Recover only the cost of reproducing, handling requests, and distributing each additional item. Marginal cost = unit revenue.)

Average cost pricing (Recover all costs associated with processing and distributing the information product or service.)

Optimum profit pricing (Select price to maximize profit.)

Fair market value (Charge what others would charge for similar information products or services.)

Price discrimination (Charge different consumers different prices.)

Price according to elasticity (Set price so that percentage of deviation from marginal cost is inversely proportional to the item's price elasticity.)

Free, or subsidized

We suggest that readers experiment with the above approaches only after they have studied the pricing, management, and other relevant literature carefully. Lamberton, quoted by Kent Hall, reminds us of a "truth" that we believe aptly sums up what information cost accountants and information economists should never lose sight of in grappling with the costing-pricing problem. That is that one can measure the number of bits or bytes of information in a message, but it is the *value of the message* which quantifies the information, not the cost or time of transmission. Messages, like art works, are viewed by people with widely different perceptions of their value. But unlike art, it is true that information is easily replicated—to allow others to "view" it is often equivalent to giving it away. As Hall puts it:

The value of a specific message is equal to the utility gained from shifting to a better choice among terminal actions. The value of an information service generating a probability distribution of messages is the expected value of the messages generated. These value calculations are, of necessity, ex post. However, the decision to seek information must be made ex ante. An ex ante valuation of a message must include the probability assumptions about the distributional (pecuniary) effects and appropriability of an (often) unknown message. In other words, an ex ante valuation is a probabilistic cost-benefit analysis.[22]

In short, the enterprise in the information economy must face up, in the end, to imperfect costing and pricing algorithms, and utilize whatever observable variables it can in the algorithms. It must utilize proxies or surrogates where directly utilizable economic attributes and variables needed to measure cost and value are unavailable.

BUDGETING INFORMATION COSTS

Let us review the sequence of topics presented in this chapter. First, we took up the broadest subject, formulating a corporate information strategy. It is there that the firm should sit back and reflect on just what role the company sees the "information resource" playing against the backdrop of its basic business, markets, and product lines. For example, maybe the company will decide that information is such a crucial resource that it should acquire an information subsidiary and thereby bring into the firm the necessary competencies to help the firm make a smooth transition to the information economy. Or perhaps the information strategy settled upon will be nothing more complicated than learning to access on-line commercial databases—a resource which most firms are just beginning to appreciate from a strategic standpoint.

Next we moved to formalizing the management of the information resource by taking up the need to evolve corporate information policies and plans. Since most companies are, as yet, just experimenting with this notion, we spent some time making an analogy to the development of other kinds of organization resource plans, and showing the parallels between them and the information plan.

We then proceeded to take up the first step of the information life cycle—the idea of planning information requirements—and suggested some approaches to fit the needs of different companies.

---

[22] Kent Hall, "The Economic Nature of Information," *The Information Society,* Vol. 1, No. 2, 1981, pp. 143–166. Reprinted with permission of *The Information Society,* Vol. 1, No. 2, 1981. © Crane, Russak & Co.

Then came the pricing-costing task. Now we move to budgeting for information resources.

Budgets, like accounting systems and plans, are nothing more than a type of management control. They are not an end unto themselves. Their value as a management instrument is in helping to illuminate for managers the best projections the company can make of what it is going to cost them to acquire and utilize all of the mainframes, minis, micros, telecommunications networks, and the other information-resource equipment they want and need.

Once again we find it useful to turn to the Diebold program in discussing the information budget.[23] Figure 7-7 is an illustration of what a company information budget might look like. The information budget should be the product of a very careful analysis of the firm's information plans. As Diebold suggests, the company's information budget should include:

The titles of all major information and information-technology collections and acquisitions proposed for the budget period (may be annually or longer), together with the collecting or acquiring department or other organizational unit

A brief (50 to 100 word) statement of the need for each such major information and information-technology acquisition: the uses to

	FY 1982	FY 1983	FY 1984
Information Resources by Purpose			
Management decision-support	$ 9	$ 10	$ 12
Corporate staff activities............	20	25	30
Marketing and sales	7	8	10
Manufacturing and production.......	9	9	12
New product development...........	6	7	8
Research and development	11	16	21
General information services.........	45	55	65
All other	2	4	6
Total........................	$109	$134	$164

[23] The Diebold Research Program, "Administration of Information Resources, Part Two: Implementing Corporate Information Policy," Report 196S49, February 1981, The Diebold Group, 475 Park Avenue South, New York, NY 10016.

	FY 1982	FY 1983	FY 1984
Information Resources by Department			
Chief executive officer	$ 2	$ 5	$ 7
Corporate staff....................	16	19	21
Marketing	23	26	28
Manufacturing....................	11	14	16
Research and Development..........	31	34	36
New product development	15	18	27
All subsidiaries	5	9	12
All other	6	9	17
Total........................	$109	$134	$164
Information Resources by Equipment and Handling Media			
Mainframe computers (excludes time share)	$ 31	$ 33	$ 36
Desktop computers and terminals	5	8	11
Telecommunications (except facsimile)	22	24	27
Microfilm and computer-output-microfilm.........................	14	17	20
Printing and reprographic	18	20	23
Facsimile	2	5	8
Word processing...................	7	9	12
Photographic	1	4	7
Time sharing.....................	6	8	11
All other	3	6	9
Total........................	$109	$134	$164
General Information Services (detail)			
Automatic data processing/ electronic data processing	$ 3.0	$ 6.0	$ 9.0
Audio-visual	.1	.2	.4
Drafting/cartography/graphics.......	.2	.4	.6
Edit/writing/translating............	.3	.5	.8
Education/training/conferences......	.5	1.1	2.1
Facilities management	6.5	9.8	11.3
Forms and publications	.8	1.4	1.9
Libraries/information centers........	7.6	9.1	10.8
Mail and delivery..................	.9	1.5	2.5
Etc. (see Figure 2-1)	25.1	25.0	25.6
Total........................	$45.0	$55.0	$65.0

Figure 7–7. Company-Wide Information-Resources Budget. *Source:* See note 23.

be made of the information collected, and the uses to be made of the information technology to be acquired; both why the information resources are needed, and how they will be used.

An identification of the cost-profit centers that will supply or provide the information products and services involved, and the cost-profit centers that are expected to make the greatest use of such products and services, along with some basis for the internal transfer pricing arrangement (if any), or the pricing policy to be followed in the case of information products and services that are to be charged to the cost of goods sold; in this regard, the acquisition (raw materials and labor) cost of information-resource inputs to the company should be clearly distinguishable from markups.

The name and other contact information for the cost-profit center that will be responsible for managing the particular information line item identified in the budget, for example: If a new database is to be developed or a new information system to be designed and developed, then the officer responsible shall be identified.

Diebold uses the term *markup* (as distinct from the term *value-added*), to mean company activities that are primarily labor-intensive or capital-intensive, and where substantial company cost-accounting experience exists (even to the extent of having available reliable standards and cost-variance thresholds), so that the price (and therefore the budget figures) can be computed using markup approaches. In contrast, the *value-added* idea comes into play in those instances where the operation is primarily information-intensive. In these instances, each department or unit adds value to the information products and services it receives from another, and passes on to yet another (for example, in the case of transfer pricing). Or, it puts a value on the cost of goods sold in the case of products and services the company sells in the marketplace.

The initial budget document is just a beginning baseline, one that inevitably shifts. Indeed, it isn't inaccurate to observe that the information budget, like all budgets, may well be obsolete a few moments after it is constructed. So it must be viewed as a dynamic, ever-changing instrument. If departments get the idea that the budget is so ephemeral as to be useless, however, then the company is in trouble. A balance must be achieved between allowing too many changes to be made, and taking too rigid and inflexible a posture in permitting changes.

This process of updating the budget baseline takes place during the year as a part of regular monthly or quarterly reviews in most companies. If the company is faced with a cashflow problem and must reduce costs, then information-resource investments and operating expenses, like any other expenses, must be curtailed. This might be accomplished by a forced ranking of all information projects. Perhaps the CIO will advise the CEO to cut back more or less equally on the level of all information services. Or perhaps, if a forced ranking approach is used and information projects are prioritized, there will be a cutoff line and those projects below the line will be dropped, deferred, cut back, or whatever.

From time to time the company's mission and goals change, or its direction changes, such that an information system or information service once thought to be perfectly indispensable must be reconsidered. The program budget reviews are the time to consider such redirections.

In the end, budgeting is a bridge between planning and performance. Without some kind of budget or plan, there is no good way of determining whether the firm is on course and moving in the right direction. Therefore, the principles of budgeting are as applicable to information resources as they are to any other organizational resource.

Budgeting for the Information-Management Function Itself

There was a time when the MIS/DP department, the library, the printing and copying plant, the message center, the files and records room, and other information-handling facilities were just cost centers, pure and simple. The idea of management dealing with them as profit centers was almost unheard of. Just four years ago, for example, in one survey of 150 industrial and nonindustrial companies, it was found that only 5 percent of the industrial groups surveyed dealt with the DP organization as a profit center. Not one of the nonindustrial groups surveyed (public utilities, banks and diversified financial firms, life insurance, retail, and transportation), considered the DP unit as a profit center!

Today, however, the pendulum has at long last begun to swing, and as companies begin to put chargeback and other self-sustaining policies into place to force information centers and other information-handling activities to stand on their own two feet, financially speaking, it becomes necessary to do more than just develop an operating-expense budget based on costs incurred. Now there is an income side of the ledger sheet as well. Information-management units in each user department must learn to project revenues from chargeback and from user fees, and from information services of all kinds, including library services.

We do not mean to imply that firms have already reached a perfectly satisfactory plateau of self-sufficiency in this area. But signs are unmistakable that the notion that information is not a free good, but is both a valuable and costly commodity that must be valued and priced for both the marketplace and for transfer purposes inside the firm (just as all manufactured goods and services of all kinds must be priced) is catching on.

That means that like other corporate activities, both line and staff, the information-management function must be a budgeted line item. Whether it is singled out as a discrete line entry or is consolidated with other related functions is a discretionary matter. Our point is simple: There are two streams of financial accountability the CIO must worry about. One is estimated costs, both capital and operating, for the corporation's purchase and use of information resources in the manufacture of its principal product lines, whatever they may be. The other is that the internal cost of operating the information-management function itself, as a corporate staff or line function (or a combination), must also be estimated and eventually find its way into accounting and budgeting machinery.

Management Controls: The Information Architecture and Corporate Database

Edward Roche believes that a comprehensive model is needed to cope with the spread of office automation and management information systems all through the corporation.[24] As he puts it:

The drive for improved reaction times of various company units and the increasing need for translation of information coming from other information pools in the firm have resulted in a natural desire that data elements in either a paper- or machine-readable mode be made consistent. Individual decision-making units within an organization, at any level, should be able to receive information or reports concerning other distinct sections of the firm without having to rely on the personnel of those other units to produce the information required. If such a horizontal and vertical reporting structure is to be possible, then the walls separating different information units must be destroyed.

Roche and others make an important distinction between the corporate information architecture, in the sense of the content of the information itself (subjects), and information architecture as that term is used in a narrower, more technical sense by the ADP community to mean file structures in computer database management systems (DBMS).

As more and more information becomes computer-based, and as more and more paper-based files become at least computer-retrievable (even though the storage medium remains paper, or microform), the problem of compatibility and consistency across departmental, subject, functional, geographic, product, and other boundary lines in the enterprise becomes more critical. There finally comes a point when, in the absence of an overall corporate architecture, the cost of transforming data from one file structure to another, from one software language to another, from one software DBMS to another, from one communications medium to another, and so on, presents a nightmare of incompatibility and inconsistency.

This is not to say that information-architecture advocates want to throw everything into one gigantic data bank, shoehorn everything into one software package, or standardize on one brand of hardware. Rather, they suggest that at the data-element level, through the use of data-element standardization programs, data-

[24] Edward Roche, "Information Architecture," *Computerworld*, October 3, 1983, In-Depth, pp. 9–26. Copyright© 1983 by CW Communications/Inc., Framingham, MA 01701. Reprinted from *Computerworld*.

element dictionaries and data directories, and the more advanced DBMSs, there is a real opportunity for at least harmonizing disparate data streams and holdings. Although a key barrier to the effective use of information architecture is politics, significant technical problems must be solved as well. The demonstration of tangible benefits that may accrue leads to a power political strategy for implementation.

When there is disagreement on the issues, political considerations tend to win out. Information architecture helps eliminate conflicting beliefs by promoting a common view of the business.

Roche sees the following benefits accruing to the enterprise that moves in this direction:

1. *Achieve Political Consensus.*   Information architecture may begin both to address and to diminish the problems of perception that are straining relations between users, management, and MIS. It does this by helping to communicate clearly how information processing and flows relate directly to specific business needs and activities.

2. *Speed and Service with Higher Revenues.*   The quickening of information velocity throughout the firm directly increases the productive capacity of each employee and business unit. Decisions are improved and customers get better service. Information technology, therefore, can become a key factor in the firm's strategic development and competitive strategy, rather than merely an overhead item.

3. *Ration Allocation of Resources.*   A comprehensive information-architecture approach should facilitate distribution of scarce information and communication resources so that they map more closely the firm's internal information structure and its associated flows.

4. *Security.*   Information and data security within corporations has long been hampered by the artificial division between the paper world and the machine world. Corporations have built up elaborate mechanisms for protecting computer-held data, only to find that once information is created in paper form, it easily flows to places where it could do potential harm to an individual or to the organization.

5. *Flexibility for Change.* The adoption of an information architecture should enhance a firm's long-term survival by adding flexibility for adjustment to severe destabilizing fluctuation in the environment. Dropping departments and divisions, cutting or adding workers, accelerating production, and stretching out activities without substantially increasing costs should be more manageable and controllable.

6. *Inventory of Systems and Identification of Backlog.* In the past, MIS used various tools for setting priorities, including project backlog lists, which indicated that the average time backlog can vary nationally from an average of 26 months to five years. The global and systematic overview of the information-architecture approach should yield a clear view of the backlog, but as defined by more comprehensive criteria than was formerly possible.

7. *A Note on Frameworks.* As there is no standardized methodology, information architecture should define an internally consistent language that bridges the communication gap between management and MIS. As it is applied to successively more detailed levels of the organization, and as the individual data-element level is approached, the fundamental properties, characteristics, and internal logic of that language should not change.[25]

Quite obviously the firm doesn't move to an overall corporate information architecture in one fell swoop. That is why we've stressed throughout this book the need for a carefully formulated transitional strategy that addresses each stage incrementally.

Management Controls: Costing and Accounting for Information Resources

For reasons mentioned earlier when we discussed budgeting, we do not propose to get into this subject in great detail. It is simply too complex and such an in-depth treatment would exceed our scope.

Strassman first suggests that modifications be made to the organization's job-classification scheme so that job categories for

[25] *Ibid.,* pp. 16, 25–26.

white-collar personnel become more detailed and comparable across organizational lines.[26] Since for accounting purposes, Strassman points out, most information-systems costs are now expensed rather than capitalized, it is important that the cost-identification process discriminate between the different classes of information costs, including the distinction between internal costs and external purchases of information resources.

Strassman suggests a scorekeeping system to track what each information transaction costs, down to the level of cost per service call, cost per page, cost per inquiry, and so forth. He then suggests establishing standard costing for each element of measured information output, and the establishment of accountability centers. Strassman was also an early advocate of a decentralized approach, and believes that information services are too important to be left entirely in the hands of suppliers. He believes the users should be in control.

So do we, but we believe the CEO needs a balanced view. Therefore, the CIO must present information costs in the same manner that the plant manager presents facility-operating costs, the personnel manager human resource costs, and so on. In short, when cost reviews are held, there should be advocates from both the supplier and the user side of the table.

Management Controls: Information Audits and Evaluations

An information audit is not much different from an environmental audit, a financial audit, or a technical audit. As Anne V. Quinn points out, the idea is to describe the present situation, point out gaps or insufficiencies, and then suggest corrective measures to augment or streamline information activities.[27]

Sometimes a company may decide that the information audit is a relatively short-term, minimal-investment, "low-hassle" alternative

---

[26] Paul Strassman, "Managing the Costs of Information," *Harvard Business Review,* September-October 1979, pp. 134–142. Reprinted by permission of the Harvard Business Review. Copyright© 1979 by the President and Fellows of Harvard College; all rights reserved.

[27] Anne V. Quinn, "The Information Audit, Is Anyone Listening?" presented at the "National Information Conference and Exposition" (NICE IV), May 30, 1980. Ms. Quinn is with Arthur D. Little, Inc., in Boston, Massachusetts.

to identify where information resources are not doing what they are supposed to do, or are inadequate. The theory behind this is simply that the other alternative—planning and launching a more ambitious, formal information-resources management program—may be more than the firm wants or can afford. They see in the audit a way to test the viability of the IRM concept itself.

As Quinn points out, many top managers don't even know how to go about evaluating the worth of information. And so, "when you start talking several thousands of dollars to conduct an information audit, it's something management can't—or doesn't know how to deal with. The proposed cost scares management, because they still don't know, or understand, the value of information and how an information resource, properly organized, staffed, and financed, can contribute to corporate objectives, and indirectly to profitability."[28]

An evaluation, in contrast to an audit, has more to do with how effectively an information-resource investment is accomplishing its purposes, rather than how efficiently it is organized, staffed, managed, directed, and controlled. Strictly speaking, an information-resource evaluation study would first examine why the resource was established in the first place, what it was expected to accomplish, and then would move on to evaluate the extent to which it is or is not accomplishing goals and objectives, and what changes might be made to strengthen and redirect its operation. The methodologies of the information audit and the information-evaluation study are overlapping, but the thrust of their underlying purpose is different. The audit has more of a "compliance-with-regulations-and-policies" overtone, while the evaluation is not so much concerned with why things may not be going well, but whether the right things are being done in the first place.

Management Controls: Eliminating Duplication and Overlap—The Data Directory and Data-Element Dictionary (DD/DED)

Leong-Hong and Plagman point out that the notion of the need to treat data as a resource is a "fundamental prerequisite to the

---

[28] *Ibid.,* pp. 1, 2.

principles of *data dictionary/Directory/Element Dictionary"*(DD/ DED). To treat data as a resource, these experts assert, requires the same degree of administration and control as is involved in the management of other resources. Data resources are managed through the administration and control of the data that describes and defines the data, or the *metadata* (a technical term meaning data about data).

Administration and control of metadata requires coordinated rules and procedures to maintain control over the integrity of the metadata. The primary tool that provides support for the administration and control of metadata is the DD/DED. It supports in a comprehensive manner the logical centralization of metadata.

The DD/DED supports the administration and control of two types of metadata, according to the above-mentioned authors, "dictionary" and "directory" metadata. In theory, these two types of metadata differ in the information each provides. Dictionary metadata provides information which describes what the data is, what it means, and what data exists. Directory metadata, on the other hand, describes where the data is located, and how it can be addressed. Current DD/DEDs contain both types of metadata, and some hybrid forms. Closely related to the kind of information a DD/DED contains is the architectural framework in which it functions, which we have described above.

In their seminal work, Leong-Hong and Plagman deal with the use of DD/DEDs as a tool in seven functional contexts:

1. Information-systems planning

2. Information-requirements definition and conversion

3. Systems and application development and conversion

4. Documentation and standards enforcement

5. Operational control of the environment

6. Distributed databases

7. End-user support[29]

[29] Belkis W. Leong-Hong and Bernard K. Plagman, *Data Dictionary/Directory Systems: Administration, Implementation and Usage,* A Wiley-Interscience publication, New York: Wiley, 1982. Reprinted with permission. Copyright© 1982 by John Wiley & Sons, Inc.

Suffice it to say for our purposes that Fortune 1000 companies today simply cannot get along without this invaluable tool. To try to do so is to invite data chaos. The point we wish to underscore most sharply here is that the DD/DED is not just a technical tool for use by database technicians, administrators, and other professionals dealing with the problem of data-element harmonization in a computer programming sense. Instead, it is an important management and research tool that can and should be used throughout the company for all of the purposes listed by the above authors, and perhaps even for additional purposes.

Management Controls: Information Standards and Guidelines

An information standard is a convention or protocol formally agreed to as a mandatory or optional (permissive) set of rules to be used in information and communication systems. For example, if a group says "we'll use the numbers 01–50 as the designations for the 50 states, that is an example of an information standard or guideline. Such information standards are often used for abbreviations, naming, representational situations to minimize space requirements, and so on. Often symbols and codes substitute for full descriptive text.

Ben H. Weil, winner of the coveted William T. Knox Award bestowed annually on the most outstanding information manager by Associated Information Managers (AIM), has been steeped in the problems of information standards and guidelines for nearly half a century. Here is what he recently had to say on this subject:

> *Whenever I discuss information standards with a person or group to whom standards are relatively unfamiliar, I invariably hear the following questions unless I have answered them in advance: "what kind of a standard is an information standard, really; since its observance isn't mandatory, why should anyone follow its rules? Why is an information standard better than a good paper or report? Is it really worth doing all that work to prepare an American National Standards Institute (ANSI) approved standard in the information field, considering*

the limited number of copies that are usually sold? Is a copy really worth what ANSI charges for it?[30]

Weil, a long-time scientific and technical information specialist employed by Exxon, and a member of various ANSI committees, believes that the fact that the observance of ANSI information standards is not mandatory places all the more stress in their preparation on the development of quality guidelines that will be used because of their sheer merits. One of these merits, he feels, is that these standards have been targeted and periodically updated to meet real needs.

Information standards are usually more authoritative than paper or reports on the same subjects, because they represent a national or international consensus and not simply the expertise of individuals or specific organizations. Information standards often start with documents resulting from local work, but the standards bodies, such as ANSI and the International Standards Organization (ISO) that draft the final standards, are usually composed of a cross-section of subject experts and concerned practitioners.

Of course standards should be dealt with in the context of internal company information standards as well as at industry, national, and international levels. They apply to virtually every information-resource area—to both the hardware and software technologies, to the systems field, and to the component disciplines that underlie the totality of IRM, including numerical data analysis, the library field, printing, and so forth.

We share Weil's conviction that a good company information standards and guidelines program, complying where applicable to appropriate industry, national, and international standards, can save the company a great deal of grief. But we also share the conviction of others who believe that standards can be carried too far, and to impose a standard just for the sake of imposing a standard may well be a mistake.

[30] Ben H. Weil, "Are Information Standards Really Worthwhile," *Bulletin of the American Society for Information Science,* Vol. 1 No. 9, April 1975, pp. 26–27. Reprinted with permission. Copyright© April 1975 by American Society for Information Science.

SUMMARY

In this chapter we moved from structure to process and endeavored to get into the functional details of information-resources management and control in sufficient depth so as to convey the importance of each stage of the information life cycle and attendant management controls. We began with top level considerations: (1) an appropriate overall corporate information strategy, (2) formulating an information plan, (3) the more detailed and technical management controls, beginning with planning information requirements, and (4) accounting and budgeting for information capital investments and operating expenses. Then we addressed auditing, standards, the notion of a corporate information architecture, the use of the DD/DED as a multifaceted information-management tool, and other controls and tools.

We eschewed an in-depth treatment of each of these topics, both because we did not want to stray very far from this book's main thrust (which is really to look at the role of the information resource at a top, strategic level), and because the technical details are far too complex to do justice to in the space we have. For those interested in pursuing the topics in detail, we urge further research and use of our bibliography. We do not mean to suggest that information managers can afford to give short shrift to these details. But there are some good texts available that probe the subjects in greater depth.

CHAPTER 8

THE KNOWLEDGE WORKER: WORKING SMARTER, NOT JUST HARDER

This chapter is divided into three parts. In the first part we discuss the job of the knowledge worker and the manager in the information age firm, and show how an entirely new set of factors must be taken into account to assess whether or not these workers and managers are "productive," and how to make them more productive. In the second part we systematically look at some major components of the human resources management function (for example, recruitment and selection), and examine how each of them is being affected by our information society. In the third and final part, we take up the question of education, training, career development, professional development, and lifelong learning in the information economy.

First, who and what is a "knowledge worker"? How do we define and measure the productivity of the knowledge worker?

DEFINING THE PERSON AND THE JOB

Although undoubtedly the terms *knowledge worker* and *information worker* were used by other writers before his classic 1962 book, Fritz Machlup, in *The Production and Distribution of Knowledge in the United States*, presents an in-depth discussion of this new kind of information age laborer. This book is usually cited as a seminal work in the field.[1] Machlup recognized that just as new occupations and new jobs had to be invented as we moved from a bow-and-arrow to an agrarian and then to an industrial society, so also will we have to invent new categories of workers in the labor force as we enter the information age, where information itself is becoming the primary source of wealth in our economy.

Machlup settled on some eight occupational categories in a classification scheme that was essentially hierarchical in design. At the bottom of his hierarchical pyramid he put those information workers that simply carry messages to and fro, without regard to the content of the messages, and with even less regard to higher-order concerns such as: "Why the message at all?" Messengers, file clerks, and the like are in his bottom group.

Next up the ladder he put information workers who perform simple chores involving the message's meaning, like secretaries who open and sort mail by category. Still further up, Machlup recognized a middle-level group who perform a wide array of content-oriented work on the information itself. Some examples of this group are: statisticians deriving a regression analysis curve, mathematicians doing a root mean square calculation, librarians developing an annotated bibliography, records analysts and archivists determining a retention schedule for company payroll and personnel records, and so forth.

Still higher up on Machlup's ladder are educators, scientists, inventors, authors, composers, and so on, whose creative input is, in his view, the highest strategic variable in his hierarchical classification analysis.

In a later work coauthored with Stephen Kagann, Machlup

---

[1] Fritz Machlup, *The Production and Distribution of Knowledge in the United States*, Princeton, N J: Princeton University Press, 1962.

focused more specifically on the changing structure of the knowl-edge-producing labor force.[2] In this study, a functional approach was also taken in studying information-worker job classifications, and the preliminary eight categories developed by Machlup in his landmark 1962 work were further refined into eight "primary functions performed in the production of knowledge," in virtually every kind of enterprise—public or private, for-profit or not.

At about the same time, another researcher, Winifred Sewell, a librarian, zeroed in on the relationship between one specific kind of information professional in one rather narrow kind of organiza-tional setting—the federal government library. She detailed the relationship between formal and official government-library pro-fessional classifications and the job functions in the federal library that they performed.[3]

In April 1976, a conference was convened at the University of Pittsburgh on "Manpower Requirements for the Information Pro-fession" which was attended by government, industry, academic, and other experts. The conference recommended the establish-ment of a consortium of professional, academic, and information-industry interests to advise the University of Pittsburgh on the implementation of research-project recommendations arising out of the discussions at the conference. This Manpower Consortium, as it came to be called, along with the University of Pittsburgh, submitted a proposal to the National Science Foundation for funding of a project designed to determine what information func-tions are performed in all sectors of the U. S. economy, and the number of professionals involved in performing each function.[4]

[2] Fritz Machlup and Stephen Kagann, "The Changing Structure of the Knowledge-Producing Labor Force," New York University, Paper No. 78-01, January 1978. Discussion Paper Series, Center for Applied Economics, New York University, Washington Square, Tisch Hall, New York, NY 10012. Reprinted with permission.

[3] Winifred Sewell, "Study of Federal Library/Information Service Staffing As Affected By Classification And Qualification Standards," Federal Library Committee, Washington, D.C., December 1977.

[4] Anthony Debons, "Final Report on the Manpower Requirements for Scientific and Technical Communication: An Occupational Survey of Information Professionals," Univer-sity of Pittsburgh, Pittsburgh, PA 15260. National Science Foundation Project DSI-7727115, in Conjunction with King Research, Inc., Rockville, MD. *The Information Professional: A Survey of an Emerging Field.* Anthony Debons, Harold W. King, Una Mansfield, and Donald L. Shiney. New York: Marcel Dekker, Inc., November 1981.

The project was undertaken by the University of Pittsburgh in conjunction with King Research, a Rockville, Maryland firm specializing in statistical and economic research in the information field. In their final report, issued June 30, 1980, six generic groups of information professionals were identified:

1. *Managers of Information.* Plan, develop, coordinate, and control information programs, and the human and material resources needed for their implementation

2. *Information-Operations Coordinators.* Perform functions with regard to (1) the data or knowledge base, and (2) the end-user, in the installation, operation, maintenance, and control of information systems, their equipment, and processes

3. *Information Systems Specialists.* Analyze information problems, and design, implement, and evaluate solutions

4. *Information Intermediaries.* Work between the end-user and the data and knowledge sources, helping the user reach an informed state

5. *Information Theorists.* Are concerned with the development of laws, theories, philosophy, and sociology of information environments

6. *Educators of Information Workers.* Provide education and/or training for the above five categories of information professionals and for nonprofessional information workers

The kinds of information workers this study *excluded* is, in our view, as important as the occupations that were included. The following groups were left out on the grounds that "nearly all white-collar workers are involved with data and information:"

Managers and administrators, (other than managers and administrators of information programs and resources) are excluded because their purpose in working with data and information is to "manage and control, not to assist a third party to become informed."

Salespersons, other than those selling information products or services, are excluded because "their dissemination of information is aimed at selling a product or service, not just helping the client to reach an informed state ('detail men' being a possible exception)."

Workers in the information field who operate below the professional level are excluded simply because "this particular project was limited to identifying information *professionals* as distinct from information workers in general."

Professionals in the information field who work only with hardware design and development are excluded because "they are not usually concerned with cognitive operations of the end-user of system output, their orientation being more towards the machine performance."

Professionals in information-intensive fields such as education, law, journalism, and the like, other than those in these fields whose primary activity is aimed at assisting a third party to reach an informed state, are excluded because "their professional activity usually involves a level of synthesis much deeper than that required of an information professional, and as such makes them 'creators of information.'"

Researchers, other than those who research with information (that is, solve research problems by gathering, analyzing, and interrelating data from a combination of sources), are excluded because "they are end-users of data and information."

Advertising professionals, other than those involved in the promotion of information products and services are excluded because "the level of persuasion in their communication with clients goes beyond merely helping them to reach an informed state."

Before commenting on these exclusions, we would like to note that this survey estimated there were over 1.64 million information professionals employed in the United States in 1980. About seven out of every ten of these were in the industrial sector, another two were in state and local governments, and the remaining one was in the federal government. The principal information functions performed by the 1.64 million information professionals were: (1) systems analysis and design (one in five), (2) management of information operations, programs, services, or databases (one in six), and (3) operational information functions (one in six).

Inappropriate Distinctions

We have some problems with this study's findings and conclusions. In the first place, the distinction between an *information professional* and an *information worker* (nonprofessional?) is a distinction that masks important factors perhaps as much, or more, than it illuminates them. Indeed, one wishes that the term *information professional* had been defined by the researchers in the broadest possible way, avoiding the industrial age distinctions of "blue collar" and "white collar." But given the scope constraints of the grantor in this case (The National Science Foundation), which insisted that the traditional definition of professional be used, we can only lament this as "water over the dam."

Our conviction is that the term *knowledge worker* needs to be very broadly defined. And terms like *information professional,* at this early stage, often tend to do more harm than good. Moreover, we believe that the knowledge worker in its broadest sense is *any* member of the labor force *who adds value to a data or information product* whether or not that added value is primarily in terms of packaging and delivering the message, or in terms of enhancing the meaning and usability of the message. In taking this stance, we hope to avoid what we consider to be a rather sterile distinction regarding the message itself and the container in which the message is placed—a distinction which Machlup found necessary to make, but which has led in directions that we feel he may not have intended.

Thus, an information or *knowledge worker* is, in our terms, a messenger, a file clerk, or a records manager who may, in the lexicon of the more academic studies cited, be simply a "carrier" rather than a content analyzer. But are they any less "professional" for having been more concerned with the container than the contents? We don't think so. Our criterion is whether or not they bring certain knowledge, competencies, and skills to their information-handling work—whatever that may be. To say, for example, that in an office context the boss is the *knowledge worker,* whereas the secretary and messenger are *support workers* and therefore (by inference), second-class citizens, is not only demeaning, but false and misleading. It is a carry-over from the industrial era, when hierarchical organization, management structures, and class distinctions between kinds of human resources were paramount.

In sum, our definition of a *knowledge worker* is anyone, in any work context (office, factory, laboratory, classroom, hospital, school, government meeting room), who adds value either to a message *or* to the message's package (container). The nature of that "added value" may be as simple as facilitating its transport from one place to another, as complex as developing some entirely new theory of information science, or contributing some entirely new form based on information processing and formatting technologies (for instance, computer art).

Needed: A New Partnership Between Human Resources Management and Information-Resources Management

If the key to exploiting the true, untapped potential of modern information-handling technologies lies not so much in simply updating and refurbishing traditional, occupational information job labels, then where does it lie? We believe the secret to unlocking the full capabilities of computers, telecommunications networks and office automation in the enterprise operating in the information economy lies in an enlightened new paradigm for the human resources-management function in the enterprise, coupled with a close partnership between these new personnel policies and attitudes, and the new information-management function we've proposed in this book.

Consider for a moment what has happened so far. First of all, we are being told that all across manufacturing and service sectors, CEOs are convinced that a shift to a more participative management style in dealing with employees is called for. Whether one agrees with a precise recipe for doing that or not, there has been a great deal of emulation for example, of the Japanese quality-control circle (QCC) idea, adapted for American workers. The essence of QCCs, whether in the classic Japanese mold, or in the Americanized version, is not just to "make employees feel good," but to harness the full potential of *all* employees of the company in trying to develop new and innovative solutions to long-standing company production and distribution problems.

Let's look at quality-control circles. According to Joji Arai, director of the Washington, D.C. office of the Japan Productivity Center, the average QCC produces fifty to sixty implemented suggestions per worker per year. The average Japanese worker receives approximately 500 days of training, including classroom instruction and on-the-job training. The difference between the Japanese and U.S. QCC approaches, according to both Arai and the American QCC expert William G. Ouchi, is that power to influence changes in the organization of work is actually delegated to production level employees, not arrogated to management.[5]

In a sense, employees in QCCs are being networked together so that the company can benefit from a much larger (deeper and wider) reservoir of ideas. The QCCs, in a sense, fly in the face of much of traditional American management theory that says that an elitist group of middle- and upper-level managers have all the brains and should operate as a corporate brain trust, while everybody else shuts up and does what they are told! In many American companies this attitude has caused problems because the company's middle- and upper-level managers have been unprepared to cope with this deluge of QCC-generated ideas, and have been unable to change their attitudes and behavioral styles to fit this new set of employee-boss roles, assumptions, and values.

Many traditionalist American managers are uncomfortable with accepting the notion that their subordinates could possibly have anything important to say or contribute. Many managers don't even know how to run and control a simple brainstorming meeting. Role playing, game playing, and other group-dynamic techniques, first advanced by the early wave of behavioral scientists such as Douglas McGregor, Warren Bennis, Kurt Lewin, Leland Bradford, and Christopher Argyris, are either unknown, discounted, or trivialized by many managers. Indeed, it can be

---

[5] William G. Ouchi, THEORY Z,© 1981, Addison-Wesley, Reading, Massachusetts. To adapt up to 250 words. Reprinted with permission.

argued that these early behavioral scientists were ahead of their time. One reason that their ideas, approaches, methods, and techniques were unexploited or even discredited is that they were inappropriate to the industrial-age conditions in which they were introduced.

Strategies for Improving Information-Worker Productivity

In Chapter 7 we looked at productivity improvements that could be effected by applying information technologies more judiciously, to streamline, speed up, and simplify factory production, office paperwork, and information handling chores. Here we look at productivity improvements that can come about by helping knowledge workers to work smarter, not just harder. In short, we believe the enlightened company is the one that pays as much attention to making sure the employee is doing the right thing, as it does to insuring that the thing is done right.

For example, if a supervisor notices that the bulk of a subordinate's time is spent changing columns of numbers into color graphic pie charts, or using the computer for electronic mail of messages that could as well be sent by manual means, there should be a question raised as to whether the assistant is using his time most "productively." Indeed, we've alluded to computer and data junkies elsewhere—a disease of the modern office that is no less *unproductive* than chronic tardiness, alcoholism or goldbricking.

It is clear that the performance and productivity of information workers can only be partially approached using the traditional definitions and yardsticks that were appropriate to the industrial age. For example, engineering standards for measuring the number of parts and subparts assembled by a worker on a production line in an automobile plant, a steel mill, or a textile factory, are partially inappropriate when it comes to deciding whether accessing and using data in a commercial database, for example, has resulted in an important breakthrough in the company's decision-making machinery—enough of a breakthrough to make a key financial-investment decision, or plant-relocation decision, and so forth.

This is not to say that such traditional measures are worthless. It means instead that for most kinds of information-handling and information-processing work done by information people (line and staff managers and other kinds of workers such as those in finance or marketing), additional approaches need to be examined.

On October 25, 1982, President Reagan signed legislation calling for a White House Conference on Productivity to develop recommendations for stimulating productivity growth in the United States.[6] Reflecting a concern about the need for greater productivity growth, the legislation specified immediate action to permit the president to submit recommendations to the Congress within twenty months. One of the areas singled out for study by this group was the need for private sector managers to develop and employ creative, innovative work practices to use fully the knowledge and talent embodied in their human resources—particularly to develop new skills to manage and guide the growing number of information and service workers.

One group focused on the problems dealing with productivity of information workers, and made these recommendations that were embodied in the conference's final report to the president:

Recognize the broad category of information workers for its critical role in productivity and provide at least the same level of attention to improving information-worker productivity as is given to production workers.

Develop specific productivity measurements, goals, and rewards for information workers' occupations and offices.

Use external market pricing and competitive assessments for evaluating the services of information workers.

In the absence of market-driven options, make information workers subject to an internal marketplace. Flexible allocation of resources should be governed by means of competitively priced payments for services and by means of competitive benchmarking of the quality of service.

[6] "Productivity Growth: A Better Life for America," White House Conference on Productivity, Report to the President of the United States, April 1984 (for sale by National Technical Information Service, Department of Commerce, 5285 Port Royal Road, Springfield, VA 22161—Report PB84-159144).

Identify the characteristics of highly productive information-worker organizations and build a strategy for improving productivity in delivery of information-worker services.

Reduce the emphasis on case-by-case justification of information-technology purchases and, instead, examine the overall effects of these investments on business-unit productivity and on the quality of services.

Develop standard productivity-reporting methods that are integrated with generally accepted financial-reporting practices.

Below the business-unit level, develop diagnostic productivity measurements that are specific to the individual operational situations, but that sum up the productivity results computed for the entire business unit.

Consider using the ratio of labor value added divided by labor costs as a measure of labor productivity at the business-unit level. At the business level of analysis, use the adjusted ratio of labor value added (after subtracting operation labor costs), divided by information-worker costs as the measure of information-worker productivity.[7]

This last recommendation seems to offer the promise of dealing head-on with the long-standing defect that existing official government productivity measures only use labor hours as a lowest common denominator approach. As we've pointed out, clearly there is a qualitative difference between hours expended by the great majority of blue-collar jobs involving physical labor almost exclusively, and so many of the white-collar information-worker jobs where brains, rather than brawn, is the crucial ingredient.

How Managers Spend Their Time

Another important stream of research on the productivity of the information worker comes from the work of Booz-Allen & Hamilton

---

[7] "Computer Conferences on Productivity," A Final Report for The White House Conference on Productivity, Computer Networks Department, American Productivity Center, 123 North Post Oak Lane, Houston, TX 77024, 1984. Reprinted with permission of American Productivity Center, Houston, TX.

Activity	Potential savings
Doing less-than-professional tasks	50–80%
Trying to find and digest the "right" information	40–70%
Unnecessary travel and time away	20–70%
Less productive meetings and telephone calls	20–50%
Expediting previously assigned tasks	20–50%
Generating and disseminating documents	10–40%
Other	0–10%

Figure 8–1. Chronic Time Wasters. *Source:* See note 8.

& Company. Figures 8-1 and 8-2 show the results of studies that examined how knowledge workers spend their time.[8] Note that a full one-quarter of the knowledge worker's time is spent in activities that this management consulting firm describes as "marginally productive." Apparently most of those activities involve information handling of one kind or another. Potential savings, according to the company, were very significant.

A second study by this firm stressed the importance of office automation as the "nerve center" of any business, and the importance of such tools as teleconferencing and intelligent workstations to improve productivity.[9]

A third study by the same company underscored the importance of information technology to the strategic planning of companies, and in particular, the need to link the uses of information technologies with the strategic business-planning function.[10] The top right quadrant of Figure 8-3, "top priority," contains four activities that over 25 percent of the firms surveyed indicated needed improvement or are gaining, in their view, importance on their "critical success factor list."[11]

[8] "Office Automation in the 1980s: The Winners and Losers," Booz-Allen & Hamilton Inc., 1980.

[9] "Office Automation in the 1980s: The Winners and Losers," Booz-Allen & Hamilton Inc., New York, NY, 1980.

[10] "Information Industry (I²)L Executive Survey of Critical Success Factors," Booz-Allen & Hamilton Inc., New York, NY, 1982.

[11] *Ibid.*, p. 8.

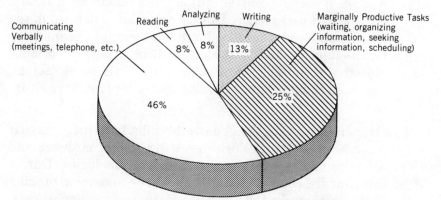

Figure 8–2. Knowledge worker. *Source:* Multi-Client Study of Managerial/ Professional Productivity, Booz-Allen & Hamilton Inc., 1980.

Unfortunately, productivity improvements traceable to knowledge-worker IQs being raised is still a very soft area, both to define and to measure. The above-cited studies and research are all quite preliminary, and do little more than to point the way. What, then, is the enterprise to do in the meantime? We suggest the following:

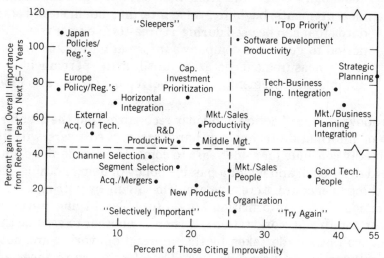

Figure 8–3. CSF's frequently cited as most in need of improvement of which are gaining importance should be high on the planning issue list. *Source: Information Industry Insights* (Booz-Allen & Hamilton Inc., 1982), p.3.

1. Approach the problem definition and measurement from a *value-added* perspective. How *value added* is defined in the personnel performance evaluation system, or the information system evaluation system, will be a mixture of both objective (countable) and subjective (qualitative) factors, that each company must develop and tailor to its own situation.

2. Deliberately establish a "controlled pilot test" program that faces head-on the explosive growth of both hardware and software (particularly end-user PC) technologies. During this time the company's policy should be to develop productivity benchmarks and a baseline for measurement purposes. The company must achieve a balance between a permissive, laissez-faire sort of corporate information-management policy on the one hand; and an unnecessarily tight and stifling policy of forcing every single piece of hardware and software to be fully justified, in a traditional cost-benefit mold, on the other.

3. At approximately six-month or annual intervals, examine the lessons learned and results derived from the controlled benchmark tests, and from that base of observations and measurements, begin to evolve interim guidelines and standards that can be used during a three-to-five-year transition period to guide the company's information-worker productivity-measurement program until more permanent and durable measurements can be evolved over a longer period.

The above course of action implicitly recognizes that the proliferation of information-technology hardware and software will undoubtedly continue for some years to come. But companies cannot afford to sit back and adopt a passive policy of doing nothing. It is one thing to encourage creative problem solving by putting a PC in the hands of every information worker (or at least tying him or her into an intelligent workstation). It is quite another to assume that all of the tasks undertaken by the information worker are, automatically, going to be productive. Therefore, performance- and productivity-measurement programs are absolutely crucial.

Strategies for Improving Managerial Productivity

We've looked at the knowledge worker as a professional, and as an occupational category, in a variety of information-economy work contexts—the office, the factory, and the laboratory. But what of the manager's job in the enterprise of the future? What are these jobs going to look like? And how do they differ from the managerial jobs in smokestack America? Here we're not just talking about *roles* as we did in Chapter 6, but of specific job responsibilities in a functional sense.

In the first place, the computer as a personal, mind-enlarging tool is having a profound effect on job definition, particularly for the manager's job. It used to be that personnel specialists set up job standards, and ultimately defined a total job primarily in terms of the percentage of time required of the incumbent in performing each of several fairly basic and commonplace tasks, such as supervising subordinates, reading and handling information, attending meetings, representing the organization, and so on. But increasingly, managers are finding that these industrial-age benchmarks as to how they should spend their time are out-of-date and not very meaningful.

For example, while "attending meetings" still constitutes a substantial fraction of the manager's total time, many managers are finding that they need to meet face-to-face with others less frequently, because they are able to mobilize needed information resources through their own PCs, and using electronic bulletin boards, computer conferencing, and teleconferencing. They also spend less time in meetings with intermediaries to explain to them what they need, why they need it, and so on. If a manager is able to solve his or her problem by relying largely on his or her own electronic information-processing capabilities, then he or she is usually (but not always) more productive. So a job standard that calls for 20 percent of time in meetings is virtually worthless. Moreover, many managers claim that they are able to do work in only a fraction of the time it used to take. Whether this applies to doing spreadsheet analysis, writing memos, updating personal files, or whatever, efficient shelf-software packages are able to speed up the pace of work substantially. Obviously this is causing a radical redistribution of the manager's budgeted time in the workday.

Additionally, managers say they can do their work with greater confidence because the machines, while certainly not faultless, are normally far more accurate in both quantitative as well as data and information-management work (for example, electronic filing of records) than any person doing the work manually. This greater reliability, stemming from machine-based calculations and operations, in turn gives knowledge workers greater confidence in themselves and in their work. They spend less time, therefore, repeating and verifying work already done.

Then there is the phenomenon of the flattening of the middle-management layer, which we touched on in Chapter 6. If, nowadays, the lower levels of workers require less supervision to do their jobs, then increasing numbers of middle management levels will be looked upon by the top level as redundant. But the returns are not yet all in on this front, as we have said. While undoubtedly many companies can slim down quite a bit by reducing the fat in this middle layer, yet, until greater experience is gained with today's participative management styles and with more flattened organizational structures, there remains a need for some middle managers to coordinate work and act as a communications bridge.

The real challenge, it seems to us, is not so much increasing the capital-to-labor ratio of office machines to knowledge workers as some management theorists would have us do (that will help, but it's not the final solution); as in finding ways to use the net gain realized from employing those technologies to increase *intellectual creativity*, not just information-processing efficiency. For example, we've suggested that the information literacy of managers can be increased by providing them with opportunities (as part of their training requirements) to enhance creative problem-solving and learning skills. This can be done at work, at home, or both. Indeed, Peter Nulty, writing in *Fortune*, tells us that most managers who use computers at work find they get hooked and buy one for their home as well. They then discover that they can spend less time at the office.[12]

[12] Peter Nulty, "How Personal Computers Change Manager's Lives," *Fortune*, September 3, 1984, pp. 38–48. Reprinted with permission. Copyright© 1984 by *Fortune* magazine.

To train these managers at home or at the office, a whole new software industry, "computer courseware," has developed. The big publishers already in the textbook training market, such as Prentice-Hall and McGraw-Hill, were among the first to jump on this bandwagon. Jeremy Main points out that programmers can create a computer-based training program for $2000 to $20,000 per hour of instruction, but videodisk courseware can cost up to five times as much.[13]

In the second part of this chapter, we examine how the various components of the traditional human resources management function, beginning with rewards and motivation, can be revitalized and reconfigured to fit the needs of today's enterprise. We'll look at several elements of the function in turn, beginning with rewarding and motivating employees.

REWARDING AND MOTIVATING EMPLOYEES

Under the Frederick Taylor model of "scientific management" that underpinned industrial-age reward and punishment systems, job satisfaction was largely limited to improved working conditions, better pay and benefits, and job tenure secured through seniority rules. Now, however, unions like the United Automobile Workers talk about a departure from the miniaturization and oversimplification of jobs, to a system that embraces broader distribution of authority—increasing rather than diminishing responsibility, engineering more interesting jobs, and creating opportunities to exercise a meaningful measure of autonomy and utilize more varied skills. It also requires tapping the creative and innovative ingenuity of the worker and soliciting his direct participation in the decisions involved in his job.[14]

Ross and Ross point out that employees are no longer content with the traditional rewards offered by the company or by labor unions, such as more pay, four-day work weeks, more fringe benefits,

[13] Jeremy Main, "New Ways to Teach Workers What's New," *Fortune*, October 1, 1984, pp. 85–94. Reprinted with permission. Copyright© 1984 by *Fortune* magazine.

[14] Joel E. Ross and William C. Ross, *Japanese Quality Circles and Productivity*, Neston, VA: Neston, 1982. Reprinted with permission. Copyright© 1982 by Neston Publishing.

and so on. What they really want is deep human satisfaction from their work. Peter Drucker, they remind us, wrote in 1939, "Any workable social order such as the corporation must confer status and function upon all its members." Is digging up the old theories all that we must do, then?[15]

No, what is needed is not just a simple revival or renaissance of first-generation (industrial-age) behavioral science, group-dynamics, and organizational-development (OD) theories and practices. Instead we need a remolding of those approaches to fit today's information-economy context.

Personnel Selection and Testing

Companies in the information age can ill afford to make too many mistakes in human capital-investment judgements. If, indeed, human resources are a company's most critical asset, along with information itself, then the enterprise operating in the information economy must take extra precautions to insure that the right peg is found for the right hole.

One approach that we believe will be increasingly valuable to the successful company is the increased use of on-the-job internships as an integral part of the selection and testing process. That is, companies should insist that both undergraduate and graduate students being eyed for recruitment spend some time within the four walls of the company prior to their matriculation and hiring, both to give them a chance to learn more about the company, and vice versa.

Such job internships are essential in enabling potential employees to really understand what the company's business is all about, and in giving the company an opportunity to influence the targeted student-employee. We believe such a policy will markedly improve the chances of finding the right people for jobs.

A second approach we believe will see increased attention is the expanded "weekend blitz," whereby company recruitment teams descend on dense urban population centers. In the future, companies will be much more competitive in zeroing in on top-flight

[15] *Ibid.*

candidates. Of course this is not a new technique. It has been used for decades, particularly in the scientific and engineering fields, in law, and in business. We will see extensions of this technique as the full strategic importance of human resources in the information age becomes widespread.

A third approach that we shall see is not just a rebirth, but an extensive overhauling and updating of the whole field of aptitude testing. Thus far, such testing has been pretty much limited to general mental or learning ability (IQ tests), simple aptitude tests, personality-trait testing, achievement-potential testing, and so forth. In the future we will be seeing more testing that focuses on the creative problem-solving and decision-making capabilities of the candidate in real-life company decision settings. In particular, companies will be putting targeted recruits through the ringer, using creative problem-solving approaches wherein information-finding, information-seeking, and information-using skills are at a premium.

Performance Evaluation: Rewards and Punishment Systems

No need is more crucial to a reinvigorated human resources function in the computer era than that of overhauling industrial-age reward and punishment systems. We've suggested that ideal information-economy working conditions do not mean mindless reversion to the behavioral-science theories and techniques of the 1940 to 1965 period. But it does mean updating and adapting many of those approaches to fit the times. Corporations, psychologists, and personnel officers alike have learned lessons from the experiences of that period. We need now to capitalize on the positive lessons learned and reject the negative ones.

For example, in the area of employee performance systems used for salary determination, promotion, training, and so forth, we believe the standards and guidelines of the enlightened enterprise should be addressed to:

Creativity and new ideas; innovation

Greater use of flex-time, including working at home and using telecommunications

Greater independence and mobility in job assignments, so that individuals are not isolated by being permanently assigned to one organizational unit

Work output measured not just quantitatively, but qualitatively as well

Lifelong learning which is formally recognized and appropriately rewarded

Greater self-direction and more use of shared team-leadership styles like those now used in project management

Improved computer and information literacy skills

Sound functional literacy (that is, reasoning ability), in both the sciences and humanities, as well as in practical problem solving on the job

By the same token, we believe there should be less emphasis addressed to:

Time clocks

Unqualified seniority, tenure rules for job retention

Unnecessary pro-forma educational and job experience requirements (that is, so many years of this kind, so many years of that kind for promotion and new assignments; so much time spent in meetings, and so forth)

Work output and productivity measured exclusively in quantitative terms

Technostress and Burnout: Health, Safety, and Security Factors in the Workplace

In an early 1985 write-up in *Business Week,* a bleak picture was printed for "a million white collar workers that are victims of smokestack America's decline." Since 1979, according to *Business-Week,* the number of white collar jobs in the steel industry alone has plunged 40 percent! In autos the figure is 15 percent. Oil companies and banks are wiping out thousands of jobs. Companies laying off these workers point to the acute need for counseling of these dis-placed, relocated, and fired employees—because of the enormous stress on the workers themselves, their marriages, and their families. It is very clear that outplacement counseling is a key fac-tor in today's highly volatile job market, as we try to get through the industrial-information economy shift.[16]

Peggy Schmidt, writing in the *New York Times* in early 1985, gave the negative consequences of using modern information tech-nologies a new, catchy label: "tech psych." Others have used the terms "technostress" and "burnout" to emphasize that the hazards of using the machines are not all physiological; many are psycho-logical.[17]

Dealing with the whole range of these problems and issues is beyond our scope. What we wish to do is identify a few selected areas and point out how the enlightened information-age corpora-tion might address them.

First, there is the question of physical discomfort. The rela-tively new field of ergonomics has grown up to deal with the prob-lems of back strain, eye strain, boredom, and other physical prob-lems reported by VDT users, and by the isolated operator in the central computer room, the PABX operator coping with message overloads, the photocopy machine operator, and many others. There is really no excuse for the company not to explore and plan carefully the physical settings of its "information factories," so that knowledge workers are better able to cope with the stresses and strains of sitting or standing six, seven, eight or more hours a day in front of a machine. A PC is not a typewriter, despite simi-larities in morphology and purpose. There are important differ-ences between them that must be taken into account when design-ing functionally comfortable work settings where these technologies are to be used.

Second, there are possible VDT health hazards. Proposed legis-lation before Congress that would control the use of VDTs in the workplace, springs from a number of legitimate user complaints

---

[16] *Source:* "Suddenly, the World Doesn't Care If You Live or Die," *BusinessWeek,* February 4, 1985, pp. 96–98.

[17] Peggy Schmidt, "What's New in Computer Psychology," *The New York Times,* January 20, 1985, p. F15.

about physical discomfort, and from fears about equipment safety. Beyond the federal government, as of early 1985, nearly two dozen states had considered legislation to restrict VDT use.

One of the most vocal critics of this proposed legislation has been the Computer Business Equipment Manufacturers Association (CBEMA). While admitting that information managers have ignored common-sense needs such as brightness controls, glare filters, tiltable screens, detachable keyboards, and other features, thereby exacerbating the present situation, CBEMA's articulate president, Vico Henriques, has been fighting VDT restrictions in states across the country for the last two years. Writing recently in *Information Management Review,* he said:

> *We intend to continue to (fight) wherever bills would unreasonably handicap users and managers who are trying to develop the best possible applications of computer technology. The proponents of restrictions are primarily unions. Assessment of their motivation varies. On the one hand, they are seen as expressing legitimate grievances that managers have failed to respond to. On the other hand, they are seen as making false claims about the negative effects of the VDT in order to win public sympathy for their drive to unionize clerical workers. I urge all responsible information managers, no matter what size your organization, first, to make sure that you have responded to legitimate user needs, and second, to voice your concerns on impending legislation to your state representatives.* [18]

Undoubtedly CBEMA and other trade associations in the electronic information-handling industries, the many hardware user groups, the many governmental bodies, as well as health organizations of various kinds, will all continue to explore the area and try to separate bona fide problems from imaginary ones. Only then can sound corporate information-policy guidance, standards, and procedures be evolved for health, safety, and security.

Third, there is the question of embarrassment and fear at having

---

[18] Vico Henriques, "Includes User Needs in Computer Planning to Avoid Restrictive Legislation in VDTS," *Information Management Review,* Vol. 1, Issue 1, July 1985, pp. 81–83. Reprinted with permission of Aspen Systems Corporation.

to learn about the new technologies in front of subordinates and peers, particularly in the over-50 age group. Most experts agree that the ultimate answer to this problem lies in creating an atmosphere of positive, supportive learning and making that atmosphere a natural part of the organizational culture. That is, if the company espouses a lifelong learning policy wherein employees of all age groups are encouraged to participate in on- and off-the-job programs, even middle and older-age people will not be so likely to feel left-out.

A fourth problem is that of stress caused by an accelerated demand for people to be highly productive, leading to a syndrome sometimes called "over-achieving." Someone once coined the word "electronwork" to describe the kind of roller-coaster that people who use electronic technologies seem to be on. As our tools become more efficient, we often feel that we're on a kind of treadmill; a race to produce more and faster than the next fellow. This compulsion often leads to anxiety and stress. The enlightened company will be the one that has access to a medically and technologically qualified in-house or external technostress consultant, who can counsel employees or refer them to other qualified experts, so that these emotional problems are effectively dealt with.

We've only dealt briefly with a few of the health, safety, and psychological problems endemic to the knowledge worker's occupation. In 1984, the Aspen Institute for Humanistic Studies mounted an international symposium called "Ancient Humans in Tomorrow's Electronic World." The conferees agreed that human beings *do* have the biological and social capacity to accommodate to our electronic world, but that they need assistance. The information-economy firm that understands the need for this help, has planned for it, and has resources on tap to bring in when needed, will be the one that succeeds in staving off counterproductive and disruptive crises at the level of the individual employee, of employee-management, and finally at the level of the company's strategic plans.

Now we move to the third main part of this chapter; education, training, career development, and professional development.

COMPUTER LITERACY VERSUS
INFORMATION LITERACY

Quinn, Kirkman, and Schultz call computer literacy a "ghost of education past." They recite the case of a Los Angeles school administrator who announced the morning after the release of the President's National Commission on Excellence in Education final report, his "enlightened" intention to add computer literacy to the core curriculum—if, that is, enough money could be found to buy the hardware and hire the teachers.[19]

Working in the context of an eleven-member network of California and Canadian school districts to guide and examine the major development issues and problems in curriculum development, the abovementioned educators and technology specialists emphasize that in the information society, students and adults alike need knowledge, skills, and attitudes that are far more generic and pervasive than simply those required to operate a computer terminal, or use a basic computer language to program a microcomputer. "Most important," they say, "they need to focus on the concepts and skills of information management rather than on a body of content reflecting today's microcomputers."[20]

One of the major issues this network is grappling with is the teaching of higher-order reasoning skills. Here is what Quinn, Kirkman, and Schultz have to say:

> As knowledge will be the capital upon which tomorrow's investments will rise or fall, and access to information or to specialized data bases is the mechanism by which knowledge can be used most productively, futurists have persuasively argued that the higher-order reasoning skills of application, analysis, synthesis, and evaluation will be the basic thinking skills of tomorrow. Moreover, the traditional reasoning models, of the logical deductive type, will not be as critical as before. What will count most in the information age is the capacity to intuit from relatively large amounts of new information those "chunks" of

[19] James Quinne, Joseph Kirkman, and Cora Jo Schultz, "Beyond Computer Literacy," *Educational Leadership*, September 1983, pp. 38–39, 67. Reprinted with permission of the Association for Supervision and Curriculum Development. Copyright© 1983 by the Association for Supervision and Curriculum Development. All rights reserved.

[20] *Ibid.*, p. 38.

information that can be related usefully to other kinds of information or to a knowledge base already stored in the brain. Reasoning skills that students can apply to the relational nature of new information and old knowledge will be at a high premium. In the intuitive or inductive reasoning process, new facts, data, or information bits are related to an already developed knowledge domain or to the working memory, and new, yet incomplete wholes are formed. Thus problems are tentatively held because they make the most sense given the amount of information at hand. [21]

The Evolution of Information Centers

Companies need not apologize for first moving to the IBM information center concept as a transitional stage between the large, centralized computer center model of the 1950s and 1960s, and the fragmented, decentralized, and networked intelligent workstation model now emerging in the 1980s. Clearly the corporation had to establish some in-house focal point to deal with the enormous demand from platoons of end-users who needed and wanted to become computer literate. We might call this stage *information-center stage one.*

The more advanced companies are now beginning to enter what we might call *stage two,* where at least an initial attempt is being made to introduce end-users to vast arrays of external databases that are available from both commercial sources and government sources, both domestically and internationally. While intermediaries are still needed as an adjunct to help end-users with on-line searches of many of these databases, or to assist with learning access protocols and command languages, slowly, larger and larger numbers of users are becoming more and more adept in searching. But there still remains the problem of enriching and enlightening end-users as to just what is available, and most importantly, how to use the information once it is retrieved. That is where *stage three* comes in.

Stage three will see the infusion of the concepts of information technology, intuitive reasoning, change, artificial intelligence, decision-support systems, expert and knowledge-based systems, and

---

[21] *Ibid.,* p. 39.

other concepts into the operating training programs of the stage three center. In short, at this point end-users will not only know which keys, and in what sequence, should be pushed on the machines, but they will also know what they don't know, what they must find, what is available, how to find it, how to access it, and above all, how to apply it to the problem at hand.

To the best of our knowledge, not a single corporation as yet has reached the stage three, and only a handful are at stage two. A few haven't even reached stage one; they are still back at a point where there isn't even a working library! There is often a dormant library that is located in a remote place, is poorly used, and functions more as a passive archive for company records than as a dynamic learning center for company employees to use.

Education and Training Programs:
The Learning Center

We've already stressed the need for lifelong learning in the new enterprise. We forecast that there will be a melding of the information-center concept, currently a place for developing computer-literacy skills, into a true learning center to which employees will come with the same high spirits and motivation as they do when they go to the gym for a workout, go jogging, or take the afternoon off for a game of golf. Learning to learn, so that nobody in the information-age enterprise stops growing, will be a first order of business.

We've also talked about the differences between computer literacy and information literacy, and the need to transform the information center of the early 1980s into the knowledge and learning center of the 1990s. But our forecast here goes even further. The knowledge center cannot just be an ivory temple of knowledge in the mode of the libraries of Alexandria, Egypt, to which access was forbidden to all except the high priest elite. It must be a populist learning center that places a premium on developing creative problem-solving abilities for all. Creative problem solving, understood comprehensively, means the ability to know what information exists, how to find it, how to access it, how to use it, and how to achieve results from it.

Many of the behavioral techniques and approaches developed by the personnel psychologists of the mid-20th century are more applicable today than they were then. For example:

Brainstorming

Buzz groups

Corporate war games

Role playing

Psychodrama

We simply suggest that instructors and consultants employing these techniques pay special attention to the information-resource component of these techniques, not just from a theoretical, but from a practical standpoint as well; that is, in the context of practical learning objectives, tied to the real world of the corporate environment.

On-the-Job and Vocational-Technical Training

In the preceding paragraphs we've paid primary attention to the primary and secondary education arenas (Kindergarten through the 12th grade), university level education, and corporate education and training programs. But, as the National Academy of Sciences has pointed out, the largest segment of the American work force consists of high-school graduates who have never attended college. In a recent report the Academy said:

The U.S. economy is expected to generate more than 25 million additional jobs between 1982 and 1995. By comparison, it added some 20 million jobs between 1969 and 1982. Americans work in hundreds of occupations; only 40 of these together will account for more than half of the expected employment growth. The projections also show relatively few young people working in new occupations. Rather, the bulk of new opportunities will exist in occupations that already are very familiar to us. Well-prepared high school graduates, therefore, can realistically hope to compete for the jobs of the future. Many people assume that advanced technology requires higher skills; in reality, it often requires different, and sometimes lesser, skills. Just as the word processor's keyboard resembles the typewriter's, the skills needed to operate both of them overlap; there is an enduring need for competence in grammar, punctuation and vocabulary.[22]

Who is training these high-school graduates without college experience? What programs are available? How good are they? How do they fit into the overall educational and training scheme we've been reviewing up to now?

In the most recent issue of the *Buyer's Guide and Consultant Directory,* published by The American Society for Training and Development (ASTD), more than 400 specialists and organizations who provide education and training products and services are listed.[23] ASTD speaks of a network of "23,000 people in the training business," and in addition to heavy involvement in the more traditional areas of career development, professional development, and organizational development, member companies offer a broad range of specialty training in community development, programs for the handicapped, industry-community college cooperation, occupational safety, public job training, quality of work life, and many others. Our purpose is simply to highlight some examples of how the commercial training business has, indeed, become a thriving industry. Much of it is directed to the vocational-technical training market, but a great deal of it complements and sometimes supplants in-house corporate training programs as well. Occasionally even staid formal institutions—the colleges and universities, for example—go to these sources to supplement their program offerings.

Another major association, The American Society for Association Executives (ASAE), also mounts strong training activities of a very wide range, including clinics, colloquia, conferences, conventions, executive development, forums, institutes, seminars, symposia, workshops, professional development, technical development, and so forth. Since the employees of many associations

---

[22] "High Schools and the Changing Workplace: The Employer's View," News Report, National Academy of Sciences, Vol. XXXIV, No. 6, June, 1984, pp. 3–12A. Reprinted with permission. Copyright© 1984 by News Report, National Research Council.

[23] 1985 Buyer's Guide and Consultant Directory, The American Society for Training and Development, Suite 305, 600 Maryland Ave. S.W., Washington, D.C. 20024. Published with the permission of the American Society for Training and Development.

and societies are people with limited college exposure, these training activities must also include basic skills and competencies.

Like so many other training organizations, the American Management Association not only offers extensive training programs and courses at selected sites, but one of its marketing pitches is "if you can't come to us, we'll come to you!" More than 2500 courses are offered per year by this one organization.[24]

Another, the Institute For Advanced Technology, headquartered in Rockville, Maryland, also offers hundreds of courses per year, both on and off-site. It's most recent listing of offerings included computer literacy for managers and business professionals, office automation concepts, voice-data integration, and dozens of other subjects.[25]

At the Federal level of government, the training challenge has been so great that a "graduate school" was established some years ago by the U. S. Department of Agriculture. This facility boasts of "over 60 years in continuing education," and offers hundreds of courses, mostly in the basic skills area, for government employees. Like so many other nonaccredited institutions, a combination of evening courses, daytime workshops and seminars, and weekend instruction is offered. Certificates in several dozen areas, including information-resources management, are offered following successful completion of a prescribed curriculum.[26]

It is clear, then, that both accredited and nonaccredited educational and training programs aimed at the vocational-technical, post-secondary-school training market, must be an equally strong component as academia, in the overall educational system of the Nation. As information technology and information-management training needs proliferate in the years ahead, we can see nothing but an expanded role for this niche of the training market. Rather than duplicate and overlap with the offerings of this sector, companies in the information economy would do well to look carefully

---

[24] Course Catalog, American Management Associations, AMA Building, 135 West 50th Street, New York, NY 10020.

[25] Catalog of Professional Development Seminars, Institute for Advanced Technology, 6003 Executive Blvd., Rockville, MD. 20852. Reprinted with permission.

[26] United States Department of Agriculture Graduate School, 600 Maryland Avenue, S.W., Room 106, Washington, D.C. 20024 (certificate in Information Resources Management program).

at what they have to offer, and build company programs and budgets to capitalize on their strengths.

Career and Professional Development: Lifelong Learning

Central to the enlargement and revitalization of the human resources management function in the information age company will be the idea of lifelong learning. Virtually every major college and university in the country today has some kind of continuing education program—oftentimes with a larger enrollment than the main undergraduate student body. Evening programs, weekend programs, on-site programs, and the like have blossomed virtually everywhere as institution after institution has found a broad new appreciative audience in adult populations already in the workforce, or in retirement. And these people are able to pay for their educational services.

The difference between what we are seeing now and what we will see, however, is that most of today's lifelong learning philosophy is based on acquiring new knowledges, and filling in gaps in both vocational and technical competencies. The spouse who neglected to take business courses and now finds him or herself as the second family breadwinner, or the frustrated middle-aged businessman who wants to brush up on a hobby like photography, are examples of people who have found gaps in their training. The "new" information-age concept of lifelong learning is based on the realization that in tomorrow's increasingly fast-moving technological settings, it is essential that education and training be appropriate to career and professional development, human resource planning, and the business plans of all corporations, as an organic, not just a "nice-to-have" element.

In a rotation program for new employees, for example, held during the first three years of the employee's tour, not only are blocs of time allocated for assignments to line and staff manufacturing and marketing jobs, staff jobs at corporate headquarters, and so forth, but recurring blocs of time are reserved for off-the-job and on-the-job education and training so that the employee's technical skills are continuously enriched and kept up-to-date. This kind of training can enable employees to meet the challenges of today's fast-moving PC software industry, for instance, where not only are new products being put on the shelf every day, but brand new techniques and new applications are constantly being evolved. It's not like buying next year's model of automobile, it's more like learning a whole new culture when taking a job overseas.

Jane F. Spivack reminds us that the information worker must make periodical sojourns back to the classroom, either in formal programs or in short-term, very specific seminars and workshops. No longer can one expect to keep up with new developments through on-the-job learning alone. Continuing education has become a fact of life. Among the choices are the continuing-education programs of colleges and universities, workshops and seminars sponsored by professional organizations, and training seminars run by vendors of automated equipment.[27]

Careers in Information: Professional, Technical, and Clerical

There are three dimensions to the subject of career opportunities in the information economy.

First, there will be brand new opportunities for entirely new kinds of jobs that aren't even in the occupational handbooks today. For example, *knowledge engineer* is an emerging category of knowledge worker composed of (as yet) a very few, highly specialized individuals working with expert systems and knowledge-based systems. Their information-processing skills overlap with, but are substantially different from, those of the systems analyst who works with large-volume-transaction information systems in such application areas as inventory control and financial accounting.

Second, there will be a continuing increase in the number of conventional information-processing jobs across the entire spectrum of information industries, including hi-tech and low-tech R&D, hardware design and development, software design and development, information systems design and development, telecommunications networks, and so forth. As these technologies proliferate and specialize, obviously the technical skills required by

---

[27] Jane F. Spivack, ed., *Careers in Information*, White Plains, NY: Knowledge Industry, 1982. Used with permission.

personnel charged with operating them will also proliferate and specialize. (*Conventional*, in this context, simply means jobs in the second, third, and fourth generation technology areas. These are technologies which won't disappear with the emergence of fifth and successive generations of technology, but which will "settle" into the labor force gradually.)

Third, virtually all existing manufacturing and service-sector jobs, as well as many agricultural jobs (particularly those involving the use of modern technologies of all kinds, not just information technologies), will involve retraining to a greater or lesser degree, to reorient incumbents to the implications and consequences of their companies' movement to embrace the new information technologies. We don't believe that any corporate job will escape—whether it be manufacturing or marketing, professional or clerical, or managerial or line worker.

Since, as we will elaborate below, academia has been so slow in responding effectively to the major transformations and dislocations taking place in the labor force, the enterprise of the future must be prepared to mount very substantial in-house education and training efforts to cope with the demands. For example, knowledge engineers, information brokers, information counselors, and marketing managers faced with the job of pricing an information product, are simply not being mass produced in colleges and universities in America today.

The Formal Educational System: How Is It Responding?

The reader may be familiar with a debate that has occupied education professionals, government, the media, parents, and students for at least a decade or more, revolving around the allegation that the decline in American productivity is related to the slow but steady deterioration of the American educational system over the last quarter century. More recently, former Secretary of Education Terrel H. Bell, who occupied that post during the first term of the Reagan Administration, has been outspoken in advancing the theme that in an era of expanding technology and changing job requirements, the nation must become a country of

learners, regardless of age and regardless of position in life.[28]
Among the oft-quoted statistics to support this thesis are:

Military services have to rewrite their technical manuals to an
8th grade level and even to 6th grade standards.

American businesses have to spend billions of dollars each year
educating, training, and retraining high-school and college graduates.

American colleges and universities are heavily involved in offering remedial courses.

Some 23 million functional illiterates are in the nation's labor
force.

In April of 1983 the National Commission on Educational Excellence released its report, indicating the above and many more
deficiencies in the educational system, and calling for a wide range
of reforms including steps to enhance competency requirements, to
introduce merit pay for teachers, to restore compulsory courses,
and reduce nonacademic electives.[29]

The above-mentioned White House Conference on Productivity
also addressed this issue, emphasizing the need for American business to adopt innovative work practices. The conference's final
report had this to say:

*In general, America's work practices have not kept pace with the
evolution of cultural and social norms. They do not recognize the
rapidly growing information worker component of the labor force, the
rising level of education attainment, and the desire of employees to
participate in their organization's decision-making. Employees at all
levels should be given the opportunity to participate in solving problems and making decisions in the organization that will lead to higher
productivity. Employees tend to know more about the machines and*

[28] Charles E. Burgess and Thomas D. Pabano, "Colleges Too Eager, Bell Says," *St. Louis
Post-Dispatch,* June 23, 1983, and Singer, Dale and Boyd, Gerald M., "Bell: Productivity,
Education Liked," *St. Louis Post Dispatch,* June 22, 1983. Used with permission.

[29] Final Report of the National Commission on Educational Excellence, April 1983,
Department of Education. See also "America's Competitive Challenge: The Need for a
National Response, Business-Higher Education Forum, Washington, D.C., April 1983.

processes they work with than do their managers. Sharing information with employees about the organization's objectives and how it is doing, in good times as well as bad, provides a basis for their contributions. Redesigning and redefining jobs, work, and organization is a second way that organizations have been successful in improving productivity and profitability. Creating smaller and leaner organizations provides an environment more conducive to innovation and superior performance. Hiring people who can adapt skills, and then teaching them more and more skills, avoids having to compartmentalize and stratify the organization. Autonomous work teams are another example of success in this area. [30]

Edward B. Fiske, writing in the January 28, 1985 *New York Times,* pointed out that educational programs run by business and industry have become a booming industry. Fiske underscored the competition between corporate education and traditional university education, drawing from findings of a 240-page study entitled *Corporate Classrooms: The Learning Business,* authored by Neil P. Eurich, and sponsored by the Carnegie Foundation for the Advancement of Teaching. [31]

Citing corporate examples like the Rand Corporation, which offers its own doctorate degree, and Wang Laboratories and Northrop Corporation, which offer master's degrees, Eurich estimated that nearly $60 billion a year is spent on corporate-run education. IBM, Xerox, RCA, Holiday Inns, and other companies have built educational facilities that look like college campuses.

In our view, the report was perhaps a bit short-sighted in calling such corporate educational programs wasteful and unacceptable "because the public pays for such education at both ends—through a tax write-off and the price of goods and services." We take a contrary view. In the information age, where increasing specialization and differentiation of products and services will be a hallmark, we cannot see how academia can possibly be fully responsive to the extraordinary proliferation of education and training requirements.

---

[30] "Productivity Growth: A Better Life for America," White House Conference on Productivity, Report to the President of the United States, April 1984 (for sale by NTIS, Department of Commerce), 5285 Port Royal Road, Springfield, VA, Report PB84-159144).

[31] Edward B. Fiske, "Booming Corporate Education Efforts Rival College Programs, Study Says," *New York Times,* January 28, 1985, p. 410.

There are too many needs, and they're coming at us too fast.

Consider computer-programming languages alone. In many undergraduate catalogs the number of courses in this one area now numbers in the dozens! Moreover, even when these students graduate, their employers must train them again in the idiosyncrasies of their own computer operating systems and environments. Moreover, today's favorite language (for instance, COBOL) will be tomorrow's "dog," as a new language or even a new generation of languages takes its place (for example, Ada).

Instead, we believe a partnership of academia and industry is a much more feasible and responsive way to deal with tomorrow's information-age challenges in the education and training arena. Just as the boundaries between multinationals and governments are becoming blurred as economic power makes inroads on a global scale, so the boundary between academia and industry is becoming blurred in the information-technology educational area. It seems to us that the colleges and universities will continue to do that which they already do very well—educate in the arts, humanities, and basic sciences. But we are convinced that corporate America is best positioned to undertake substantial training and retraining programs in the applied-technology area, to supplement university training—particularly in the explosive field of information technology. We don't offer a black-and-white recipe, just a realization that the shift to corporate education-academia education mixes will be gradual, but inexorable, over a long period of time. What would be tragic is if both sides battled over turf instead of collaborating in some kind of a partnership arrangement.

SUMMARY

In this chapter we have tried to identify just who knowledge workers are, what they do, how their jobs fit into the context of the enterprise in the information economy, and some of the attributes, consequences, and impacts of this new role in the information economy. We've tried to do the same with managers.

We have argued that in one sense, in the information age, virtually every employee is a knowledge worker, and every job is a knowledge worker job. We feel that trying to make too fine a distinction between professional, technical, clerical, managerial, and other traditional occupational classifications is counterproductive. While these traditional differentiations do have their place in formal personnel job-classification schemes and in scholarly occupational studies, what is far more important to our context is the need for the enlightened corporation to create conditions for an involved, committed, and participative workforce. Creativity, innovation, problem solving, reasoning ability, and teamwork in that environment are, by definition, at a premium.

The information economy will require substantial investments, both at the level of the firm, and in terms of governmental policies and assistance, to cope with job dislocations and the shock of retraining for large segments of the labor force that are not equipped, intellectually or emotionally, to deal with working in electronic information work environments. A partnership between academia, industry, government, and social institutions is called for, since no single institution or sector of society can possibly cope with the multiple challenges single-handedly.

The information economy is bringing with it personal health, safety, and psychological stress factors that are no less real than the business, commercial, and economic factors. Both sets of factors are woven into the same socio-business fabric that every CEO must address. The wise company is one that will have planned for these human factors and has available to it, both in-house, and from external sources, professional assistance to bring in when needed. Organizational development and team bonding will be important once again.

It is our conviction that at the heart of the knowledge worker and manager's job is the forging of a new partnership between information management and human resource management. This is critical to a firm's viable competitive strategy in the information economy.

CHAPTER 9

THE CHANGING ROLE OF
BUSINESS IN THE
INFORMATION SOCIETY

Throughout this book, we have shown how the information economy and information-processing industry affect every major aspect of business management. Moreover, we have emphasized that no level of business strategy—whether corporate, business unit, or functional—can afford not to account for and reflect the growing importance of information resources on competitive strategy. Not all manufacturing or service firms, industries, or markets will be equally affected by the changing context of business in the information economy. It is difficult, however, to imagine any firm, be it large or small, traditional or emerging, which can totally exclude itself from the effects of this structural economic change over the next five to 10 years, and still survive and prosper.

In this chapter, we extend our concern with business management in the information economy to focus on the changing role of business in the information society: That is, on the governmental and social changes to which managers and executives must respond in designing and implementing effective business strategies. How are businesses affected by political and social changes in the information society? How can executives and managers develop constructive approaches to public-policy issues and debates which will continue to influence business success or failure in the information economy?

At the outset, we assume that businesses cannot take a purely reactive role in dealing with political, social, and cultural changes occurring in the information society. A major part of the external business environment is indeed shaped and influenced by social conditions and values, and shifts in political and regulatory approaches. Thus, a business which has a laissez-faire attitude toward such changes runs the significant risk of being blind-sided by forces or changes that were not anticipated or planned for. In addition, a firm's ability to sustain a competitive strategy over time, may increasingly be influenced not just by purely economic or business trends, but by shifts in regulatory, social, and cultural attitudes. In sum, it seems to make good business sense to adopt a constructive and anticipatory attitude toward social and political changes brought on by the evolution of the information economy.[1]

In this final chapter, our intent is to center on those key features of the information economy that are likely to significantly impact the public-policy agenda and responsibilities of business. In so doing, it is important to recall that as advanced economies like the United States evolved from the agrarian to industrial age, the complex fabric of economic, political, and social institutions and values was dramatically and irrevocably affected. Over the last 80 years in the United States, our political and social environment has gone through major upheavals as the industrial economy has matured from the early 1900s, because of the growth of the great syndicates and corporations in the railroad, oil, and steel industries throughout the 1920s and 1930s, and the unionization, trustbusting, and depression periods and up to the eras of the New Deal, New Frontier, Great Society, and environmental movements. These and

---

[1] Michael Rogers Rubin, *Information Economics and Policy in the United States,* Littleton, CO: Libraries Unlimited, 1983, pp. 8–11.

so many other changes have redefined the context of business in society, as well as changed our conceptions of the responsibilities and roles of business in dealing with political and social changes.

THE INFORMATION ECONOMY IS A POLITICAL AND SOCIAL REALITY

Today, the emergence of the information economy, its impact on the public-policy agenda and on the role of business, is no less dramatic. Therefore, the first salient point concerning the information economy's effect on the *public* role of business is that the information economy is not simply a business reality, but is also a political and social reality. That is, business, economic, and even technological issues alone do not define the contours and evolution of the information economy, but rather, the *interactions* and *interdependence* between these issues and changing social and political concerns and values exhibited on a national and international scale, are what result in the positive and negative consequences of the information economy on society.[2]

These interactions and interdependencies are clearly exhibited in a report entitled *Computer-Based National Information Systems: Technology and Public Policy Issues,* published by the Office of Technology Assessment of the U.S. Congress in 1981. In this report, OTA identified 14 areas of law and regulation that affect information systems or are affected by them. (See Table 9-1.)[3] Not only do these 14 issue areas involve multiple participants in government at the state, federal, and even international levels, but, more importantly, each area directly or indirectly affects business users of information resources and technology. The applicable laws, regulations, and court decisions vary according to particular business sectors (such as banking, insurance, retailing, real estate), and represent a diverse and complex fabric of public- and private-sector interactions.

[2] David M. O'Brien and Donald A. Marchand, eds., *The Politics of Technology Assessment,* Lexington, MA: D.C. Heath, 1982, pp. 6–11.

[3] U.S. Congress, Office of Technology Assessment, *Computer-Based National Information Systems: Technology and Public Policy Issues,* Washington, D.C.: U.S. Government Printing Office, 1981, p. 55.

TABLE 9–1. Principal Areas of Law and Regulation Regarding Information Systems

Area of Concern	State	Federal	Regulatory	Court[a]	International
Privacy	X	X		X	X
Freedom of information	X	X		X	X
First amendment		X	X	X	
Fourth amendment		X		X	
Due Process	X	X	X	X	
Communications regulations	X	X	X	X	X
Computer crime	X	X		X	
Proprietary rights		X		X	
Evidence	X	X	X	X	
Liability	X	X		X	
Antitrust		X	X	X	
Taxation	X	X			X
Government provision of information	X	X			X
Government procurement of information systems	X	X			

Source: OTA working paper on "The Legal/Regulatory Environment of Information Systems." June 1980. See note 3.

[a] Involvement that creates new law or interpretation.

In addition, information-policy issues affect the firm's internal and external information-systems environment. To illustrate these internal and external impacts of information-policy issues, OTA defined four levels of issues and indicated the specific relations between the character of the issues and their potential impacts on a firm's information-systems strategies and operations. (See Table 9-2.)[4] At the systems level, social issues include the impacts of systems on individuals, work groups, or organizations. Technical,

[4] *Ibid.,* p. 57.

TABLE 9–2.   Structure of Information-Policy Issues

Level of Issues	Character of Issues	Example Issues
System level	Relate to the design, implementation, and operation of particular information systems	Government procurement policy Efficiency and economy of operation Security of information systems
Information level	Relate to the handling of data: collection, storage, use, and dissemination	Privacy (recordkeeping) Freedom of Information regulations Copyright and patents as related to computer programs
Secondary policy impacts	Exist independent of the particular information systems, but are changed in magnitude or character by use of technology	Privacy (surveillance) First admendment rights Fourth amendment rights Social vulnerability Federal-State relations
Long-term societal effects	Long-range societal impacts that are not currently reflected in specific policy problems, but which may ultimately affect the nature of U.S. society.	Privacy (social attitudes) Psychological self-image of humans Education needs Social-political effects Cultural impacts

Source: Office of Technology Assessment. See note 4.

operational, and reliability factors all can have broader societal significance, even though they originate in the operational uses of specific information systems. In recent years, public and regulatory attention has focused on areas such as:

Airline reservation systems and possible unfair competitive practices

The changing impacts on the banking system of electronic funds-transfer technologies

The capacity for international financial and investment companies such as E.F. Hutton to invent new and legally questionable ways of engaging in thousands of funds transfers in the banking and investment communities

As privately operated information systems affect potentially millions of people, and impact the use of financial and other resources, there is likely to be more societal interest focused on the operational objectives and accountability of such systems and the businesses that control them.

At the information-issue level, a complex combination of state and federal laws and regulations govern the use of business or consumer information, and the privacy and confidentiality interests of individuals and corporations. Freedom of information laws can and do conflict with individual or proprietary concerns of businesses. Copyright and patent laws become outmoded with the appearance of new technologies such as personal-computer software or videotape players. Laws protecting the confidentiality of banking, credit records, and medical records conflict with either the needs of law enforcement, the changing nature of computer and communications technologies, and/or the operational efficiencies of private firms intent on providing more comprehensive services to individuals which in turn require increasing amounts of sensitive individual record information.

At the secondary-policy input level, the use of information technology can have impacts on policy issues that have existed for years, and are to a degree independent of the technologies used. Will the inviolability of the mail service be retained in an era of electronic mail and document-distribution services? Will First Amendment rights enjoyed by the print media be protected adequately in an era of electronic publishing, distribution, and access? Can electronic ID cards and computers on a card assist in reducing fraud in the credit card, banking, and financial-services industries? Will companies be allowed to file their taxes, tariffs, and schedules with the government electronically? Clearly, the products and services of the information-processing industry will raise concerns both about the negative social impacts of their uses, and about their constructive uses to reduce fraud, increase information security, and provide other social benefits.

Finally, at the level of long-term societal effects, the increasing uses of information resources and technology by business on a national and international (or multinational) scale, will effect longer-term changes in individual values, social attitudes, and cultural perceptions. While these effects may arise over long periods of time (decades versus years), and be difficult to detect and measure precisely, they nevertheless represent important trends in the external business environment that must be perceived and valued at the level of corporate strategy. Some of these trends are:

The cultural sovereignty of nations, and the concerns over international broadcasting by satellites

Transborder dataflow regulations and the management of information resources and technology in the multinational business arena

The changing information and computer literacy of the young versus the middle-aged population, and the growing competition for jobs

The cultural adjustments being made by individuals and businesses because of the pervasive impacts of the information-processing industry's products and services on the home, office, factory, school, and even church

As the information economy continues to mature and evolve, it is clear that executives and managers cannot afford to be unaware of both the internal versus external, and short- versus long-term issues raised in doing business. They must adjust to the mutual dependencies created by the social and political changes affecting economic and business trends.

BLURRING DEFINITIONS AND BOUNDARIES OF LAW AND CUSTOM

A second important impact of the evolution of the information economy on the public responsibilities of business, are the modifications of legal definitions and laws such as privacy, copyright, and disclosure, and the blurring of boundaries between areas of regulatory jurisdiction in fields like banking, retailing, financial services, credit cards, and real estate, or in the computer, communications, information, and broadcasting industries.

The products and technologies of the information-processing industry have in recent years had an unprecedented impact on traditional notions of intellectual property, privacy, and related information-ownership and control issues that more and more companies must address in the information economy. These include, for example, liability for the credibility of information (that is, accuracy) that is sold in the information marketplace or used to make decisions about other businesses or consumers, the legality of electronic images of legal documents, the problem of software piracy, and the issue of the rights of individuals to see and know what data is being held about them (such as in the use of banking, credit-reporting, insurance, and medical records).[5]

The worth of an information product or service in the marketplace is directly related to what is coming to be called *value added*. Historically, we are familiar with the value coming from the *creation* of intellectual property like the works of authors, composers, and patent holders. However, value added to information does not come solely from the creation of any information product or service. It also arises from that product's conversion to more readily accessible electronic and photonic media, pricing, or valuation, and from many other events during the entire life cycle of that product or service.

For example, at the *conversion* stage in the life cycle of information, information value stems from several sources:

Conversion from manual to automated media

Translation into another language or format

Presentation in a more appropriate, timely, or entertaining manner

Validation by a more authoritative and creditable party

---

[5] See Forest W. Horton, Jr., ed., *Understanding U.S. Information Policy*, Washington, D.C.: Information Industry Association, 1982, *The Information Policy Primer*, Vol. 1.

Embodiment in multiple storage and distribution media

Construction of access aids, such as indexes or abstracts

Reorganization into a more usable form, such as portability

Within the information economy, individual firms can pursue a conversion strategy in many different ways. For example, Mead Data Central retypes the text of all federal and state court decisions to make them available on-line (through a fee service known as LEXIS) to lawyers who are then able to automatically search the U.S. case law for precedents that apply to a current case. Congressional Information Services provides federal documents in microfilm, along with a complete index and on-line electronic database, in order to help users gain access to government information more efficiently. Disclosure, Inc., microfilms all basic Securities and Exchange Commission documents and sells the microfilm to libraries, enabling them to add this important information to their collection at a fraction of what it would cost in paper form.

At the *distribution* stage in the information life cycle, added information value may arise from still other sources and in other ways:

Increased availability to accessibility by vertical markets adds value.

The value of information varies for every user.

Information value originates not simply from its content, but also from how the content is packaged.

The packaging of information content is a process of reconstructing new information packages with higher value from lower-valued information packages.

As we suggested in Chapter 4, a major source of competitive advantage today arises from the packaging and repackaging of information products and services directly, or in packaging information in a product or service and thus adding value to the latter.

At the valuation or pricing stage of the information life cycle, rewards for intellectual property may arise from many sources, like:

Retail Sales.   Books, records, movies, videocassettes, audiocassettes, and computer software are sold directly to the consumer.

Subscriptions.   Magazines, newspapers, newsletters, and business investment and other information services, both in print form and electronic form, are paid for by the user in advance to gain regular and timely access to a compilation of information products which may vary in value to the user.

Sponsored Information.   Television and radio broadcasts, direct mail and outdoor advertising, are free to those who have invested in the necessary receiving equipment. The producer is paid not by the consumer, but by a third party—the advertiser—who wants an opportunity to reach an audience.

Publicly Funded Information.   Health and Safety information, libraries and clearinghouses, public television, and even some on-line databases, are offered free or subsidized at marginal cost by federal, state and local governments and nonprofit institutions, to achieve particular public-interest objectives.

Finally, when files and databases are purged of obsolete and unused data, value is added to the residual collection because the user does not have to pay for and cope with unnecessary and irrelevant materials that can clog information channels.

Thus, it is clear that our traditional definitions and notions of intellectual property embodied in information products or services are being directly affected, as they should be, by the evolution of the information economy. Similarly, as we will illustrate below, our traditional notions of copyright and intellectual ownership are also undergoing significant changes.

For example, until the 1960s when use of copying machines became widespread, our notion of what was legal or illegal to copy were fairly clear. When all information was in book, magazine, article (that is, print form), the problem of copying was relatively controllable. But, with the advent of electronic publishing, coupled with the increasing power and lower prices of copying technologies including electronic, microfilm and facsimile (FAX)—many new challenges to copyright standards have cropped up. Today, headlines do not just announce bank robberies, thefts of jewels, or embezzlement of funds; instead, they announce "software piracy," "video cassette recorder copying," "computer hacking," "automatic teller machine thefts," and "credit-card fraud." Electronic thievery, in short, is becoming as lucrative or perhaps even more so than the theft of physical objects.

Another intellectual-property doctrine that has been significantly challenged by the ease of electronic copying is the "fair use" doctrine. In the past, school teachers, librarians, and students had an easy time deciding what and how much to copy for use in class assignments or research. But as electronic copiers and video-cassette technologies have spread throughout the school, library, and home, intellectual-property owners have become concerned that their returns from creating, producing, and distributing their works are being eroded by the wholesale and indiscriminate copying of materials. There are many categories of intellectual-property ownership fixed in tangible forms, such as:

Literary works

Musical compositions

Dramatic presentations

Pantomines and choreographic presentations

Pictorial, graphic, and sculptural works

Motion pictures and other audio visual works

Sound recordings of all kinds

Each of these traditional forms of intellectual property can be digitized and automated so that their conversion, distribution, and valuation (as mentioned earlier) is dramatically changed. In recent years, software as a form of intellectual property has raised significant and difficult challenges to the "ownership" and "fair use" issues. In 1984, the U.S. Congress passed an important piece of legislation entitled the Computer Software Copyright Act, which amended an earlier law to include a definition of "computer program" (software) into our traditional notion of copyrightable work. While the intent of the new law seems relatively clear where the creative software work matches fairly closely the above-listed "original works of authorship," there remain major areas of ambiguity with software programs that are largely "invisible" to the computer user, such as operating systems and "utility" programs.

Thus, not only are traditional concepts of law being transformed in the information economy, but new legal definitions and concepts must be created to cope with the shifting of boundaries between print forms and electronic information forms. This shifting of legal boundaries is originating in the tendency within the information economy, as we pointed out in Chapters 1 and 2, for whole industries and sectors of the economy to deliberately alter traditional marketplace boundaries for competitive advantage. This produces significant pressures on legislatures, courts, and regulatory agencies to adjust the traditional laws and regulations governing these sectors. The pressures on traditional legal concepts such as copyright, patent, and fair use are but a manifestation of the larger pressures in the information society to redraw the laws and regulations affecting whole industries and sectors of the economy. Some good examples are the 1984 divestiture of AT&T, and the current turmoil in the banking, financial services, and retailing sectors.

THE GROWING ROLE OF INFORMATION AS AN ECONOMIC RESOURCE AND COMMODITY

A third feature of the information economy which directly affects the role of business in society is the growing role of information as an economic resource and commodity. As we noted in Chapter 2, while it is true that information has always been the basis of numerous industries, such as the printing and publishing trades, it is increasingly apparent that the production, storage, transmission, and use of information has been radically transformed by the evolution over the last 15 years of new electronic-based information products and services. The information-industry sector is still a relatively small one in terms of the total revenues of the entire information-processing industry. However, the current emphasis on software, database management systems, and end-user tools in the computer and communications industries, tends to reenforce the increasing importance of information content and innovative

information packaging and distribution. Finally, as the information-processing industry matures and converges with the broadcasting industry, more and more emphasis will be placed on information as an economic resource and commodity—a concept which
is at the center of profitability in broadcasting.

As these changes in the commercial value of information come
about, the lines between the public and private sectors in the
electronic-information marketplace will need to be redrawn. As a
major producer and distributor of information resources, government's presence in the information marketplace is becoming increasingly contentious. In part this is because it is almost impossible for government officials to avoid pressures to manipulate prices
for information services and products, for a variety of political
purposes that go beyond marketplace considerations. As a result,
government ends up with a wide variety of apparently inconsistent
and capricious pricing policies that range from giving government
information away free, solicited or unsolicited, to selling government information for a fee that is, indeed, sometimes even beyond
what industry competitive-pricing practice might suggest.

In recent years there appears to be increasing dissension between the public and private sectors over their respective roles in
disseminating information. The core problem seems to be that
certain information the government collects or produces has both
social and economic value. It has social value, and therefore can be
considered a "public good" like education, welfare services, and
defense programs, in the sense that it helps citizens determine what
government services they are entitled to, and find out what government is doing so as too permit them to become more informed. It has
economic value precisely because businesses, citizens, academic
and other institutions, foreign governments, and other foreign
enterprises are willing to pay marketplace prices for the information good or service.

In 1985, the Reagan Administration promulgated an important
but controversial policy on the management of federal information
resources, that sharpened the public-private sector debate on the
dissemination of government information.[6] The policy instructs

---

[6] Proposed OMB Circular "Management of Federal Information Resources," *Federal
Register,* March 15, 1985, pp. 10734–10747.

agencies to also satisfy conditions regarding the manner of dissemination even after they have justified and made the basic decision to disseminate information in the first place.

First, agencies must act in the most cost-effective manner, which includes maximum reliance on the private sector. This is an application of another, broader policy on the general subject of performance of commercial activities (Office of Management and Budget Circular A-76), wherein it is stated that government's preferred policy is to rely on the private sector wherever possible to provide the products and services the government needs, in lieu of manufacturing such products in-house. For example, before an agency establishes a service for electronic dissemination of government information via an on-line computer system, the agency should compare the cost of contracting the service versus in-house performance, and determine whether in-house performance is less costly.

Second, agencies must avoid creating information-technology monopolies. Many agencies operate one or more central information-technology facilities to support their programs. In these agencies, program managers are often required to use the central facilities. The manager of such a monopoly facility has a lesser incentive to control costs, since he or she has a captive clientele. The program manager has little leverage to ensure that information-processing resources are efficiently allocated, since he or she cannot seek, or can seek only with great difficulty, alternative sources of supply. To provide incentives conducive to more businesslike procedures in these facilities, Reagan's policy admonishes agencies to avoid monopolistic information-processing arrangements. These should be entered into only if their cost-effectiveness is clear and they are subject to periodic review.

Third, Federal agencies are admonished by the Reagan policy to recover the full costs of information–processing support to internal programs, and, furthermore, to *allocate* such costs and eventually recover them from the program users. In private-sector parlance this is often called *chargeback*. Office of Management and Budget Circular A-121 is the authority in this area, but it was revised with the issuance of the new directive we are currently reviewing here.

Fourth, Federal agencies are advised that they must keep up with state-of-the-art technologies. Two broad areas are singled out for special mention in this context: electronic-information collection and dissemination, and end-user computing. In the case of the former, it is pointed out that many agencies, such as regulatory commissions like the Securities and Exchange Commission (SEC) are rapidly moving to position themselves so as to be able to receive electronic filings instead of paper filings from the private sector. However, the Office of Management and Budget (OMB) points out that agencies must take special care to rethink how to strengthen privacy, confidentiality, and security measures. Electronic information seems to be more vulnerable to theft than manually handled information, although an argument can be made that either mode is subject to fraud, abuse, and misuse.

With respect to end-user computing, there is clearly some danger that downloading files from central-agency corporate databases, offloading them, manipulating the data, and then uploading them back into the central-agency database, could cause unforeseen difficulties unless appropriate controls were in effect.

Leading the drive, within and without the Reagan Administration, to "privatise" government information holdings, access, and dissemination, are strong forces who favor restricting the role of government. They point out that:

Our society is founded on the traditional view that individual freedom and initiative, expressed through competitive private enterprise, are the best means of supplying the products and services needed by society.

Government entry into the marketplace can have a chilling effect on private sector investment in the generation, collection, and distribution of information.

When government enters the marketplace, it interferes with the ability of the market mechanism to allocate resources to the optimum production of goods and services.

The private sector, if not threatened by the anticompetitive effects of government in the marketplace, can widen the distribution of information from government as well as from other sources.

Counterbalancing the Reagan initiatives in this area are those who would favor *not* restricting the role of government, and who point out:

> There is a need to ensure equitable, open access by the public in general to information which has been generated, collected, processed, or distributed with taxpayer funds.
>
> To participate fully in our democratic society, citizens must be informed and aware regardless of their individual ability to pay for needed information.
>
> Information needs that are not served by the marketplace must be met by the government.
>
> The government has a role to play in stimulating the development of information as a resource for dealing with societal problems.

Horton puts forward a possible model that attempts to bridge the social and economic dimensions of this private-public sector debate, based on the intrinsic value of the information and the purposes to be served by it, and a pricing policy deemed "fair." For example, a clear distinction is made between police, fire, emergency, and other health and safety information needs on the one hand, and relatively less critical ("edifying") information requirements on the other.[7]

Some political scientists and sociologists have entered the debate pointing out that government intervention to deal with market failures is nothing new. Public education is a prime example. Richard M. Neustadt of the Carter White House Domestic Policy Staff underscored the notion that what is new is not the very notion of intervention, but rather that for the first time all of us are beginning to think of all those different kinds of interventions— post office (for example, electronic computer-originated mail or ECOM, new defunct), education, disclosure, and so on—as pieces of one puzzle. They are not, Neustadt emphasizes, separate issues.

---

[7] Forest W. Horton, Jr., "The Public-Private Sector Controversy Over Disseminating Government Information," *Journal of Public Communication*, Vol. 6, No. 1, pp. 21–25.

They all tie together around the idea of government intervention in the information marketplace to produce social benefits.[8]

The information industry sees at least two alternative approaches to the role of government in information dissemination. A choice, in other words, exists between an approach based on "market-failure" analysis, subject to such rules as the policies enumerated in the above mentioned OMB policy circulars, on the one hand, and an approach based on an all-out commitment to the stimulation of an information industry, on the other. Robert Willard, former vice-president for Government Relations and Paul Zurkowski, president, of the Information Industry Association (IIA), would like to see Congress enact legislation that directs and clarifies government reliance on the private sector, believing that existing Administration policy directives, rules, and regulations are not enough, and, moreover, are often confusing and contradictory.[9]

IIA believes the "sunset idea" should be applied to government projects and programs where internal government creation of information was the initial plan, but where the policy should be automatically and periodically reviewed in the light of changing circumstances. This would be the case, they contend, for example, with large information systems and databases like MEDLARS (Medical Library Automation Retrieval System), operated by the National Library of Medicine.

There can be no question that government's participation in the electronic information-handling marketplace will have far-reaching impacts and consequences on virtually every company that does business with the government, and on those that are regulated by it. Therefore every enterprise in the information economy has a stake in the outcome of this ongoing debate. Regulation, antitrust activities, deregulation, censorship, the Freedom of Information Act, and even foreign-trade export controls (precluding the shipment of high-tech equipment to the Soviet Union and its allies), all comprise pieces in this complicated process of redefining the roles of the private and public sectors in the information marketplace.

[8] Forest W. Horton, ed., *Understanding U.S. Information Policy*, Washington, D.C.: Information Industry Association, 1982, *Information Policy Primer*, Vol. 1, p. 30.

[9] *Ibid.*, pp. 28–38.

THE GROWING ROLE OF INFORMATION AS A SOURCE OF SOCIAL AND POLITICAL POWER

Just as information and knowledge resources have become critical to business in the information economy, these resources have also become growing sources of social and political power. Historically, information and knowledge have always been important to the rulers of nations and to military forces. Indeed, the origin of the phrase "information is power," is the application of information and knowledge resources in political and military settings. Moreover, as we noted in Chapter 3, the pragmatic use of information and knowledge in commerce and trade did not arise in the twentieth century, but in the Middle Ages. So it can be said that information and knowledge in the sense of strategic intelligence has been part of the working capital of political, military, and even religious leaders throughout Western history. What distinguishes the modern era of information economies from other periods, however, is that information and knowledge can be organized and used on a scale never before considered possible, with the use of new information and communication technologies. Possession and use of these technologies is considered the distinguishing criteria for the success or failure of individuals, groups, and social institutions in the diverse contexts of individual action, religious development, and social interaction. Moreover, an important criteria of success or failure in the modern world—for individuals, institutions, and even nations—is how well or poorly they use, organize, distribute, and control information and knowledge resources to serve their diverse goals and objectives. Thus, it is not surprising that as the information economy of the United States and other advanced nations has matured, issues related to information as a source of political, social, and even individual power have reached public and governmental decision-making agencies more and more frequently.

For example, while concern in the United States over individual privacy dates back many years, it has only been since the 1960s, as Table 9-3 suggests, that privacy as a political issue emerged on the national scene, and significant legislative and regulatory activity arose to deal with it.[10] In part, the appearance of the privacy

[10] U.S. Congress, Office of Technology Assessment, *Computer-Based National Information Systems*, p. 73.

TABLE 9–3. Significant Milestones in the Development of the Privacy and Computer Issues[a]

C. 1964	Proposal for a National Statistical Center and the resulting public debate on privacy and Government data systems—culminating in a series of congressional hearings.
1967	Alan Westin's influential book *Privacy and Freedom.* [b]
1970	Fair Credit Reporting Act—provisions regarding credit records on individuals.[c]
1971	Arthur R. Miller's book *The Assault on Privacy: Computers, Data Banks, and Dossiers.* [d]
1972	National Academy of Sciences report: *Databanks in a Free Society.*[e]
1973	Health, Education, and Welfare Secretary's Advisory Committee on Automated Personal Data Systems report: *Records, Computers, and the Rights of Citizens.*[f]
1974	Family Educational Rights and Privacy Act controlling access to educational records.[g]
1974	Privacy Act of 1974 enacted.[h]
1977	Privacy Protection Study Commission report: *Personal Privacy in an Information Society.*[i]
1978	Right to Financial Privacy Act of 1978 enacted to provide controls on release of bank information.[j]

Source: Office of Technology Assessment.

[a] Note: There were also numerous hearings and reports by Senate and House congressional committees during this period, which are not listed here. James Rule and collaborators list 60 major Committee hearings and reports dealing with information privacy from 1966 to 1977.[k]

[b] Alan Westin, *Privacy and Freedom*, New York Atheneum, 1967.

[c] Fair Credit Reporting Act, 15 U.S.C. 1681(1970).

[d] Arthur R. Miller, *The Assault on Privacy: Computers, Databanks, and Dossiers* (Ann Arbor: University of Michigan Press, 1971).

[e] Alan Westin and Michael Baker, *Databanks in a Free Society*, (New York: Quadrangle/New York Times Book Co., 1972).

[f] Department of Health, Education, and Welfare, Secretary's Advisory Committee on Automated Personal Data Systems, *Records, Computers and the Rights of Citizens*, Washington, D.C., 1973.

[g] Public Law 93-568.

[h] Public Law 93-579.

[i] Privacy Protection Study Commission, *Personal Privacy in an Information Society*, Washington, D.C., 1977.

[j] Right to Financial Privacy Act of 1978 (Public Law 95-630).

[k] James Rule, et .al., *The Politics of Privacy* (New York: Elsevier-North Holland, 1980).

concern was closely connected with the appearance of computers in large government and private organizations capable of processing millions of individual records. The issue also appeared at a time when more and more individuals perceived the computer as a symbol for the dehumanization and alienation they feel when dealing with large public and private organizations. Moreover, as the information-processing industry evolves, it is not likely that the issue of privacy will go away. Rather, it will become an expression of the concerns individuals in the information society have with defining the basis on which they will interact with record-keeping institutions, and negotiate their rights and remedies.

Underlying the issue of privacy is the larger question of equity embodied in the uneven distribution of knowledge and information resources in the society. As we noted in Chapter 8, the information economy increasingly demands individuals who at a minimum, can read, write, and count, and who can assume a variety of jobs demanding various skills in using information resources and computers. However, as we also noted, there is growing concern today that the schools are increasingly failing in these basic tasks. When fully 20 percent of the people in the world's most advanced information economy can not read or write or handle the most basic arithmetic exercises, a potentially explosive and fundamental issue looms on the horizon: How will these information-poor individuals be accommodated in the information society? Will there be in the United States, as well as in other economies, a permanent information-poor class, disenfranchised from productive work by their lack of basic educational skills, or will programs be devised in both the public and private sectors to help the information poor achieve the basic intellectual tools necessary for effective work and an adequate standard of living in the information economy?

Clearly, there are no simple answers to these fundamental questions. As we suggested in Chapter 8, business will play a critical role in providing the illiterate and information poor with remedial educational opportunities, that will supplement the programs of government and educational institutions. If fairness or equity are to be achieved in dealing with the issue of the information poor and uneducated in our society, these social values will need to be pursued by business executives and managers aware of the social conditions required for their firm's long-term prosperity in the information economy, as well as their short-term public or civic responsibilities. In short, the growing importance of information resources as sources of social and political power is a two-edged sword—offering significant opportunities to achieve economic growth and prosperity while at the time providing real challenges for managers and executives in providing enlightened solutions to vexing social and political information-age issues.

THE IMPACTS OF THE INFORMATION ECONOMY AND INFORMATION-PROCESSING INDUSTRY IN BUSINESS ARE INCREASINGLY INTERNATIONAL

A fifth salient feature of the role of business in the information society is the increasing internationalization of public issues. Indeed, all of the public policy issues and concerns which we have discussed thus far have a clear international dimension. For example, in Chapter 1 we noted that the information economy is a growing international phenomenon which more and more differentiates the advanced from the less advanced nations in the world. Moreover, as more and more countries have come to realize that the information-processing industry is emerging as the world's largest industry, and as a critical engine for future wealth creation, the stance that a particular country takes in relation to its national economic and social goals has increasingly resulted in laws, regulations, tariffs, and general social policies which emphasize a diversity of approaches toward information policies or information. This is taking place in both developed and undeveloped nations. The outcome of these actions by individual nations has been to increase the complexity of international business decisions, as well as to raise the level of risk or uncertainty in dealing with nations whose goals and objectives in coping with the information economy and information-processing industry are also just emerging and are by no means stable, or, in some cases, clearly defined.

Thus, doing business in the international economy today requires attention to a broad range of information-policy issues that affect both the internal and external environment of firms. As Figure 9-1

General Impacts of Country Diversity on Doing Business
  Sociopolitical climate
  Language differences
  Local cultural and attitudinal constraints
  Availability of human talent and skills
  Ability of and variations in currency exchange
  Availability of a national infrastructure for communications, trans-
    portation, and mail
  Attitudes toward technology in workplace
Specific Impacts of Country Diversity on Information Management
  Availability of knowledge workers
  The telecommunication infrastructure—prices, quality, attitude to-
    ward business users, and technical standards
  The informatics strategy of the country
  Sophistication and type of information-processing industry in the
    country
  Transborder dataflow regulations
  Worker attitudes and cultural perceptions toward information tech-
    nology in the workplace

Figure 9–1.   Impacts of Country Diversity on Strategic Information
Management

suggests, any firm engaged in international trade and commerce must address a broad range of concerns arising from the diversity of individual countries in terms of sociopolitical and economic factors.[11] Language and cultural differences will have an important influence on the extent to which a business can establish information-management strategies that are consistent for all the countries in which it operates. General attitudes on the part of workers toward technology in the workplace will also influence the specific information-technology approaches individual businesses can pursue in offices or plants. The educational level and literacy of workers coupled with the publicly provided or private means available for training and remedial education, will influence the extent to which a firm pursues information resources strategies that are comparable across foreign subsidiaries or in diverse foreign markets.

Moreover, country diversity will affect the specific approaches

[11] See, James I. Cash, Jr., F. Warren McFarland, and James L. McKenney, *Corporate Information Systems Management: Text and Cases,* Homewood, IL: Richard D. Irwin, 1983, pp. 459–474.

businesses pursue to strategic information management. Variations in the information strategies of national governments will determine whether a firm purchases information technology that is "home grown" or generally available form multinational vendors. Differences in telecommunications infrastructures may influence a business's decision to process its subsidiary data in the native country rather than in centralized data centers outside a specific country. Increasingly, both developed and undeveloped nations have sought to regulate the transfer of personal-record or other sensitive financial data outside their borders by multinational businesses. Finally, worker attitudes, traditions of unionization, and cultural perceptions toward the use of information resources and technology in factories, offices, and homes will differentiate the strategies that companies can adopt to information management in diverse national contexts. Thus, there exist many constraints on the capabilities of firms intending to use information resources for competitive advantage on a multinational scale, that vary significantly from country to country in the world on both the north-south and east-west axes. The internationalization of the information economy and information-processing industry represent a major challenge to business to effectively respond to both the business and sociopolitical dimensions of this phenomenon.

IN THE INFORMATION SOCIETY, BUSINESS ORGANIZATIONS MUST BE FLEXIBLE AND ADAPTIVE

We have emphasized throughout this book the need for business organizations to be flexible and adaptive in providing products and services, in deciding what markets or industry sectors in which to play, and in developing competitive strategies that respond to increasing complexity and dynamic shifts in the information economy. We have also noted that these shifts in business strategy also require flexibility and adaptability in designing organizational structures and forms. The traditional model of the closed hierarchical pyramid has given way to the extended enterprise. The debate over centralization versus decentralization has given way to distributed and matrix forms of organization. And finally, the traditional limitations of time and geography have given way in the face of advances in communications and computer technologies.

Furthermore, as the boundaries between services and manufacturing, and between various service sectors, continue to collapse due to the increasing "informationalization" of business, it is no longer necessary to think of designing business organizations as if function followed form. That is, perceived limitations in the way businesses can be organized no longer have to constrain or delineate the business goals or objectives a firm wishes to pursue. Indeed, more than ever before, the form or structure a firm takes on can follow directly from its specific business objectives and strategies. Thus, the flexibility of a firm's products or services must also be reflected in its structure and functions. For example, banks and financial services firms are using information technology to promote increased customer services and decentralization of branch office operations. Therefore, they are no longer required to process all information in a centrally controlled MIS/DP group.

In addition, the requirement that a firm be able to adapt or "readapt" to its external as well as internal business environment, necessitates flexibility not only in the face of economic or technological changes, but also in the face of very dynamic social, political, and cultural changes on a national and international scale. For example, how a multinational organizes its plants or marketing offices internationally will be determined by the sociopolitical factors of worker values and education and the attitude of government toward business, as well as by traditional business criteria of location of plant relative to distribution outlets and the need for direct marketing presence in specific countries.

AN ESSENTIAL FEATURE OF THE INFORMATION SOCIETY IS LEARNING, NOT JUST DOING

At the beginning of this book, we emphasized that the evolutionary path of the information economy and society are not inevitable or foreordained. More than ever before, a key ingredient of management in dealing with organized social complexity and dynamic changes will be the capability to learn and not just to act.[12] As the complex business environment makes action more error prone and risky, learning will be an essential part of all action. A competitive and productive firm will create an active learning environment and will constantly examine the appropriateness of its corporate vision and the requirements of the business environment in which it operates. If business is to become smarter, management styles must be geared to learning and doing. In many ways, this shift is at the heart of the changing role of business in the information society.

Managers in the modern enterprise must be attuned to the political, social, and cultural environments in which the firm exists, as well as to the economic and technological factors that influence the firm's markets, products, and services. It is no longer possible, if it ever was, to draw clear lines of demarcation between business issues and the political and social realities within which business must operate. Doing business in the information society requires the self-discipline to learn before one acts.[13] It is perhaps ironic that as the information society matures, we return to a basic theme of Western intellectual and philosophical thought—the need for knowledge to inform the use of power. Today, we possess the technology and institutions to literally transform the way business and commerce are transacted on a national and global scale. The real challenge is to possess the knowledge and creativity to illuminate the paths in which we exercise the power embodied in our tools and employees. The firms that just survive in the information economy will be the ones that use information resources and computer technologies only as cost-displacement and labor-saving tools. The firms that compete effectively and flourish in the information economy will be the ones that use information technologies and information resources in strategic ways to manufacture new and better products, find new markets and enlarge their shares of existing markets, and distribute products and services in creative ways. These will be the intelligent organizations of the future.

[12] Todd R. LaPorte, "Complexity and Uncertainty: Challenge to Action," in Todd R. LaPorte, ed., *Organized Social Complexity*, Princeton, NJ: Princeton University Press, 1975, pp. 348–349.

[13] Peter F. Drucker, "Playing in the Information-Based 'Orchestra,'" *The Wall Street Journal*, June 4, 1985.

BIBLIOGRAPHY

Abarbanel, Karin, "Industry Outlook," *The Executive Female,* November–December 1984, pp. 24–28.

Abetti, Pier A., "Technology: A Challenge to Planners," *Planning Review,* July 1984, pp. 24–25, 45.

"A Nation Bets Its Future on 'Informatics,'" *Modern Office Procedures,* December 1982, pp. 46, 48.

"A New Marketing Blitz in the War of the Plastic Cards," *Business Week,* July 23, 1984, pp. 126–128.

Alexander, Tom, "Computing with Light at Lightning Speeds," *Fortune,* July 23, 1984, pp. 82–84, 86, 88.

Alexander, Tom, "Cray's Way of Staying Super-Duper," *Fortune,* March 18, 1985, pp. 66–76.

Alexander, Tom, "The Next Revolution in Computer Programming," *Fortune,* October 29, 1984, pp. 81–82, 84, 86.

Alexander, Tom, "Why Computers Can't Outthink the Experts," *Fortune,* August 20, 1984, pp. 105–106, 108, 112, 114–116, 118.

"America Rushes to High Tech for Growth," *BusinessWeek*, March 28, 1983, pp. 84–88, 90.

Arnold, Bob, "The Information Revolution Yet to Come," *BusinessWeek*, February 4, 1985, pp. 12–14.

Arnold, Bob, "Why Can't a Woman's Pay Be More Like a Man's?", *BusinessWeek*, January 28, 1985, pp. 82–83.

"Artificial Intelligence Machines Burst out of the Lab," *BusinessWeek*, October 1, 1984, p. 109.

"Artificial Intelligence Is Here," *BusinessWeek*, July 9, 1984, pp. 54–57, 60–62.

"Automated Service Stations Aid Credit Card Processing," *Gulf Oilmanac*, August 1984, pp. 1, 5.

"A Videotex Pioneer Pushes into the U.S. Market," *BusinessWeek*, April 16, 1984, pp. 62, 66.

Ayres, Robert V., *The Next Industrial Revolution*, Cambridge, MA: Ballinger, 1984.

Baker, Michael, "Making a Business of Information," September 1983, London: Her Majesty's Stationery Office.

"Bank's Service Firm Cuts Costs with Communications Link," *Computerworld*, July 9, 1984, p. 34.

Barty-King, Hugh, *Girdle round the Earth, the Story of Cable and Wireless*, London: Heinemann, 1979.

Batt, Robert, "Bank of America Launches $200 Million Worldwide Link," *Computerworld*, June 25, 1984, p. 9.

Batt, Robert, "MIS Scope Seen Altered as Store-Level Systems Abound," *Computerworld*, June 18, 1984, p. 21.

Bell, Daniel, *The Coming of Post-Industrial Society*, New York: Basic, 1973.

Bell, Daniel, "The Third Technical Revolution," *Business Quarterly*, Summer 1982, pp. 33–37.

Bemelmans, Th. M. A., ed., *Beyond Productivity: Information Systems Development for Organizational Effectiveness*, Amsterdam: Elsevier Science, 1984.

Benjamin, Robert I., John F. Rockart, Michael S. Scott Morton, and John Wyman, "Information Technology as a Strategic Opportunity," *Sloan Management Review*, 25, Spring 1984, pp. 3–10.

Benson, Dan, "Connecticut Mutual Life Creates an 'Oasis' in the Information Desert," *Management Technology*, October 1983, pp. 85–96.

Berke, Leslie M., "Increased Productivity: The Source of Office Systems," *Computer Decisions*, September 15, 1984, pp. 33–34, 38, 40.

"Better Late than Never," *Forbes*, July 2, 1984, p. 129.

"Bill Marriott's Grand Design for Growth: Upscale and Down in the Lodging Market," *BusinessWeek*, October 1, 1984, pp. 60–62.

Blank, Edward, "Telemarketing: The Key Element of the Direct Marketing Matrix," *Telemarketing*, April 1984, pp. 46–48.

Blumenthal, Marcia, "Mobil Considering IRM As Separate Line Entity," *Computerworld*, February 9, 1981, pp. 27–28.

Blyskal, Jeff, "Mail Order for the Masses," *Forbes*, July 16, 1984, pp. 35–36.

Booker, Ellis, "Decision-Support Systems: Computers Help You Win the Game," *Computer Decisions*, September 15, 1984, pp. 15, 17–18, 20, 24, 28.

Booz, Allen and Hamilton, Inc., *Information Industry Executive Survey of Critical Success Factors.*

Borbely, Jack, "Chief Information Officer: What's in a Title?", *Online*, May 1985, pp. 91–93.

Botkin, James, D. Dimancescu, D., and R. Stata, *Global Stakes*, Cambridge, MA: Ballinger, 1982.

Boulding, Kenneth E., and Lawrence Senesh, eds., *The Optimum Utilization of Knowledge*, Boulder, CO: Westview Press, 1983.

Bowles, John, "The Search for a New Engine of Growth," *BusinessWeek*, January 17, 1983, p. 10.

Bradley, Robert J. and Stan E. Williams, "Educating Society for the Information Age." *Data Management*, November 1982, pp. 28–33.

Braunstein, Yale M., "Information As a Factor of Production: Substitutability and Productivity," Vol. 3, No. 3, *The Information Society*, (1985), pp. 261–273.

Brief of Information Industry Association, Amicus Cureae, in Support of Reversal in the Case of Dun & Bradstreet vs. Greenmoss Builders, Inc., No. 83–18 in the Supreme Court of the United States, October Term 1984.

Brinberg, Herbert R., "Effective Management of Information: How to Meet the Needs of All the Users," *Management Review,* February 1984, pp. 8–13.

Brinberg, Herbert R., "Content, Not Quantity . . . Tailor Specific Data to Specific Needs—New Thrust of Information Management," *Management Review,* December 1981, pp. 8–11.

Brinberg, Herbert R., "Let's Put the Information Function in Its Place— but Where Is It?" Presentation to the Conference Board, New York, April 13, 1983.

Brose, Michael E., "The Technology Factor in Corporate Planning," *Planning Review,* July 1984, pp. 10–14.

Buell, Barbara, "Big Brother Gets a Job in Market Research," *Business-Week,* April 8, 1985, pp. 96–97.

Burns, Christopher, "Copyright and the Information Industry," *Information Times,* Spring 1984, pp. 31–33.

"Business Is Turning Data into a Potent Strategic Weapon," *Business-Week,* August 22, 1983, pp. 92, 94, 98.

Buzzell, Robert D., ed., *Marketing in An Electronic Age,* Boston: Harvard Business School Press, 1985.

Bylinsky, Gene, "America's Best-Managed Factories," *Fortune,* May 28, 1984, pp. 16–24.

Bylinsky, Gene, "The Holes in AT&T's Computer Strategy," *Fortune,* September 17, 1984, pp. 68–70, 74, 78, 82.

"Californians Buy Gasoline with ATM Bank Cards at Mobil Stations," *Computerworld,* September 10, 1984, p. 38.

Calvin, Geoffrey, "What the Baby-Boomers Will Buy Next," *Fortune,* October 15, 1984, pp. 28–34.

Canten, Irving D., "Learning to Love the Service Economy," *Harvard Business Review,* 84, May-June 1984, pp. 89–97.

Cash, James I., Jr., "Interorganizational Systems: An Information Society, Opportunity or Threat?" *The Information Society,* Vol. 3, No. 3, (1985), pp. 199–228.

Cash, James I., Jr., and Benn R. Konsynski, "IS Redraws Competitive Boundaries," *Harvard Business Review*, 85, March-April 1985, pp. 134–142.

Cash, James I., Jr., F. Warren McFarland, and James L. McKenney, *Corporation Information Systems Management: Text and Cases*, Homewood, IL: Irwin, 1983.

Charnes, A., and W. W. Cooper, eds., *Creative and Innovative Management*, Cambridge, MA: Ballinger, 1984.

Chick, Morey J., "Information Value and Cost Measures for Use As Management Tools," *Information Executive*, 1, 1984, pp. 47–66.

Cleveland, Harlan, *The Knowledge Executive*, New York: Dutton, 1985.

Compaine, Benjamin M., ed., *Understanding the New Media*, Cambridge, MA: Ballinger, 1984.

"Compugraphic: Trying to Move Typesetting from the Shop to the Office," *BusinessWeek*, July 2, 1984, p. 89.

Connolly, James, "Firm Plans Off-Line Based Nationwide POS Net," *Computerworld*, September 10, 1984, p. 87.

Connolly, James, "Two Banks Close to Full Micro-Based EFT," *Computerworld*, June 18, 1984, p. 19.

Cook, James, "You Mean We've Been Speaking Prose All These Years," *Forbes*, April 11, 1983, pp. 142–149.

Cook, Jay, IV., "Bank of America Builds Financial Services Around XT's," *Business Computing*, July 1984, pp. 34–47.

Coopers and Lybrand, "The Information Industry: Doing Business during the Revolution," Monograph, New York: Coopers and Lybrand, 1984.

Cordell, Arthur J., *The Uneasy Eighties*, Background Study 53, Ottawa, Canada: Science Council of Canada, 1985.

Cutaia, Jane H., "Pharmaceutical Makers May Get a Shot in the Arm," *BusinessWeek*, January 14, 1985, p. 98.

Darst, Steven U., "The Information Age: Can We Come to Grips with It?" *Office*, January 1983, pp. 186–191.

Davidson, William H., *The Amazing Race*, New York: Wiley, 1984.

Davis, Dwight, "Workplace High Tech Spurs Retraining Efforts," *High Technology*, November 1984, pp. 60–62, 64–65.

Dertouzos, Michael L., and Joel Moses, eds., *The Computer Age: A Twenty-Year View,* Cambridge, MA: MIT Press, 1979.

"Dial-Up Inquiry System Helps Firm's Salesmen," *Computerworld,* May 28, 1984, p. SR/13.

Diebold, John, "IRM: New Directions in Management," *Infosystems,* October 1979, pp. 41–42.

Diebold, John, "Six Issues That Will Affect the Future of Information Management," *Data Management,* July 1984, pp. 10–12, 14.

Diebold, John, *Making the Future Work,* New York: Simon & Schuster, 1984.

Dix, John and Susan Blakeney, "Open Market: New Services, Lower Prices," *Computerworld,* June 25, 1984, pp. 1, 8.

Dizard, John W., "Machines That Look for a Market," *Fortune,* September 17, 1984, pp. 87–88, 92, 96, 100, 104.

Donaldson, Gordon and Jerry W. Lorsch, *Decision Making at the Top,* New York: Basic Books, 1983.

Dreyfuss, Joel, "Reach Out and Sell Something," *Fortune,* November 26, 1984, pp. 127, 132.

Drucker, Peter F., "Growing Mismatch between Jobs and Job Seekers," *The Wall Street Journal,* Editorial, March 26, 1985.

Drucker, Peter F., "Out of the Depression Cycle," *The Wall Street Journal,* January 9, 1985.

Drucker, Peter F., *The Age of Discontinuity,* New York: Harper & Row, 1968.

Dumaine, Brian, "Tailor-Made Keys to Corporate Data Troves," *Fortune,* October 1, 1984, p. 129.

Edelhart, Michael, "Information Can Give Your Company a Competitive Edge," *Management Technology,* November 1983, pp. 29–33.

Fay, Stephen, "Central Bankers Have a Hot Line Too," *Fortune,* October 1, 1984, pp. 138, 140, 142.

Feigenbaum, Edward A., and Pamela McCorduck, *The Fifth Generation,* Reading, MA: Addison-Wesley, 1983.

Field, Anne R., "Programs That Make Managers Face the Facts," *BusinessWeek,* April 8, 1985, p. 74.

Field, Anne R. "Software for the Common Man," *Business Week*, March 18, 1985, pp. 94–100.

Finney, Paul, "Two-Way Street: An IBM Network Keeps Toyota on Its Toes," *Management Technology*, November 1984, pp. 34–40.

Flax, Steven, "Whirlwinds Hit the Yellow Pages," *Fortune*, October 1, 1984, pp. 113–114.

Flaherty, David H., *Protecting Privacy in Two-Way Electronic Services*, White Plains, NY: Knowledge Industry, 1985.

Fombrun, Charles, N. M. Tichy and M. A. DeVanna, *Strategic Human Resource Management*, New York: Wiley, 1984.

"Ford Aerospace Tries a Risky New Orbit: Satellite Communications," *Business Week*, August 20, 1984, pp. 111, 114.

Forman, Crain, "Executives Emphasize Improving Productivity of White Collar Staff," *Wall Street Journal*, July 19, 1984.

Fishman, Alan L., "Putting Technology into Strategy," *The Journal of Business Strategy*, 5, Spring 1985, pp. 54–65.

Fuller, Catherine and Barry L. Parr, "Consumer Videotex: Information for Everyone," *Information Times*, Spring 1985, pp. 33–36.

Ganley, Oswald H., and Gladys D. Ganley, *To Inform or to Control?*, New York: McGraw-Hill, 1982.

"GE Gambles on the Home of the Future," *Business Week*, August 27, 1984, p. 36.

Gerrity, Thomas P., "The Role of the CEO in Managing Information Technology," *Information Strategy*, Fall 1984, p. 4–9.

Gessner, Robert A., *Manufacturing Information Systems*, New York: Wiley, 1984.

Gifford, David and Alfred Spector, "The TWA Reservation System," *Communications of the ACM*, July 1984, pp. 650–665.

Gillin, Paul, "Information Seen As Strategic Weapon for Business," *Computerworld*, June 18, 1984, p. 12.

Gillin, Paul, "Merrill Lynch Breaks Ground with Prototyping Effort," *Computerworld*, June 25, 1984, p. 6.

Gingrich, Newt and Marianne Gingrich, "Post-Industrial Politics: The Leader as Learner," *The Futurist,* December 1981, pp. 29–32.

"GM Moves into a New Era," *BusinessWeek,* July 16, 1984, pp. 48–52, 54.

Goldstein, Mitchell, "Wiring the Automated Office," *National Productivity Review,* 3, Summer 1984, pp. 337–342.

Gottschalk, Earl C., "Allied Unit, Free of Red Tape, Seeks to Develop Orphan Technologies," *The Wall Street Journal,* September 13, 1984, Sec. 2, p. 31.

Greenther, Robert, "Computer System for Brokers Shows Buyers Views of Houses," *The Wall Street Journal,* July 18, 1984, sec. 2, p. 29.

Guimaraes, Tor, "IRM Revisited," *Datamation,* March 1, 1985, pp. 130–134.

Hall, Alan, "Deregulation Drags Bell Labs out of Its Ivory Tower," *BusinessWeek,* December 3, 1984, pp. 116–124.

Harris, Marilyn A., "Electronic Retailing Goes to the Supermarket," *BusinessWeek,* March 25, 1985, pp. 78–79.

Harris, Marilyn A., "Will Today's Stock Quote Machines Go the Way of Ticker Tape?" *BusinessWeek,* March 18, 1985, pp. 144, 148.

Harris, Marilyn A., "Computer Makers Plug into the Customer," *BusinessWeek,* January 14, 1985, pp. 96–97.

Harris, Marilyn A., "IBM: More Worlds to Conquer," *BusinessWeek,* February 18, 1985, pp. 84–98.

Harrison, F. L., "Microcomputers—the Breakthrough in Computer Modelling," *Long Range Planning,* October 16, 1983, pp. 94–99.

Hart, Gary, "Investing in People for the Information Age," *The Futurist,* February 1983, pp. 10–14.

Hawken, Paul, *The Next Economy,* New York: Holt, 1983.

Hax, Arnoldo, ed., *Readings on Strategic Management,* Cambridge, MA: Ballinger, 1984.

Hax, Arnoldo C., and Nicolas S. Majluf, *Strategic Management,* Englewood Cliffs, NJ: Prentice-Hall, 1984.

Hayes, Robert H., and Steven C. Wheelwright, *Restoring Our Competitive Edge,* New York: Wiley, 1984.

Heijn, H., "Automate the Organization, or Organize the Automation?", Productivity Brief No. 14, Houston, TX: American Productivity Center, June 1982.

Helm, Leslie and Rebecca Aikman, "Office Products: A Japanese Slugfest for U.S. Turf," *BusinessWeek,* May 13, 1985, pp. 98–99.

Helm, Leslie and Sarah Bartlett, "Now Japan Wants to Conquer Global Finance," *BusinessWeek,* April 8, 1985, pp. 58–59.

Herrman, John, "Computerized Swapping: Mercedes Gets a Grip on Inventory Control," *Management Technology,* November 1984, pp. 26–31.

Herrman, John, "How Chemical Bank Uses Computers to Drive Hard Bargains," *Management Technology,* March 1984, pp. 42–44, 46.

Herrman, John, "Pay as You Go: Cutting the High Cost of Ordinary Sales Calls," *Management Technology,* September 1984, pp. 46–50.

Hershey, Robert, "Commercial Intelligence on a Shoestring," *Harvard Business Review,* 58, September-October 1980, pp. 22–24, 28, 30.

Hirschheim, R. A., "Data Base—a Neglected Corporate Resource?" *Long Range Planning,* October 16, 1983, pp. 79–88.

Holloway, Clark, "Strategic Management and Artificial Intelligence," *Long Range Planning,* October 16, 1983, pp. 89–93.

Horton, Forest W., "Economic Thought Must Adjust to Information Age," *MIS Week,* November 12, 1980, p. 26.

Horton, Forest W., "Information Age Gives Productivity New Slant," *Computerworld,* May 4, 1981, p. 65.

Horton, Forest W., *Information Resources Management,* Englewood Cliffs, NJ: Prentice-Hall, 1985.

Horton, Forest W., "Redefining Productivity for the Information Age," *Information Management,* January 1983, pp. 26–27.

Horton, Forest W., "Software's Next Dimension," *Computerworld,* June 25, 1984, pp. ID/7–ID/11.

Horton, Forest W., "Tapping External Data Sources," *Computerworld,* August 15, 1983, pp. ID/1–3, ID/7–8, ID/10.

Horton, Forest W., *The Information Management Workbook: IRM Made Simple.* Washington, D.C.: Information Management, 1981.

Horton, Forest W., "The Knowledge Gateway System to Information Access," *Computerworld,* December 5, 1983, pp. ID/9–18.

"How Brokers Avoid Drowning in Data," *BusinessWeek,* November 15, 1982, p. 135.

"How Business Is Joining the Fight against Functional Illiteracy," *BusinessWeek,* April 16, 1984, pp. 94, 98.

"How Computers Remake the Manager's Job," *BusinessWeek,* April 25, 1983, pp. 68–80.

"How Personal Computers Are Changing the Forecaster's Job," *BusinessWeek,* October 1, 1984, pp. 123–124.

"How 'Smart Cards' Can Outwit the Credit Crooks," *BusinessWeek,* October 15, 1984, pp. 105, 108, 112, 116.

Hyer, Nancy L. and Urban Wemmerlov, "Group Technology and Productivity," *Harvard Business Review,* 62, July-August 1984, pp. 140–149.

"IBM's Big Leap onto the Factory Floor," *BusinessWeek,* September 17, 1984, p. 50.

"Information Management in the Insurance Industry," *Information Management,* December 1983, pp. 16–18, 36.

"Information Managers Called on to Set Trends," *Information Management,* June 1983, p. 28–29.

Ingrassia, Paul, "Industry Is Shopping Abroad for Good Ideas to Apply to Products," *The Wall Street Journal,* April 29, 1985, pp. 1, 16.

"Inside Information: A Green Light for Analysts?" *Institutional Investor,* August 1983, p. 94.

"Insurance Companies Adjust to Neic Claims Processing Network," *Computerworld,* September 10, 1984, p. 43.

Ives, Blake and Gerard P. Learmonth, "The Information System As a Competitive Weapon," *Communications of the ACM,* December 27, 1984, pp. 1193–1201.

Ivey, Mark and Geoffrey C. Lewis, "Computerphones: The Heavyweights Could Start Bells Ringing," *BusinessWeek,* March 4, 1985, pp. 110–111.

Jackson, Leon, "OA Forcing Organizational Change," *Computerworld,* April 9, 1984, pp. ID/43–ID/48.

Jacobs, Sanford L., "Software Is a Cheap Business to Get into—but Many Fail," *The Wall Street Journal,* April 29, 1985, p. 27.

Janulaitis, M. Victor, "Gaining Competitive Advantage with Computer and Communication Technology," *Spectrum,* December 1, 1984, pp. 1–4.

"Japan's Push to Write 'World-Class' Software," *Business Week,* February 27, 1984, pp. 96, 98.

"Japan's Strategy for the '80's," *Business Week,* (Special Issue), December 14, 1981, pp. 39–120.

Jelinek, Mariann and Joel D. Goldhar, "The Strategic Implications of the Factory of the Future," *Sloan Management Review,* 25, Summer 1984, pp. 29–38.

Johnson, Edward N., "The Document As An Information Source," *Information Management,* May 1983, pp. 21–22, 25.

Jones, Alex S., "And Now, the Media Mega-Merger," *The New York Times,* March 24, 1985, Sec. 3, pp. 1, 8–9.

Jonscher, Charles, "Information Resources and Economic Productivity," *Information Economics and Policy,* 1, 1983, pp. 13–35.

Karten, Howard A., "Getting Smart: Public Data Bases, Part II," *Management Technology,* September 1983, pp. 34, 36–39.

Kearns, David T., "Xerox's Productivity Plan Is Worth Copying," *Planning Review,* May 1985, pp. 14–31.

Kelley, Robert E., *The Gold-Collar Worker,* Reading, MA: Addison-Wesley, 1985.

Kessler, Felix, "Here Come the Regional Superbanks," *Fortune,* December 10, 1984, pp. 137–144.

Kester, Denise, "Telemarketing in the Insurance Industry," *Telemarketing,* October 1984, pp. 12–14.

King, William R., "Information As a Strategic Resource," *MIS Quarterly,* 1983, pp. iii–iv.

King, William R. "Planning for Strategic Decision Support Systems," *Long Range Planning,* October 16, 1983, pp. 73–78.

Kizilos, Tolly, "Kratylus Automates His Iron Works," *Harvard Business Review,* 84, May-June 1984, pp. 136–144.

Koff, Richard M., *Using Small Computers to Make Your Business Strategy Work,* New York: Wiley, 1984.

Kundert, Rick, "Information Management," *Production Engineering,* March 1984, pp. 85–95.

Lacob, Miriam, "Computers Put Corporate Cash to Work," *Computer Decisions,* September 15, 1984, pp. 108–110, 114–117.

Landis, Laura, "Time Inc. to Buy a Publisher for $480 Million," *The Wall Street Journal,* February 22, 1985, p. 2.

LaPorte, Todd R., ed., *Organized Social Complexity,* Princeton, NJ: Princeton, 1975.

Leff, Nathaniel H., "What You Don't Know Can Hurt You," *Business Week,* March 14, 1983, p. 12.

Lehner, Urban C., and Amal Nag, "GM Says Its Acquisition Strategy Targets Several Non-Auto Areas," *The Wall Street Journal,* January 21, 1985.

Leinster, Colin, "Mobile Phones: Hot New Industry," *Fortune,* August 6, 1984, pp. 108–113.

Lervin, Leonard, ed., *Telecommunications in the United States: Trends and Policies,* Washington, D.C.: Artech, 1981.

Levine, Jonathan B., "Bank of America Pushes into the Information Age," *Business Week,* April 15, 1985, pp. 110–112.

Levine, Jonathan B., "Tiny Satellite Dishes Are Serving Up a Hot New Market," *Business Week,* March 11, 1985, pp. 102, 106.

"Life Card May Aid Doctors, Patients," *The Columbia Record,* May 9, 1985, Sec. A, p. 8.

Loomis, Carol J., "How the Service Stars Managed to Sparkle," *Fortune,* June 11, 1984, pp. 158–166.

Loomis, Carol J., "The Earnings Magic at American Express," *Fortune,* June 25, 1984, pp. 58–61.

Lord, W. J., Jr., "Information Analysis," *Journal of Business Communication,* 21, Winter 1984, pp. 7–18.

Louis, Arthur M., "The Great Electronic Mail Shootout," *Fortune,* August 20, 1984, pp. 167–168, 170, 172.

"Low-Tech Education Threatens the High-Tech Future," *Business Week,* March 28, 1983, pp. 95, 98.

Lueck, Thomas J., "Why Jack Welch Is Changing G.E.," *The New York Times,* Sec. F., pp. 1, 8.

MacGregor, John M., "What Users Think About Computer Models," *Long Range Planning,* October 16, 1983, pp. 45–57.

Mackulak, Gerald T., "Planning Techniques for Computer Integrated Manufacturing," *National Productivity Review,* 3, Summer 1984, pp. 315–333.

Magazine, Ira C., and Robert B. Reich, *Minding America's Business,* New York: Harcourt, 1982.

Main, Jeremy, "New Ways to Teach Workers What's New," *Fortune,* October 1, 1984, pp. 85–86, 90, 92, 94.

"Making Office Systems Pay Off," *EDP Analyzer,* February 23, 1985, pp. 1–16.

Malik, Rex, "Communism vs the Computer," *Computerworld,* July 9, 1984, pp. ID/36, ID/38–ID/48.

"Management Warms Up to Computer Graphics," *Business Week,* August 13, 1984, pp. 96–97, 101.

"Managers Are Reluctant to Try Innovative Productivity Techniques," *Wall Street Journal,* July 19, 1984.

"Mapping System Helps Insurance Firm Assess Its Markets," *Computerworld,* June 25, 1984, p. SR/19.

Martin, James, *Telematic Society,* Englewood Cliffs, NJ: Prentice-Hall, 1981.

Massey, Thomas P., "Japan Goes On-Line in the U.S. Market," *Management Technology,* March 1984, pp. 31–36.

Massey, Thomas P. "NEC's Enormous and Expanding Niche," *Management Technology,* March 1984, pp. 37–39.

Masuda, Yoneji, *The Information Society as Post-Industrial Society,* Tokyo, Japan: Institute for the Information Society, 1980.

McCauley, Herbert N., "Developing a Corporate Private Network," *MIS Quarterly,* December 7, 1983, pp. 19–33.

McClellan, Stephen T., *The Coming Computer Industry Shakeout,* New York: Wiley, 1984.

McComas, Maggie, "The Hard Sell Comes to Software," *Fortune,* September 17, 1984, pp. 59–60, 64.

McDowell, Edwin, "The New Reach of Random House," *The New York Times,* May 5, 1985, Sec. F, pp. 1, 23.

McFadden, Michael, "The Master Builder of Mammoth Tools," *Fortune,* September 3, 1984, pp. 58–60, 62, 64.

McFarlan, F. Warren, "Information Technology Changes the Way You Compete," *Harvard Business Review,* 62, May-June 1984, pp. 98–103.

McLaughlin, John F., and Anne E. Dirinyi, *Mapping the Information Business,* Cambridge, MA: Harvard, Center for Information Policy Research, 1980.

McLeod, Raymond Jr., and John C. Rogers, "Marketing Information Systems: Their Current Status in Fortune 1000 Companies," *Journal of Management Information Systems,* 1, Spring 1985, pp. 57–75.

Methlie, Leif B., and Alf M. Tverstol, "External Information Services: A Survey of Behavioral Aspects of Demand," *Information and Management,* 5, September 1982, pp. 269–277.

Miller, Michael, "Computers Keep Eye on Workers and See If They Perform Well," *The Wall Street Journal,* June 3, 1985, pp. 1, 16.

Miller, Victor E., "The Emergence of the Chief Information Officer," *AMA Forum,* February 1983, pp. 29–31.

Miller, Michael W., "U. S. Software Firms Try to Curb Foreign Pirates to Protect Big American Share of World Market," *The Wall Street Journal,* April 18, 1985, p. 34.

Molitor, Graham T. T., "The Information Society: The Path to Post-Industrial Growth," *The Futurist,* April 1981, pp. 23–30.

Montgomery, David B., and Charles B. Weinberg, "Toward Strategic Intelligence Systems," *Journal of Marketing,* 43, Fall 1979, pp. 41–52.

"Morgan-Stanley's High-Tech Boot Camp," *Business Week,* December 24, 1984, pp. 79, 82.

Moriarty, Rowland T., Jr., and Robert E. Spekman, "An Empirical Investigation of the Information Sources Used during the Industrial Buying Process," *Journal of Marketing Research,* May 21, 1984, pp. 137–147.

Moss, Mitchell L., ed., *Telecommunications and Productivity,* Reading, MA: Addison-Wesley, 1981.

Mueller, Robert R., "Training the Next Generation of Information Managers," *Information and Records Management,* October 1982, pp. 20–25.

Murphy, Cornelius J., "Kodak's 'Global Factory,'" *Planning Review,* May 1985, pp. 32–34.

Myers, Virgil, "What Executives Should Know before Endorsing the Next Generation of Manufacturing Systems," *Infosystems,* October 1979, pp. 42–43.

Naisbitt, John, *Megatrends,* New York: Warner, 1982.

Naisbitt, John and Patricia Aburdene, *Re-inventing the Corporation,* New York: Warner, 1985.

A. C. Neilsen Company, *The Business of Information 1983,* Washington, D.C.: Information Industry Association, 1983, Volume I: "Data and Analysis," Vol. II: The Outlook for the Information Industry 1983.

Nicholas, Henry, *Copyright, Information Technology and Public Policy,* New York: Dekker, 1975.

Norton, Robert, "Scovill's Smart Locks Click," *Fortune,* September 17, 1984, pp. 51–54.

Norton, Robert E., "The Best of the Biggest Banks," *Fortune,* August 20, 1984, pp. 193–194, 196.

November, Robert S., "Impact of Information Technology on the Home Market," *Information Times,* Spring 1985, pp. 16–18.

Nulty, Peter, "How Personal Computers Change Manager's Lives," *Fortune,* September 3, 1984, pp. 38–40, 44, 48.

O'Connell, Joan, "Cutting the Guesswork out of Surgery," *Business Week,* April 8, 1985, p. 80.

"Office Automation Restructures Business," *Business Week,* October 8, 1984, pp. 118–121, 124–125.

O'Flaherty, Tom, "The Many Corporate Uses of Personal Computers," *Management Technology,* October 1983, pp. 54–58.

Ohmal, Kenichi, *The Mind of the Strategist,* New York: Penguin, 1982.

"On-Line Management Package Keeps Avco Informed," *Computerworld,* July 9, 1984, p. 49.

Organization for Economic Cooperation and Development, *Information Activities, Electronics and Telecommunications Technologies,* Paris: OECD, 1981.

Otten, Klaus W., "Information Resources Management: Management Focus on the Value of Information and Information Work," *Journal of Information and Image Management,* August 1984, pp. 9–14.

Otten, Klaus W., "Personal Information Tools (Personal Computers): The Changing Environment and Its Management," *Journal of Information and Image Management,* June 1984, pp. 21–23.

Paine, Webber, Mitchell, Hutchins Inc., "The Information Industry," A first quantitative analysis prepared with the cooperation of the Information Industry Association, March 12, 1984.

Parsons, Gregory L., "Information Technology: A New Competitive Weapon," *Sloan Management Review,* Fall 1983, pp. 1–13.

Patterson, William Pat, "Corporations in Crisis: Coming to Grips with the Information Age," *Industry Week,* March 5, 1984, pp. 57–62.

Paul, Bill, "Eastman Kodak Is Planning to Market Its Communications System to Business," *The Wall Street Journal,* November 21, 1984, p. 6.

Pearson, William H., "Information: Using It As a Profitable Strategic Asset," *MIS Week,* 28 April 1983, p. 32.

Pool, Ithiel De Sola, *Forecasting the Telephone: A Retrospective Technology Assessment,* Norwood, NJ: Ablex, 1983.

Port, Otis, "Here Comes the Fastest Chip on Earth," *Business Week,* March 4, 1985, pp. 104, 106.

"Portables Help Grocery Chain Manage Perishables," *Computerworld,* July 9, 1984, p. 53.

Porter, Michael E., *Competitive Advantage,* New York: Free Press, 1985.

Porter, Michael E., *Competitive Strategy,* New York: Free Press, 1980.

Porter, Michael E. and V. E. Millar, "How Information Gives You Competitive Advantage," *Harvard Business Review,* Vol. 63, No. 4, pp. 149–160.

Posey, Bruce G., and Harold T. Smith, "The Third Era of Work," *Management World,* January 1983, pp. 12.

Power, Daniel J., "The Impact of Information Management on the Organization: Two Scenarios," *MIS Quarterly,* September 7, 1983, pp. 13–20.

Productivity Growth, A Better Life For America: A Report to the President of The United States, White House Conference on Productivity, April 1984.

"Publishers Go Electronic: An Industry Races to Relearn the Information Business," *BusinessWeek,* June 11, 1984, pp. 84–87, 90, 92, 97.

Raia, Ernst, "Helping Machine Tools Help Themselves," *High Technology,* June 1985, pp. 45–58.

Raimondi, Donna, "Neic System Speeds Processing of Health Insurance Claims," *Computerworld,* September 10, 1984, p. 42.

Ramirez, Anthony, "A New Industry Is Fixing to Fix Your Personal Computer," *Fortune,* March 18, 1985, pp. 150–156.

Reich, Robert B., *The Next American Frontier,* New York: Time, 1983.

Reitman, Walter, ed., *Artificial Intelligence Applications for Business,* Norwood, NJ: Ablex, 1984.

"Reshaping the Computer Industry," *BusinessWeek* (Special Report), July 16, 1984, pp. 84–87, 90–92, 94, 98, 103–106, 111.

"Retailer Uses Integration As Tactic to Battle Data Flow Bottleneck," *Computerworld,* July 16, 1984, pp. 81, 93.

Richman, Tom, "What America Needs Is a Few Good Failures," *Inc.,* September 1983, pp. 63–72.

Riggs, Henry E., *Managing High-Technology Companies,* Belmont, CA: Lifetime Learning, 1983.

Robinson, David G., "Managing the Value of Information Systems," *Spectrum,* June 1, 1984.

Robinson, W. Dorin, "The Bank That Banked on Telemarketing," *Telemarketing,* October 1984, pp. 16, 18, 19.

Roche, Edward, "Information Architecture," *Computerworld,* October 3, 1983, pp. ID/9–ID/26.

Rochester, Jack, "The Advice Industry: Pat McGovern's Amazing Computer Counting House," *Management Technology,* November 1984, pp. 34–40.

Rockart, John F., and Adam D. Crescenzi, "Engaging Top Management in Information Technology," *Sloan Management Review,* 25, Summer 1984, pp. 3–16.

Rockart, J. F., and M. S. Scott Morton, Arnold C. Hax, ed., "Implications of Changes in Information Technology for Corporate Strategy," *Readings on Strategic Management,* Cambridge, MA: Bollinger, 1984.

Roman, Daniel D., and Joseph F. Pruett, Jr., *International Business and Technological Innovation,* New York: North-Holland, 1983.

Rubeyser, William S., ed., *Working Smarter,* New York: Penguin, 1982.

Russell, Judith C., "All the Information, All the Time—Online," *Data Management,* February 1983, pp. 41–42.

Russell, Robert Arnold, "Repealing Parkinson's Law: The Information Revolution, What Should We Be Doing?", *Productivity Brief No. 26,* Houston, TX: The American Productivity Center, June 1983.

Saddler, Jeanne, "Comsat Holiday Inns Set Venture for TV, Teleconferencing," *The Wall Street Journal,* October 30, 1984, p. 12.

Samiee, Saeed, "Transitional Data Flow Constraints: A New Challenge for Multinational Corporations," *Journal of International Business Studies,* XV, Spring-Summer 1984, pp. 141–150.

Sammon, William L., Kurland, Mark A., and Robert Spitalnic, ed., *Business Competitor Intelligence,* New York: Wiley, 1984.

Sanger, David E., "Lotus Said to Seek Dataspeed," *The New York Times,* April 25, 1985, Sec. D., pp. 20–21.

Saporito, Bill, "Allegheny Ludlum Has Steel Figured Out," *Fortune,* June 25, 1984, pp. 40–41, 44.

Schement, Jorge Reina, Leah A. Lievrouw, and Herbert S. Dordick, "The Information Society in California: Social Factors Influencing Its Emergence," *Telecommunications Policy,* March 1983, pp. 64–72.

Schrage, Michael, "McGraw-Hill Aims to Blend Print, Computer," *The New York Times,* October 14, 1984, Sec. F., pp. 1, 5, 6.

Seiler, Robert E., "Creative Development of Computerized Information Systems," *Long Range Planning*, October 16, 1983, pp. 100–106.

Selig, Gad, "A Framework for Multi-National Information Systems Planning," *Information and Management*, June 5, 1982, pp. 95–115.

Shamoon, Sherrie, "Fast Computerized Feedback: How Columbia Pictures Markets Movies Better," *Management Technology*, January 1985, pp. 44–47.

Shamoon, Sherrie, "Turnkey Systems for Industry: McDonnel Douglas Builds An Information Business," *Management Technology*, September 1984, pp. 40–45.

Shelton, E. Kirk, "Transactional Services on Videotex," *Information Times*, Spring 1985, pp. 12–14.

Sherman, Stratford P., "Eight Big Masters of Innovation," *Fortune*, October 15, 1984, pp. 66–68, 72, 76, 80, 84.

Sieck, Steven K., "Artificial Intelligence: Its Promises for the Information Industry," *Information Times*, Spring 1985, pp. 6–10.

Singleton, Loy A., *Telecommunications in the Information Age*, Cambridge, MA: Ballinger, 1983.

Sizer, Richard, "Key Issues in Managing Information," *Long Range Planning*, October 16, 1983, pp. 10–18.

Smith, Dr. Harold T., "Who Will Manage Information—the Generalist or the Specialist?" *Management World*, March 1980, pp. 8–10, 36.

"Software Moves to Center Stage in the Office," *Business Week*, February 27, 1984, p. 92.

"Software Publishing: Now the Agents Are Moving In," *Business Week*, August 6, 1984, pp. 84–85.

Stillman, Stanley, "On-Line Data Bases: The Facts You Want Are At Your Fingertips," *Management Technology*, November 1984, pp. 58–64.

Stipp, David, "Computer-Models Help Speed the Search for Useful Drugs," *The Wall Street Journal*, March 22, 1985, p. 27.

Stix, Gary, "Building in Efficiency: Computers Accelerate Manufacturing," *Computer Decisions*, September 15, 1984, pp. 45–46, 48, 53–54, 56, 58.

Stone, Philip J., and Robert Luchetti, "Your Office Is Where You Are," *Harvard Business Review,* 85, March-April 1985, pp. 102–117.

Strassman, Paul A., *Information Payoff,* New York: Free Press, 1985.

Strauss, Lawrence, *Electronic Marketing,* White Plains, NY: Knowledge Industry, 1983.

"Successful Information Systems Are Linked to Overall Business Plans," *Information Management,* May 1983, p. 28.

Sullivan, Kathleen, "Paper Firm Relies on Voice-Based Inventory System," *Computerworld,* September 19, 1984, p. 44.

Synnott, William R., and William H. Gruber, *Information Resource Management: Opportunities and Strategies for the 1980's,* New York: Wiley, 1981.

"System Beefs Up Hardee's DP Operations," *Computerworld,* May 28, 1984, p. SR/41.

Tietelman, Robert, "Physician, Teach Thyself," *Forbes,* May 21, 1984, pp. 220, 222.

"Telecommunications Equipment Sales: A Revolution in Progress," *Telemarketing,* April 1984, pp. 32–35, 49–52.

"Teleports: Grand Bypasses for Big-City Markets," *Business Week,* August 27, 1984, p. 91.

"The Banks' Great Struggle to Master a Tangle of Data," *Business Week,* December 10, 1984, pp. 106, 108.

"The Business Intelligence Beehive," *Business Week,* December 14, 1981, p. 52.

"The 'Chief Information Officer' Role," *EDP Analyzer,* November 22, 1984, pp. 1–12.

"The Golden Plan of American Express," *Business Week,* April 30, 1984, pp. 118–122.

"The High-Tech Renaissance in Southern California," *Business Week,* September 17, 1984, pp. 142–144, 148.

Toffler, Alvin, *The Adaptive Corporation,* New York: McGraw-Hill, 1985.

Toffler, Alvin, *The Third Wave,* New York: Morrow, 1980.

"The Man who Computerized Bargain Hunting," *Fortune,* July 9, 1984, p. 137.

"The Medicare Squeeze Pushes Hospitals into the Information Age," *Business Week,* June 18, 1984, pp. 87–90.

"The New Breed of Strategic Planners," *Business Week,* September 17, 1984, pp. 62–66, 68.

"The New Economy," *Time,* May 30, 1983, pp. 62–70.

"The New Entrepreneurs: How Startup Companies Give America a Competitive Edge," *Business Week,* April 18, 1983, pp. 78–87.

"The New Shape of Banking," *Business Week,* June 18, 1984, pp. 104–108, 110.

"The New World of Corporate Finance," *Forbes,* June 18, 1984, pp. 93–94, 96, 100.

"The New York Colossus," *Business Week,* July 23, 1984, pp. 98–99.

"The Revival of Productivity," *Business Week,* February 13, 1984, pp. 92–100.

"The Super Services that Time-Sharers Provide," *Management Technology,* September 1984, p. 44.

Thompson, Albert J., "Financial Information Services in the Information Age," *Information Times,* Spring 1985, pp. 25–26.

"Trends in Computing: Systems and Services for the '80's," *Fortune,* July 9, 1984, pp. 65–128.

Tricker, R. I., *Effective Information Management,* Oxford: Beaumont, 1982.

Tucker, Elizabeth, "Fiber Optics Speeding Information Revolution," *The Washington Post,* November 4, 1984, Sec. K, pp. 1, 4.

Tucker, R. U., "How to Plan Information Strategy," *Management Today,* September 1982, pp. 62–65, 124.

"Turning Information into Profits," *Gulf Oilmanac,* 5, 1983.

U. S. Congress, Office of Technology Assessment, *Computer-Based National Information Systems, Technology and Public Policy Issues,* Washington, D.C.: U.S. Government Printing Office 1981.

Vamos, Mark N., John Wilke, Elizabeth Ames, James E. Ellis, and Karen Pennar, "Rupert Murdoch's Big Move," *Business Week*, May 20, 1985, pp. 104–108.

"Video Conferencing: No Longer Just a Sideshow," *Business Week*, November 12, 1984, pp. 116–120.

Vincent, David R., "Information As Corporate Asset," *Computerworld*, September 26, 1983, pp. ID/1–ID/8, ID/12.

Vise, David A., "Federal Express Takes New Gamble: 2-Hour 'Zap Mail,'" *The Washington Post*, November 4, 1984, Sec. K, pp. 1–3, 7.

Vlasho, Louis, "How to Use Information in Shaping Your Business," *The Office*, February 1983, p. 44.

Vogel, Ezra F., *Japan as Number 1*, New York: Harper & Row, 1979.

Walker, Ruth, "'Entrapreneurs' Sprouting New Ventures Within," *The Christian Science Monitor*, January 14, 1985, p. 19.

Walter, Stephanie K., "Full-Function Folksiness: How Computers Led L. L. Bean out of the Maine Woods," *Management Technology*, February 1985, pp. 26–32.

Wayne, Leslie, "Citi's Soaring Ambition," *New York Times*, June 24, 1984, Sec. 3, pp. 1, 8, 9.

Wayne, Leslie, "The Big Board's Fight to Stay on Top," *The New York Times*, October 14, 1984, Sec. F, pp. 1, 12.

Weil, Ulric, *Information Systems in the 80's*, Englewood Cliffs, NJ: Prentice-Hall, 1982.

Westin, Alan F., H. A. Scheweder, M. A. Baker, and Shiela Lehman, *The Changing Workplace*, White Plains, NY: Knowledge Industry, 1985.

"What Made Reed Wriston's Choice at Citicorp," *Business Week*, July 2, 1984, pp. 25–27.

Whitehead, Ralph, Jr., "Planning for 'The Next Economy,'" *Inc.*, June 1984, pp. 44–53.

"Who's Excellent Now?" *Business Week*, November 5, 1984, pp. 76–88.

"Why IBM Snapped Up the Rest of Rolm," *Business Week*, October 8, 1984, p. 48.

"Why MIS Specialists Keep Getting Mixed Reviews," *Management Technology*, August 1984, pp. 11–12, 14.

"Why Sears Chose Another Retailing Man," *Business Week,* August 27, 1984, pp. 27–28.

"Why the Big Apple Shines in the World's Markets." *Business Week,* July 23, 1984, pp. 100–102, 104, 108.

"Will IBM Climb to the Top in Software, Too?" *Business Week,* October 22, 1984, pp. 100–109.

Williams, Frederick, and Herbert S. Dordick, *The Executive's Guide to Information Technology,* New York: Wiley, 1983.

Williams, John D., "Gulf and Western Gets Pact to Buy Prentice-Hall," *The Wall Street Journal,* November 27, 1984, p. 4.

Winston, Patrick H., and Karen A. Pendergast, eds., *The AI Business,* Cambridge, MA: MIT, 1984.

Wiseman, Charles, *Strategy and Computers,* Homewood, IL: Dow Jones-Irwin, 1985.

Wiseman, Charles and Ian C. MacMillan, "Creating Competitive Weapons from Information Systems," *The Journal of Business Strategy,* 5, Fall 1984, pp. 42–49.

Wood, Lamont, "Computerized Distribution: Directing the Flow of Goods," *Computer Decisions,* September 15, 1984, pp. 63–64, 68, 72–73.

Wood, Lamont, "Ringing in the New Retail Technology," *Computer Decisions,* September 15, 1984, pp. 76, 78, 82, 84.

"Would You Buy a Car from This Computer?" *Business Week,* December 17, 1984, pp. 93–97.

Young, Earl C., and Harold P. Welsch, "Information Source Selection Patterns As Determined by Small Business Problems," *American Journal of Small Business,* 7, Spring 1983, pp. 42–49.

Young, Lawrence F., "The Information System As a Corporate Strategic Weapon," *Information Strategy,* 1, Fall 1984, pp. 21–26.

Zurkowski, Paul G., "Integrating America's Infostructure: An Article Explaining the Information Industry Map," Reprint, New York: Wiley, 1983.

Zygmont, Jeffrey, "The Truck of the Future," *High Technology,* June 1985, pp. 28–35.